THE PRESIDENT AS ARCHITECT:
FRANKLIN D. ROOSEVELT'S
TOP COTTAGE

THE PRESIDENT AS ARCHITECT:
FRANKLIN D. ROOSEVELT'S
TOP COTTAGE

John G. Waite Associates, Architects

Mount Ida Press  Albany, New York

Printed in the United States of America
ISBN 0-9625368-3-0

John G. Waite Associates, Architects, PLLC
384 Broadway
Albany, New York 12207
518.449.5440

Mount Ida Press
152 Washington Avenue
Albany, New York 12210
518.426.5935

Design: The Market Street Group
Printing: Fort Orange Press

Front cover: Franklin D. Roosevelt inspecting construction work at Top Cottage, October 1938. Reprinted, by permission, from New York Times Pictures.

Back cover: President Roosevelt on the west porch of Top Cottage, June 2, 1941. Photograph by Margaret Suckley. Courtesy of the Franklin D. Roosevelt Library, Hyde Park, New York.

Renderings on inside covers: Vladislav Yeliseyev

CONTENTS

6 Foreword

9 Preface

12 Acknowledgments

14 Introduction

16 Construction History

74 Architectural Description

130 Conservation Assessment

144 Restoration

156 Index

FOREWORD

President Franklin D. Roosevelt with Ruthie Bie and Fala on the west porch of Top Cottage, February 1941. Photograph by Margaret Suckley, courtesy of the Franklin D. Roosevelt Library, Hyde Park, New York.

ABOUT 2:30 IN THE AFTERNOON, JULY 1, 1938, the traveling White House press corps was assembled on a wooded hilltop overlooking Franklin D. Roosevelt's mother's place at Hyde Park. They had been summoned to a most unusual press conference. The President himself soon arrived, driving up the steep hillside at the wheel of his hand-controlled Ford. This was "Dutchess Hill," he told the reporters—"Don't leave out the 't,' " he said—and he wanted them to know that he was planning to build himself a small cottage on its summit. The walls were to be built from fieldstone taken from the old walls that twisted through his woods. He'd been thinking of building here for twenty years, he said. It was the spectacular views that had drawn him. "Right there," he said, gesturing across the slow-moving Hudson, 410 feet below, "is the north of the Catskill Range. This is the south of the Catskill. This is the Shawangunk, through there. That, south through the fields, is the Hudson Highlands and northeast. Back here, is the Berkshires. I can actually see into Connecticut and Massachusetts."

Over the ensuing weeks, as construction continued, he doled out more information about his plans to eager reporters. He was himself the architect, he said, though he'd had an "associate," Henry Toombs of Georgia. The cost would be no more than $16,000. There would be no air conditioning, no telephone, no screens on the porch, no formal landscaping —"just the trees" and the tranquil view.

No decision made by a President, no matter how apparently trivial, goes uncriticized. Despite the lengths to which FDR felt he had gone to impress the press with the modest scale of his plans, some members of the press angered him by insisting on calling the finished cottage his "Dream House." Licensed architects denounced the President for claiming to be an architect when he had no license. Margaret L. Suckley, the president's devoted and unmarried cousin, had hoped to share the cottage with him one day; so had his long-time secretary, Marguerite LeHand; both had to overcome their disappointment. And there was controversy within the President's family, as well: Sara Delano Roosevelt, already appalled that her daughter-in-law had felt it necessary to build herself a cottage at Val-Kill at the foot of Dutchess Hill, was wounded to learn of her son's plan for a retreat of his own and is said to have exacted a pledge from him that he would never spend a night there so long as she lived; so far as anyone knows, he never did, either before her death or after it.

Still, FDR loved the time he found to spend in the small stone structure he called variously "Dutchess Cottage," "hilltop cottage," and "Top Cottage." It was initially meant to be his private retreat after he left the presidency in 1940, a place to write his memoirs without fear of interruption from the people who invariably clamored to see him at his mother's home. And even after world events intervened, compelling him to run for a third, and then a fourth term, he always hoped to work there quietly after he finally did retire.

That, of course, was not to be, and Top Cottage saw a great deal of history being made between its completion in 1939 and the President's death in 1945. Just weeks before the world went to war, it was officially opened with a picnic for King George VI and Queen Elizabeth of England, marking the climax of the first visit by a British monarch to the United States and meant to strengthen ties with Britain in the coming struggle with Hitler. It was on its open flagstone porch that the King and Queen were offered their very first hot dogs, chosen by Eleanor Roosevelt over her mother-in-law's strenuous objections to demonstrate to royalty that Americans had their own cuisine. (The King savored his and asked for a second; the Queen is said to have thought her mouth too tiny to even take one bite.)

Winston Churchill came to the cottage several times during the war; on a warm afternoon in the spring of 1942 he and FDR may have discussed the possibility of working together toward making an atomic bomb. Madame Chiang Kai-shek visited Roosevelt on his hilltop. So did Crown Princess Louise of Sweden, Queen Wilhemina and Princess Juliana of the Netherlands, Princess Martha of Norway, Canadian premier MacKenzie King, Henry Wallace, Harry

Hopkins, and scores of other important figures in the Roosevelt administration and the Allied leadership.

Still more history was made here when Roosevelt was alone or with one or two old friends who could be counted on not to interrupt as he mulled over his next move in the greatest war in history while gazing through the trees at the slow-moving Hudson and the blue hills beyond.

The President's hilltop retreat is, so far as I am aware, the only presidential home ever designed by a President other than the two designed by one of Roosevelt's heroes, Thomas Jefferson—Monticello and the more modest dwelling Jefferson called Poplar Forest. The restoration of Top Cottage, now completed, will help visitors understand more fully the complex dynamics of the Roosevelt family, whose three strong-minded personalities in the end each required a separate dwelling of his or her own.

And the cottage has still more symbolic importance. More than half a century after FDR's death most people still don't fully grasp the fact that he was unable to stand, let alone walk, unaided, entirely dependent on his valet for his most basic needs. Determined to be more independent in the privacy of his own cottage, he carefully designed it all on one floor with no threshold barriers in the doorways so that he would need no help moving about in his wheelchair. It was a point of special pride to him that he was able personally to serve the guests he invited to his new cottage; at teatime a toaster was set up on a card table within easy reach in front of the stone fireplace so that he could toast bread, then butter it with a flourish and hand it to his guests without anyone's help. So far as I know, there is no other historic structure anywhere in the United States that specifically commemorates the achievements of a disabled person. As someone who had polio myself, I can imagine few things more inspiring for young disabled people than to be able to see for themselves this eloquent symbol of the heights to which a paraplegic was able to rise in America.

Geoffrey C. Ward

PREFACE

FEW AMERICANS DURING HIS PRESIDENCY WERE EVER AWARE of the fact that Franklin Delano Roosevelt, their charismatic, charming, confident, energetic President, was disabled—paralyzed from the waist down, largely confined to a wheelchair and unable to stand unassisted by braces, crutches, or a combination of the two and, sometimes, one of his strapping, young sons, Jimmy, Elliott, Franklin, Jr., or John.

Yet, it is undeniable that FDR was one of this country's greatest and most beloved leaders during times that held some of the greatest challenges to our society and all that it stands for. And, from those closest to FDR (from Eleanor Roosevelt to Steve Early to Frances Perkins) to later-day, award-winning historians (Doris Kearns Goodwin and Geoffrey Ward), we have learned that the experience of polio and his learning to live with constant pain and crippling disability most likely gave FDR much of the strength, courage, determination, and compassion that made him the great President and leader he was.

During his second term, in all likelihood in anticipation of retirement from the White House and looking ahead to a treasured time of reflection and quietude, writing his memoirs, meeting with world leaders, and editing his presidential papers, FDR started noodling and drawing on the back of an envelope a hideaway cottage to be nestled among his trees, high atop one of Dutchess County's highest hills, with a view through those trees to the Hudson River Valley.

What he designed and built (with the assistance of architect Henry J. Toombs) was a very simple and modest two-bedroom cottage with a great living room and a wonderful open porch. One bedroom was for himself and the other for an aide or manservant to provide the necessary assistance with virtually every detail of his daily living. In keeping with his earlier designs for "Stone Cottage" at Val-Kill and "The Little White House" in Warm Springs, Georgia, his hilltop cottage, Top Cottage as it came to be known, was a very personal and intimate place, one without grandeur or pretension. Apparently he innately knew he needed little of elaborate edifices and grandiose structures: his confidence and presence were sufficient.

Importantly, FDR designed the cottage primarily for himself—as a disabled person, mostly confined to a wheelchair—with lowered windows that allowed views of the outdoors and his favorite trees while sitting, doors without raised saddles or sills, entries to the house without barriers or steps, a ramp from the porch to the grounds beyond, and little conveniences to serve his need for independence, such as an electric outlet near his favorite chair in the living room so that he could personally provide toast to his guests for hors d'oeuvres at tea or cocktail time. As a tool for educating the public about FDR's disability and about the needs of disabled persons and accessibility in general, Top Cottage provides an opportunity of unparalleled proportions.

As the historians and architectural sleuths tell us in the report that follows, FDR never spent a night at Top Cottage. He used it mostly for meetings with other world leaders; strategy sessions with his World War II partner, Winston Churchill; and wonderful family and extended family events such as picnics, teas, and cocktail parties, sometimes with royalty, where he would reign enthusiastically with his ebullient personality and infectious charm.

After FDR's death in 1945, Eleanor gave Top Cottage to their son Elliott, who lived there with his then-wife Faye Emerson. Elliott sold Top Cottage to the Philip S. Potter, Sr., family of Poughkeepsie, along with approximately 118 acres in December 1952. Several times during the Potter family's ownership, efforts were made to sell Top Cottage. For whatever reasons, those efforts were unsuccessful. Top Cottage remained in the Potter family's hands for almost 44 years, a blessing that helped to preserve so much of the original fabric that was essential to its ultimate restoration. We are grateful to all the wonderful Potter family!

In the mid-1990s a more serious effort to sell Top Cottage arose. Key people at the U. S. National Park Service's Roosevelt-Vanderbilt National Historic Sites, particularly Facilities

Manager Henry van Brookhoven, became aware of the efforts and contacted several Roosevelt grandchildren, as well as J. Winthrop Aldrich, Jr., the Deputy Commissioner for Historic Preservation at the New York State Office of Parks, Recreation and Historic Preservation. Many telephone calls later, all with a sense of urgency and crisis (with the potential that Top Cottage would be sold quickly on the open market to the highest bidder), a critical decision was made to approach the Open Space Institute in New York City to see if they could become interested in an effort to save Top Cottage for preservation and ultimately public use. The Open Space Institute, with funding support from the Lila Acheson and DeWitt Wallace Fund for the Hudson Highlands, was developing a strong track record for purchasing and setting aside, for public access and recreational use, tracts of open space or "green" areas along the Hudson River. It was felt that Top Cottage, because of its natural affinity with the main Roosevelt home, Springwood, and with the Eleanor Roosevelt site of Val-Kill, both under active management as National Historic Sites by the National Park Service, would be a likely and critical addition to the public experience at Hyde Park.

An initial meeting was held by two Roosevelt grandchildren and "Winty" Aldrich with the Open Space Institute. The response was not encouraging. Nevertheless, Aldrich and the two grandchildren persisted, even going to the length of proposing a walking trail from the banks of the Hudson River through Springwood to Val-Kill that would continue up Dutchess Hill to Top Cottage from the Val-Kill site, much as Top Cottage was connected to Val-Kill by a narrow, winding, steep cinder road when FDR built and used Top Cottage. That key link of a public-access walking trail from the river all the way to Top Cottage may have been the critical element that finally convinced the Open Space Institute to go to bat with the Wallace Fund for support for the acquisition of Top Cottage. They were successful!

What followed was a lengthy series of negotiations back and forth between the current representative of the Potter family, Owen Potter, who himself had lived at Top Cottage, and Joe Martens, an attorney for the Open Space Institute (now its president). Joe devoted countless hours getting to know the property, walking almost every inch of the property and its borders (including probably a bit of trespassing on some neighbors' lands!), getting surveys done (including locating the boundaries of wetlands on the property), developing maps, and getting title searches done, among other activities. Importantly, Joe also began the sensitive task of contacting adjoining landowners about the possibility of deeding parts of their property to the Open Space Institute so that a walking connection could be reestablished between Val-Kill and Top Cottage. Throughout the process, Joe's patience, thoroughness, professionalism, and persistence kept us all on track and moving forward.

Also deeply involved was Dr. John F. Sears, the executive director of the Franklin and Eleanor Roosevelt Institute (FERI), which was brought in as an existing, capable, tax-exempt, nonprofit organization that would manage the restoration of Top Cottage and hold a lease until such time as Top Cottage could be turned over to the U. S. Government as an important addition to the Roosevelt-Vanderbilt National Historic Sites at Hyde Park.

Ultimately, a deal was struck between Owen Potter and the Open Space Institute. Like all good deals, both sides thought they had gotten most of what they had wanted and given up only a little more than they had planned! But it was all done amicably, and the real winner was Top Cottage.

At the closing, actual title to Top Cottage was taken in the name of the Beaverkill Conservancy, a subsidiary of the Open Space Institute, which then entered into a lease and management agreement with FERI. FERI and various members of the Roosevelt family then committed themselves to a fundraising effort to support the restoration of Top Cottage.

Concurrently, with the generous support of a very few anonymous donors and an anonymous foundation, key Roosevelt family members and Dr. Sears sought out John G. Waite Associates, Architects, a firm of nationally known historic-preservation architects. Jack Waite had been an informal member of a small advisory group, the Top Cottage Committee, that initially evaluated Top Cottage and its architectural and historic importance and made the initial determination that Top Cottage was of such historic and architectural significance that it had to be saved. Other key members of that committee were George Knox, Geoffrey Ward, and grandchildren Kate Roosevelt Whitney and Chris Roosevelt. Knowing, with Jack's good advice, that restoration of such a structure should not and must not be undertaken without thorough, professional research and investigation, FERI commissioned the Waite firm to conduct a historic structure study in August 1996.

The historic structure report resulting from that study, completed in January 1997, reflects the love of the subject, enthusiasm, experience, and professionalism of Jack Waite, his wife, Diana S. Waite (who was the research historian for the project), project manager Clay S. Palazzo, and the entire team at the Waite firm. Largely as a result of those talents and the personal devotion of every member of that team, the report has been the true and proper foundation for the restoration of Top Cottage—and, best of all, it is a great read!

Kate Roosevelt Whitney and Christopher du P. Roosevelt
April 2001

ACKNOWLEDGMENTS

THE TOP COTTAGE HISTORIC STRUCTURE REPORT that formed the basis for this book was completed by John G. Waite Associates, Architects, in 1997. The firm then prepared construction documents for the restoration of Top Cottage during 1998, supervised the restoration construction from 1999 through 2000, and, in conjunction with the Elmore Design Collaborative, prepared a cultural landscape report in 2001. We would like to thank the following groups and individuals for their assistance in the preparation of this book and for their efforts in supporting the restoration of Franklin D. Roosevelt's Top Cottage.

Christopher du Pont Roosevelt and Kate Roosevelt Whitney, individually and as representatives of the Roosevelt Family Committee, provided the vision, leadership, and support necessary for the acquisition, scholarly study, and restoration of Top Cottage. This work would not have been possible without their efforts.

Geoffrey C. Ward, Roosevelt biographer and consultant to the Franklin and Eleanor Roosevelt Institute, was a strong advocate of the restoration process and generously offered advice regarding sources of historical information.

J. Winthrop Aldrich, Deputy Commissioner for Historic Preservation, New York State Office of Parks, Recreation, and Historic Preservation, offered insight and encouragement on both personal and professional levels, throughout the property-acquisition and building-restoration process.

The Open Space Institute, through its land-acquisition affiliate, the Beaverkill Conservancy, purchased Top Cottage from the Potter estate with a $750,000 grant from the Lila Acheson and DeWitt Wallace Fund for the Hudson Highlands, thereby assuring the long-term preservation of the property. In assuming responsibility for fundraising, restoration, and programming, the Franklin and Eleanor Roosevelt Institute became the agent for the immediate work and created an endowment for the future preservation of the site.

William J. vanden Heuvel, Chairman of the Franklin and Eleanor Roosevelt Institute, guided the Institute in its role as guardian of Franklin D. Roosevelt's personal and public legacy through the acquisition and restoration of the President's Hyde Park retreat. John F. Sears, as the Executive Director (retired) of the Franklin and Eleanor Roosevelt Institute, assumed the responsibility for the daily management of projects and grants associated with Top Cottage. His tireless enthusiasm for this work has seen the restoration to a successful completion. Elaine Murphy, Associate Director for Programs of the Franklin and Eleanor Roosevelt Institute, ably assisted John in these efforts.

Congressman Gerald Solomon was instrumental in returning Top Cottage to the original enclave of Roosevelt holdings at Hyde Park by arranging National Park Service acceptance of the restored cottage. Congressman John Sweeney has enthusiastically supported Congressman Solomon's initiative.

The National Park Service has recognized Top Cottage as a National Historic Landmark, largely through the efforts of architectural historian Carolyn Pitts of the History Division, National Park Service. Paul (Skip) Cole, former National Park Service Superintendent for the Roosevelt-Vanderbilt National Historic Sites, encouraged the development of a private-public partnership for the advancement of the Top Cottage project. With Skip's departure for his new role as Superintendent of the Roosevelt Campobello International Park, Bruce D. McKeeman, the Deputy Superintendent for the Roosevelt-Vanderbilt National Historic Sites, and Henry J. van Brookhoven, the Facility Manager for the Roosevelt-Vanderbilt National Historic Sites, continued to support the restoration of Top Cottage through their thoughtful advice and review of the project's development. Sarah Olson, the recently appointed Superintendent for the Roosevelt-Vanderbilt National Historic Sites, has advanced the cordial working relationship established between the Franklin and Eleanor Roosevelt Institute, the Open Space Institute, and the National Park Service.

The director and staff of the Franklin D. Roosevelt Library generously gave their time in support of the restoration research for Top Cottage. Cynthia Koch, Director of the Franklin D. Roosevelt Library, made the resources and staff of the library readily available. George Norton, Facility Manager at the library, shared information and documents at his disposal. Raymond Teichman, Supervisory Archivist at the library, shared his intimate knowledge of the library's collections. The entire library staff offered prompt, professional assistance in response to our many and varied requests.

Owen Potter, as executor of his mother's estate, managed the sale of the Top Cottage property to the Open Space Institute, so that the property could be acquired for the benefit of the public. Owen generously recounted his knowledge of Potter family history at Top Cottage.

Upon learning of the effort to restore the property, William A. Faber, son of the original builder John Faber, came forward with photographs, drawings, newspaper articles, and correspondence regarding the Adams-Faber Construction Company and its participation in the original construction. The Faber family generously donated much of this material to the Franklin D. Roosevelt Library.

The restoration construction was undertaken by Magic General Contracting of Salem, New York. The general contractor was supported by the following subcontractors and consultants: Western Building Restoration, the masonry contractor; Wm. Keith Rich, the electrical contractor; Associated Lightning Rod Company; Eastern State Well Drillers; Phillip Sanzo Plastering; Spectrum Painting and Paper Hanging; Hammond Security; and civil engineers Smith & Mahoney, P.C.

This book was produced with the assistance of the staff at Mount Ida Press: Diana S. Waite, President; Erin Johncox, Editorial Assistant; and Pearl Weisinger, Managing Editor. Constance Timm of the Market Street Group provided the graphic design.

John G. Waite Associates, Architects

Senior Principal
John G. Waite, FAIA

Project Manager
Clay S. Palazzo

Architectural Staff
Douglas G. Bucher
Chelle M. Jenkins
Nancy A. Rankin
Arik W. Mathison
Carrie M. Britt
Michele M. Kohut

Consultants
Elmore Design Collaborative, landscape architect
Mount Ida Press, architectural historian
Preservation Specs Group, specification writer
Schaefer Associates, mechanical, electrical, plumbing engineer

INTRODUCTION

View looking west from Top Cottage, June 1939. Photograph by Von Knoblauch, courtesy of the Franklin D. Roosevelt Library, Hyde Park, New York.

TOP COTTAGE IS AN IMPORTANT HISTORIC BUILDING that is too little known. Planned by President Franklin Delano Roosevelt (with the assistance of Henry J. Toombs, who was listed as associate architect), Top Cottage is unusual as one of the few buildings designed by a U. S. President while in office. In this respect, it is comparable to Poplar Forest, Thomas Jefferson's rural retreat near Lynchburg, Virginia, constructed between 1806 and 1819. Like Poplar Forest, Top Cottage was the expression of a President's clearly thought-out architectural ideas for his own house. Top Cottage also embodied Roosevelt's ideas about the appropriate architectural style for the Hudson Valley and the importance of the valley's Dutch heritage.

Although one of America's first barrier-free buildings when it was constructed in 1938, Top Cottage has received little recognition. As a result of recent research and particularly with the publication of Geoffrey C. Ward's *Closest Companion*, its significance is at last beginning to be realized. FDR's lifelong efforts in overcoming the effects of polio helped to change the attitude of the American public toward people with disabilities, and the home that he designed to accommodate his disability is a symbol of his determination and independence.

Because of its significance, Top Cottage was acquired by the Open Space Institute and leased to the Franklin and Eleanor Roosevelt Institute (FERI) in 1996. As the first step in adopting a disciplined approach to the restoration of Top Cottage, FERI commissioned John G. Waite Associates, Architects, to prepare a historic structure report for the building. This book has been developed from that report.

A team of architects, architectural historians, building conservators, and decorative-arts specialists, under the direction of Clay S. Palazzo, project manager for the restoration, produced a historic structure report on Top Cottage. The activities involved in the preparation of the historic structure report may be broadly described as surveying, recording, and analysis. All of the existing building fabric was examined to determine its date of origin and to assess its current condition. A permanent graphic and written record of the building was compiled as part of the process.

Researching the Franklin Delano Roosevelt papers and other contemporary archival materials and gathering the recollections of those associated with Top Cottage made it possible to assemble a history of the building's design, construction, and subsequent alterations. Careful measurement of the building resulted in the creation of an accurate set of measured floor plans, sections, and elevations. At the same time, a detailed architectural description of the entire structure, including all exterior features and room-by-room descriptions of the interior, was compiled. All of the constituent parts of the building's fabric were examined to determine the nature of physical problems that had occurred over the decades, as well as the existing conditions and the scope of needed repairs. A preliminary investigation of paint layers proved invaluable in dating various elements and in gaining an understanding of the original decorative schemes.

A historic structure report is essential in developing a responsible stewardship program based on the adoption of a curatorial approach to the problems of maintenance, restoration, and reuse of a historic building. Just as an art conservator should not intervene in the life of an artistic artifact before obtaining a thorough knowledge of its history, significance, and composition, so those engaged in the preservation of buildings and landscapes should proceed only from a basis of knowledge. Too often in the past, the cultural integrity of buildings and their settings has been compromised by approaches to restoration grounded on personal whims, willful romanticism, inadequate research, and expedient notions of repair.

Assembling the details of Top Cottage's history and current condition in a historic structure report established a benchmark that not only provided a guide for the recently completed restoration work but will also furnish future generations with a clear picture of what was found in our time. This approach will help ensure the long-term preservation of Top Cottage in the form intended by Franklin D. Roosevelt.

CONSTRUCTION HISTORY

President Franklin D. Roosevelt showing Mayor Fiorello LaGuardia Top Cottage under construction, August 7, 1938. Courtesy of the Franklin D. Roosevelt Library, Hyde Park, New York.

SOON AFTER HIS ELECTION to his first term as President, Franklin D. Roosevelt realized that Springwood, his mother's home, did not provide him with sufficient privacy during his visits to Hyde Park. The problem was, he wrote, that

> I found that on my trips to Hyde Park from Washington, it was almost impossible to have any time to myself in the big house. The trips were intended primarily for a holiday—a chance to read, to sort my books, and to make plans for roads, tree plantings, etc. This was seemingly impossible because of
>
> (a) visitors in the house
> (b) telephone calls
> (c) visits from Dutchess County neighbors
> (d) visits from various people who, knowing I was going to be in Hyde Park, thought it an opportune time to seek some interview.

"Therefore," Roosevelt continued, "I began talking about building a small place to go to escape the mob."[1]

The property that the President selected for his retreat included Dutchess Hill, one of the highest points in the county; from the summit magnificent views extended west across the Hudson River to the Catskill and Shawangunk mountains, and to the east there were glimpses of Connecticut and Massachusetts.[2] It was an area that Roosevelt knew well, for he had roamed its woods as a boy. He had sometimes taken Margaret (Daisy) Suckley, his neighbor and cousin, for long drives through the back roads of Dutchess County, and they had stopped to talk on the crest of Dutchess Hill. In 1937 he was finally able to purchase the property.[3]

In a memorandum that he drafted in 1942, Roosevelt recalled that his initial thoughts about developing the site had been very modest. There would be "only a terrace on the top of Dutchess Hill-in what formerly was known as 'the Chestnut Woods'," he wrote; the terrace would include only "a lean-to shelter large enough to go under in case it rained," with an attached "fireplace and kitchenette."[4]

With Daisy Suckley, though, Roosevelt discussed more ambitious plans, even before he had purchased the land. In September 1935, after one of their country drives, she wrote him about his plans for what she had come to call Our Hill: "Are you going to put up any kind of log cabin?" she asked. "It would be such a perfect place for you to write your detective stories, when you can get around to them." She had also mailed him a sketch of the proposed cottage.[5] But Roosevelt's response, written in October, indicates that he already had a local Dutch vernacular aesthetic in mind:

> You said once "log cabin"—But I don't think so—even John Burroughs's—across the [Hudson] River—looked very artificial. They all do unless they are a hundred years old—& then they are full of...crawly bugs—No, I think a one-story fieldstone two room house—just like the one William (or was it Gerardus?) Beekman lived in (without doubt) when he (or they) first went to Esopus— one with very thick walls to protect us against the Indians and a little porch on the West side. Do you mind—*then*—if I tell you fairy stories till it gets very late?
>
> Yes I know the house below Poughkeepsie very well—but it has been added to—and some day you shall do me a water-color of the house on the Hill—In the Old Houses book there are some pictures that are a little like what I mean—[6]

In her sketch Daisy Suckley had evidently shown a cultivated landscape around the cottage, for Roosevelt also remarked that "Yes—I like it very much—and I can understand the garden if I translate the flowers in part at least in terms of trees." He also mentioned a porch where the two of them would sit "after sundown and look at the Catskills and all the things in between."[7]

Roosevelt made some sketches of the house during 1937, and Daisy Suckley was preparing some drawings as well: "I have the plans here, and pictures of the house too! And perhaps I shall *have* to take them down to show to the architect! Who knows?"[8] On September 21 she wrote enthusiastically to Roosevelt, who had just embarked on a campaign trip in the West: "That plan you made has tremendous possibilities—I wonder if you have thought out any details—such as where the front door is—where the fireplace—What to do with that 3-sided space in the back!! I can think of lots of things! In fact, I have the furniture *placed*! Subject to change!"[9] The plan that Roosevelt had shown her may have been very similar to the one that he had sketched in one of his stamp catalogs that had a "3-sided space in the back" and failed to indicate the location of the front door or the fireplace.[10]

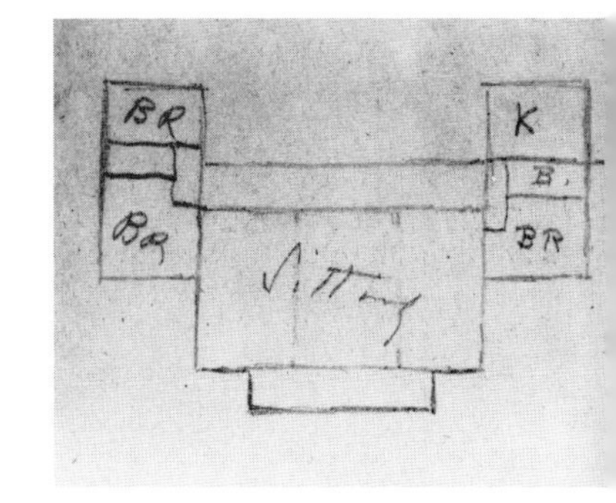

Sketch plan for Top Cottage by President Franklin D. Roosevelt, found in his 1928 *Standard Postage and Stamps Catalogue.* Courtesy of the Franklin D. Roosevelt Library, Hyde Park.

As Roosevelt was busy campaigning in October, Daisy Suckley daydreamed about the cottage: "I was some 12 miles from here, on a Hill, sitting before a fire also—very near the corner of a sofa. Someone was reading aloud—two french windows on each side of the fireplace, opened onto a porch . . . Across the length of the back of the room were book shelves right up to the ceiling—In the middle, a door opening onto a terrace facing East!"[11]

induced by the open fire, I don't know —
I was some 12 miles from here, on a
Hill, sitting before a fire also - very near
the corner of a sofa - Someone was
reading aloud - two french windows
on each side of the fire place, opened
onto a porch - Outside - it was dark
under the trees & a wind rustled what
remained of autumn leaves — Across
the length of the back of the room were
book shelves right up to the ceiling - In
the middle, a door opening onto a
terrace facing East!

Sunday night. I made a quite perfect (?)
floor plan - but suddenly realize that the
chimney will stick up in a very queer
place

It wont do at all!

View from the south

How's This?

other wing behind

road

Kitchen porch

view from the west

Sketch elevations for Top Cottage by Margaret Suckley, 1937. Courtesy of Wilderstein Preservation.

She prepared a new drawing of the cottage for him: "I made quite a perfect floorplan—but suddenly realize that the chimney will stick up in a very queer place," she told the President. Her plan maintained the basic arrangement that Roosevelt proposed in his stamp-catalog sketch: a central block with a porch extending across its west facade and two smaller wings set back from the central block. Her plan placed the kitchen and other service areas in the south wing, and a large bedroom, with a fireplace, filled the full width of the north wing. In one elevation she illustrated the problem with placing the chimney on the west side of the central block (her drawing may even show it between the two French doors she mentioned) and noted on the drawing that "It won't do at all!" She then sketched a second elevation in which there were two inside-end chimneys rising above the roof ridge. She positioned a driveway along the east side of the house, where it is today.[12]

In conversations and correspondence FDR and Daisy continued to revise the arrangements at the cottage during the fall of 1937. Her letters indicate how much the scheme was still evolving but also show that many features were already determined. "I've been studying the plans" for the cottage, she wrote the President,

> & longing to discuss certain variations from mine—I think that 'porch recess' is a splendid idea—also those little corner fireplaces—in fact I must confess that it all seems *better* than mine!
>
> You have made the wings much bigger than I, & we've both planned for lots of book space! Do you think it might be a good idea to have windows on the north & south ends of the living room? There would be such lovely vistas to look through!
>
> Just one thing *really* worries me! And that is the angle of the attic floor!! The trunks will be continually coasting down to the eaves . . . But that is probably just a minor detail which can be easily arranged! I'll bring all these plans down to W. We can argue about them, & I can be just as facetious as I wish—You won't mind—will you!

"I've spent ages on the plans," she continued, "& *think* I have the south wing perfected. We'll see if you agree, or if I'm all wrong! It's all done to scale too!"[13]

At some point that fall Roosevelt relocated the kitchen to the north wing and the bedrooms to the south wing. Daisy had refined the arrangement of the bedroom wing, and during a visit to Washington, she wrote of her expectations that she would be sharing those quarters:

> But, upstairs in my bag, are plans for a Dutch house—just as comfortable & convenient and cheerful—but surrounded by trees and distance and peace and a glow of an open fire. Did you think the south wing plan good—really? Of course, the middle room has the bigger closet—and the eastern room is the larger—But, you see, the occupant of the middle room would probably spend a *lot* of time in the eastern room & she *needs* a big closet! How is this for a name: "O.

House on O.H." and for that entrance, there could be quite a large glass square room which could be used in the mornings as a sun porch—[14]

Another letter from Daisy, written on December 5, 1937, hints that FDR may now have been thinking of scaling the project back to a more modest scheme:

What an excellent idea, for you to have a "Retreat" on the top of your wooded hill—I have worked out a possible plan which would allow of future improvement & enlarging—& would lay pipes where they might be most useful—Doors, also, in three directions—

"Exploration of the Terrain" would show where a cellar could be dug, without disturbing the most important rocks—Perhaps you would need only a small cellar under part of it—[15]

In any case, Roosevelt intended the building mainly for seasonal use, from spring through fall. "This cottage will probably be unoccupied most of the time in the winter," he wrote late in 1938 as construction was nearing completion: "And if occupied it would only be for a few hours or for a day or for a Saturday-Sunday at the most."[16]

In his 1942 memorandum Roosevelt provided an explanation of how the plan had evolved. The scheme for a simple terrace and lean-to with attached fireplace and kitchenette, he wrote, had "gradually" grown,

first into a large terrace and a large living room which could be used in colder weather; thence into a plan for a small cottage, and, finally, into the adopted plan of a wide porch, a living room, two bedrooms and a bath, and a wing large enough for a pantry, kitchen and double bedroom. This was called for in order to have someone take care of the place and prevent theft, etc.

I did not personally expect to occupy the bedrooms but thought that they could be used by the children in case any of them wished to move there for a holiday or for the summer.

The house was, therefore, designed by me and the detailed plans were worked up by Henry Toombs.[17]

President Roosevelt and Architect Henry Toombs

When Henry Toombs began to draw up the detailed plans for the President's cottage early in 1938, he and Roosevelt had already been working together for well over a decade. During the mid-1920s Toombs had met Eleanor Roosevelt and her friends Nancy Cook and Marion Dickerman at the home of Caroline O'Day, who was Toombs's cousin and was then serving in Congress as a representative-at-large from New York. The four women, Toombs wrote, had "become fast friends," and the occasion of Toombs's visit was "the scene of an excited discussion of a proposed cottage, financed by the four to be built on FDR's property near Hyde Park on Hudson." The women had been planning the cottage themselves, with Nancy Cook as "their chief designer." Now they were confronted with what Toombs termed "a classic, if minor, architectural dilemma": how could they "get a stair up without running it into the chimney." Barely realizing that this was the opportunity to secure his first independent commission, Toombs recalled, "I... rushed to their rescue....The transition of their status from that of delightful ladies being architecturally advised to that of clients was, as I remember, swiftly ... made." This project was the cottage that became known as Val-Kill.[18]

Margaret Suckley with Fala on the west porch of Top Cottage, June 2, 1941. Photograph by Franklin D. Roosevelt, courtesy of the Franklin D. Roosevelt Library, Hyde Park.

Toombs's engagement as the architect for Val-Kill was, he later wrote, a "heady experience for me." He was then a "young architect," just 28 years old and "only recently the possessor of a very junior job in the most honored firm of McKim, Mead and White." He had earned a bachelor's degree in architecture in 1921 and a master's in 1923, both from the University of Pennsylvania, worked in Philadelphia as a draftsman for architect Paul Cret, and recently returned from two years of study abroad. His new job in New York was "vastly important to me for I was happy in believing architecture was a great profession," although, he frankly admitted, "My inexperience was equalized by my enthusiasm."[19]

Toombs had daydreamed at work about "how a junior draftsman could get a client," and with Val-Kill he now had his chance. He developed the design and the working drawings after work. It was, he recalled many years later, "the hardest job I've ever done." He convinced two friends, architects Joseph Kellum Smith and William J. Creighton, to stamp the drawings, since Toombs did not yet have an architectural license. Franklin Roosevelt took on the role of advisor and contractor for the cottage. Toombs was enormously grateful to the Roosevelts for the opportunity that the design of Val-Kill had presented: "I do not recall that any question was raised by my clients as to my experience or competence. This was fortunate. I was a young fellow they were pleased to help. An interest truly characteristic of the Roosevelts. Maybe it wasn't shrewd but somebody always has to take a chance with a young fellow. They bore the burden easily."[20]

Henry Toombs displaying a model of Top Cottage. Reprinted, by permission, from the *Atlanta Journal-Constitution*, October 16, 1938.

Toombs believed that the creation of the Val-Kill cottage was an "absorbing interest" for Franklin Roosevelt and a "relieving" one as well, turning his mind away from the rigors of dealing with infantile paralysis. Toombs wrote, "truly" Roosevelt "loved to build, and had persistent interest in the details of building."[21] Toombs elaborated on another occasion:

> I would say that the President had a definite architectural sense. He quickly grasps the implications of plans and elevations and, while his sketches from the point of view of a trained architect are rather crude, they nevertheless show a sense of proportion.
>
> Most of the sketches which I have and which he has done in connection with Warm Springs or various houses are rough, free-hand outlines. It is pertinent to note that in explaining a plan the President more often than not, and like a trained architect, takes a pencil to sketch what he is explaining. This is, I would say, habitual with him. . . .
>
> So far as I know he has never used any regular drafting equipment, generally putting things to a scale by using an ordinary foot rule, but the drawings which he would so make are definitely more adept than those which would be made by the average layman.[22]

Toombs enjoyed working with Franklin Roosevelt. In 1926 two other significant commissions from the Roosevelts followed the work at Val-Kill: the James Roosevelt Memorial Library in Hyde Park, named for FDR's father and financed by his mother, and the Val-Kill Shop for Eleanor Roosevelt.[23]

Meanwhile, FDR had become involved with the Georgia Warm Springs Foundation, and, as Toombs explained, "its gradual development into a significant medical institution, its policies, medical progress and physical plant and environment were a continuing care and interest to him." During the late 1920s and the 1930s Toombs worked with Roosevelt on construction projects at Warm Springs. "Each building as it was undertaken, was a matter for his particular interest and decision," Toombs wrote. "He concerned himself with the plans in detail; was quick in understanding, and fertile in suggestion." Roosevelt purchased land at Warm Springs in 1926, and Toombs collaborated with him on the design of a cottage, whose exterior FDR had "wanted to follow the lines of an old antebellum house in a neighboring town." This house was built in 1932 and later became known as the Little White House. A garage and a guest house were also constructed.[24]

Toombs drafted an essay entitled "Doing Architecture with F. D. R." about Roosevelt's architectural interests. Toombs's analysis of Roosevelt's stylistic preferences for buildings at Warm Springs applies as well to Top Cottage. "His taste was for the simple," Toombs recalled. "He liked the word 'homey.' He was loath to accept anything which in appearance suggested sophistication, richness in detail, or elaborateness." "This love of simple surroundings," Toombs wrote, "a bright fire, always a cluttered room of books, papers, a few ship models & odds & ends, sometimes a curious but seldom a really fine thing, formed the unstudied background he liked to live in. I cannot imagine either he or Mrs. Roosevelt employing a decorator 'to do' a room or house for them. They would use what they had, add without much bother other necessaries. The results were homelike, personal, unpretending, livable."[25]

Meanwhile, in 1927 Toombs had helped Roosevelt with an "odd job" at Hyde Park. The assignment was "to surround the walls of a little room in the first floor of his mother's house with carefully arranged cabinets to house his collection of papers." Toombs recalled that "We went to considerable trouble to get the cabinets and shelves the exact sizes for different categories of papers" and that "after it was completed he spent much time in working there with his collections."[26]

Toombs later viewed this small commission as a possible link to another project in which Roosevelt needed help with his much larger collections—the Franklin D. Roosevelt Library at Hyde Park. As the two men began planning the library in the fall of 1937, Roosevelt loaned Toombs books on the "Hudson River Dutch tradition." He urged Toombs to "study them" and proposed "that we stick to that tradition." Toombs prepared some preliminary designs and obtained some construction estimates, but in 1939 the project was turned over to the Procurement Division of the Treasury Department. Toombs first learned from newspaper stories that he was no longer being consulted on the project.[27] Nevertheless, Toombs maintained a friendly relationship with the President. Toombs and his wife Tanya were guests at the White

Section and plan for Top Cottage, sketched by President Roosevelt on back of a Budget Bureau memorandum dated February 3, 1938. Courtesy of the Franklin D. Roosevelt Library, Hyde Park.

House in 1941, and Eleanor Roosevelt befriended Tanya and their son, Michael, while Toombs served in the war.[28]

Toombs also enjoyed an ongoing, easy friendship with Nancy Cook and Marion Dickerman, and they frequently helped him with professional contacts and with insights into the President's expectations and dreams. Toombs later shared with them a common concern for Roosevelt's architectural legacy. In 1961 Toombs returned to Marion Dickerman an original drawing of Top Cottage that Roosevelt had sketched in 1938, and she later presented it to the Presidential Library in Hyde Park, where it remains today. Toombs's papers are preserved in the Georgia Department of Archives and History, and they include valuable documentation on Roosevelt's architectural projects, including Top Cottage.[29]

Designing the Cottage

Top Cottage was the third of three houses in which, as Toombs put it, FDR had "helped as architect." All were "small houses for occasional use." At Warm Springs and Top Cottage the functions of the living and dining rooms were combined. Toombs called the President "an early enthusiast over that idea—liked its simplicity, informality and lack of pretension."[30]

In the drafts of "Doing Architecture with F.D.R.," Toombs related how he first became involved with Top Cottage: "This project I did not know of until [Roosevelt] showed me the floor plan which he had studied out and wanted me to translate into working drawings." The President had prepared "sketches, plans, and section," and Toombs noted that they had been drawn "on pieces of linen-backed paper of lasting quality." He was not certain whether this style of presentation had been "suggested by the President's historical sense, or by one of his circle of admiring friends." Roosevelt's floor plan, dated February 1938, was reproduced and widely published later that year when a public announcement was made about the house.[31]

Toombs probably saw these drawings for the first time during a weekend meeting with the President in mid-February 1938. In January Roosevelt had asked whether Toombs

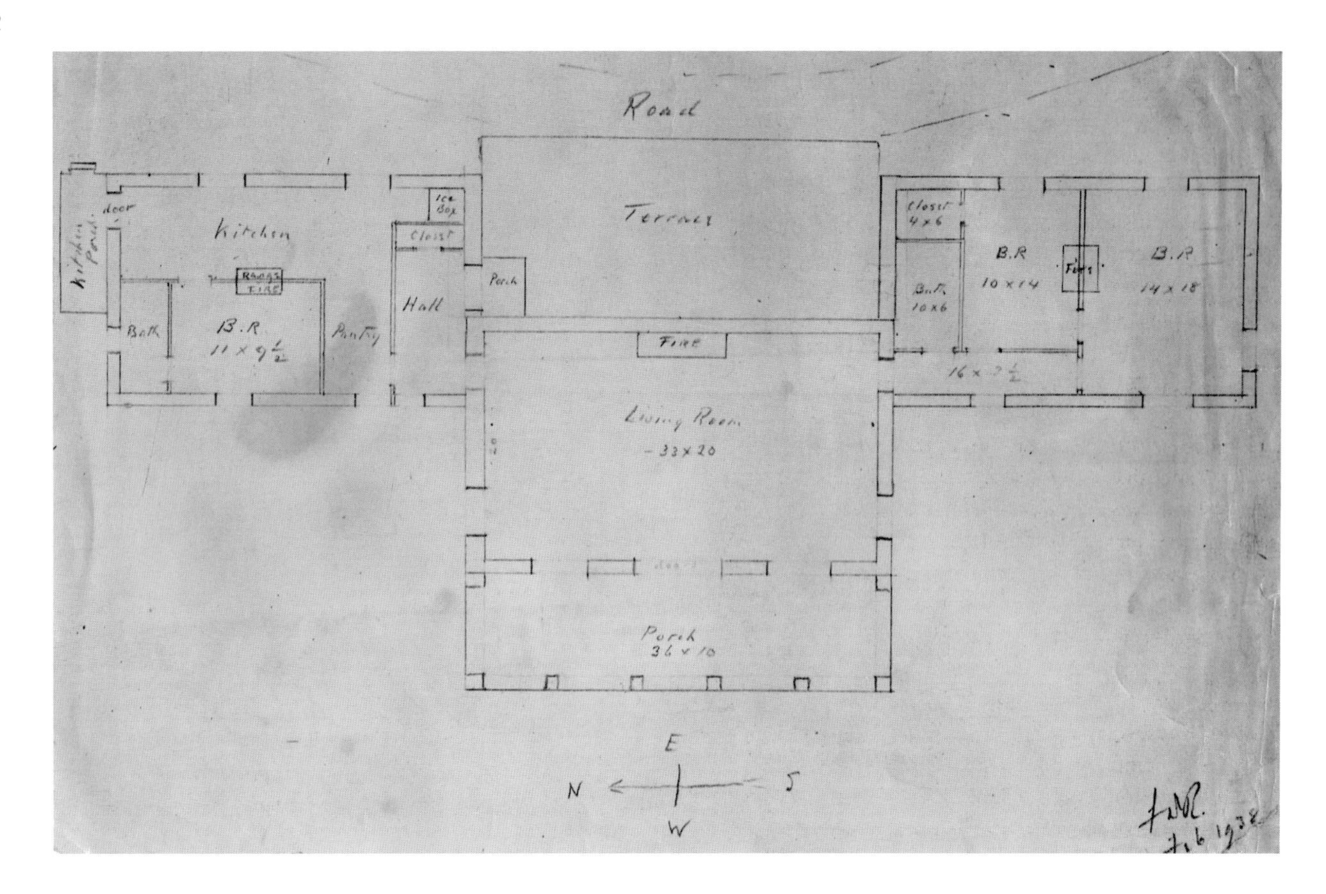

Floor plan of Top Cottage by President Roosevelt, February 1938. Courtesy of the Georgia Department of Archives and History, Atlanta.

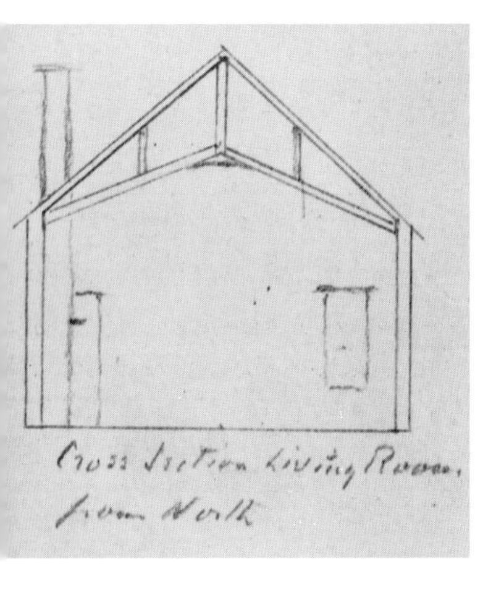

Section drawn by President Roosevelt, February 1938. Courtesy of the Franklin D. Roosevelt Library, Hyde Park.

was "coming North soon." Toombs replied that he was planning to be in New York around the middle of February, as soon as he had finished the drawings for a Federal Reserve bank and for new buildings at Warm Springs but promised that "If for any reason this is not soon enough," he would "strain something and come sooner."[32]

Toombs had planned this trip in order to meet with Dorothy and George Backer, friends of Roosevelt who were then living at Oyster Bay, Long Island, but planning to build a house in Hyde Park. In the fall of 1937 Nancy Cook and Marion Dickerman had encouraged the Backers to engage Toombs as their architect. "That was a magnificent piece of press-agenting you did in my behalf," Toombs wrote in a note thanking the two women, "It quite took my breath away." He thought that it "would certainly be fun to do a house for them" near Val-Kill and called the Backers "grand people." "As you know," he continued, "doing a house is fun for me anyway, but it is particularly so when you like the people." During this trip Toombs had visited at Val-Kill with Nancy Cook and Missy LeHand, Roosevelt's private secretary.[33]

Early in 1938 FDR had been making inquiries about the actual construction of the cottage. In response to a request from the President, John Cutter, a Boston contractor, sent a circular on a patented "trick fire-place," some sort of "contraption to go in a fire-place to increase [its] heating capacity." This letter probably did not reach Roosevelt until the February meeting with Toombs. Nevertheless, the two men must have spoken about the possibility of using such a fireplace at the cottage, for Roosevelt forwarded the literature to Toombs on February 24 along with a note commenting that "I agree with you that it is doubtful if we should try anything like that in such a big room."[34]

In his thank-you note to Cutter, also dated February 24, Roosevelt mentioned that he was passing the material on to Henry Toombs, and this comment suggests that Roosevelt had by then formally asked Toombs to begin work on the cottage. The President would later explain that what he had done "was to draw the plan and Henry Toombs did the real job. I have to be careful about that because I haven't the license to practice architecture in this State."[35]

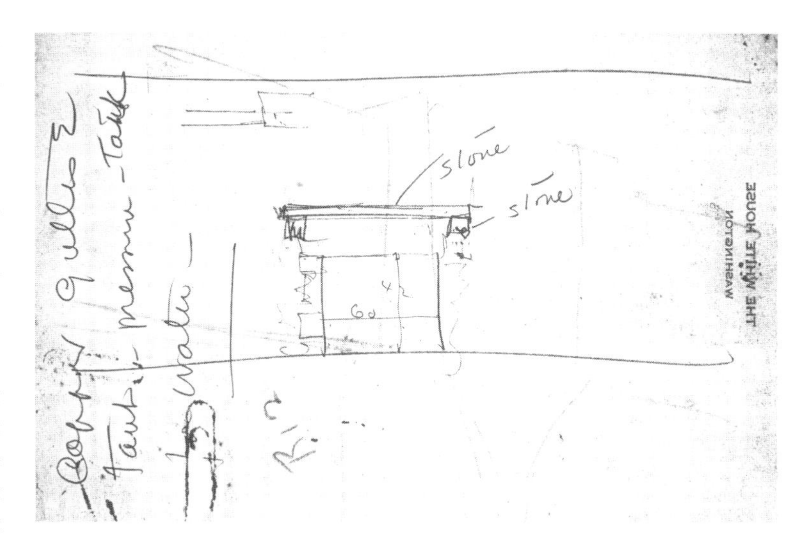

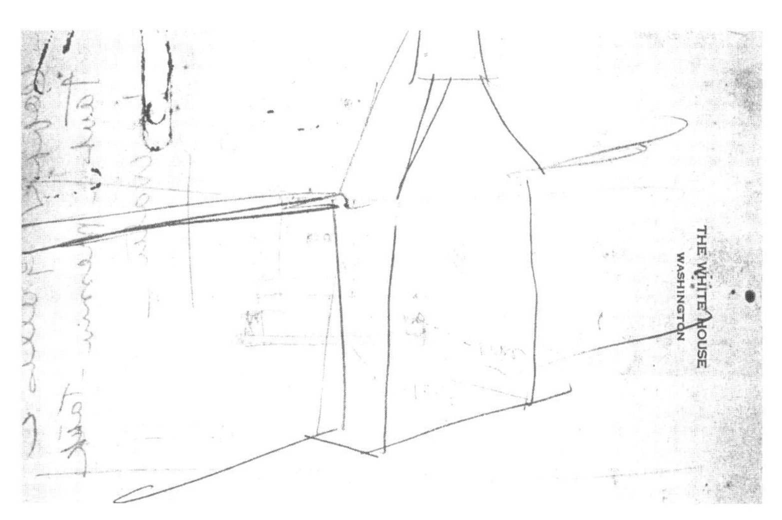

Sketch for fireplace in living room by Henry J. Toombs. Courtesy of the Georgia Department of Archives and History, Atlanta.

Sketch of chimney mass by Henry J. Toombs. Courtesy of the Georgia Department of Archives and History, Atlanta.

While Cutter was not enthusiastic about the patent fireplace, he did strongly recommend insulation. Cutter prepared what he called "an extremely crude sketch representing an 'end-on' view peak of a building," in order to illustrate that insulation should be placed "between the ceiling of the room and the attic floor." He recommended using bats of rock wool or similar substance "cut to fit the space between the floor or ceiling joists." He explained that insulation would keep the room "10 degrees cooler in summer," make it much easier to heat in cold weather, but not be "an expensive job." Cutter told Roosevelt that "The louvers, which you talked about placing at either end of the building, will not keep the building cool, according to my experience." Cutter's drawing and text indicate that the cottage was to be a one-story structure.[36]

Toombs was scheduled to meet again with the President on March 31 in Warm Springs. Eleanor Roosevelt was also in Georgia at this time, and Frank Neely, the head of Rich's Department Store in Atlanta, had invited Mrs. Roosevelt to visit his farm, where Toombs had designed the house and grounds. Neely, who had met Toombs through Mrs. Roosevelt and Nancy Cook, now told the First Lady that "aside from our pleasure in your visit it would add prestige to Henry's work which he is trying to establish in Atlanta." Mrs. Roosevelt not only accepted the Neelys' invitation but also paid Toombs an important tribute by featuring him in her "My Day" column of March 30. She cited his designs for Val-Kill, the local library at Hyde Park, and Warm Springs and called Toombs "an artist to his finger tips."[37]

Meanwhile, after the February meeting in Hyde Park with the President, Toombs had prepared a set of ⅛-inch-scale drawings for the cottage. They included an east elevation, a west elevation with a five-bay-wide center section, an alternate west elevation with a wide center doorway and flanking single windows, a north elevation, and a section looking south through the center of the building showing the basement and trusses over the living room. He also prepared a plan of the first floor, in which the bedrooms, located in the south wing, were arranged quite differently from what Roosevelt had shown in his February drawing. In Toombs's plan the larger bedroom had two closets on the east wall, which created a deep recess around the east window, and the bathroom was placed in between the bedrooms. On March 24 Toombs drew up an alternate bedroom-wing plan, which closely followed Roosevelt's original scheme, and this was the one used in the bidding documents. In this scheme Toombs also tucked a corner fireplace into the servants' bedroom, located in the north wing.[38]

An envelope imprinted with the name of the Georgia Warm Springs Foundation carries what are probably Toomb's notes from the March 31 meeting with the President. Some items were simply listed on the envelope ("Driveway," "Heating," "Electricity," "Gas for cooking," "Elec. fixtures," "All plaster interior," "windows small"), but other notes seem to reflect Roosevelt's responses. A "no" followed notations about air conditioning and wide-board floors, while "yes" followed notes about a septic tank and "linoleum on B.R. Flrs."

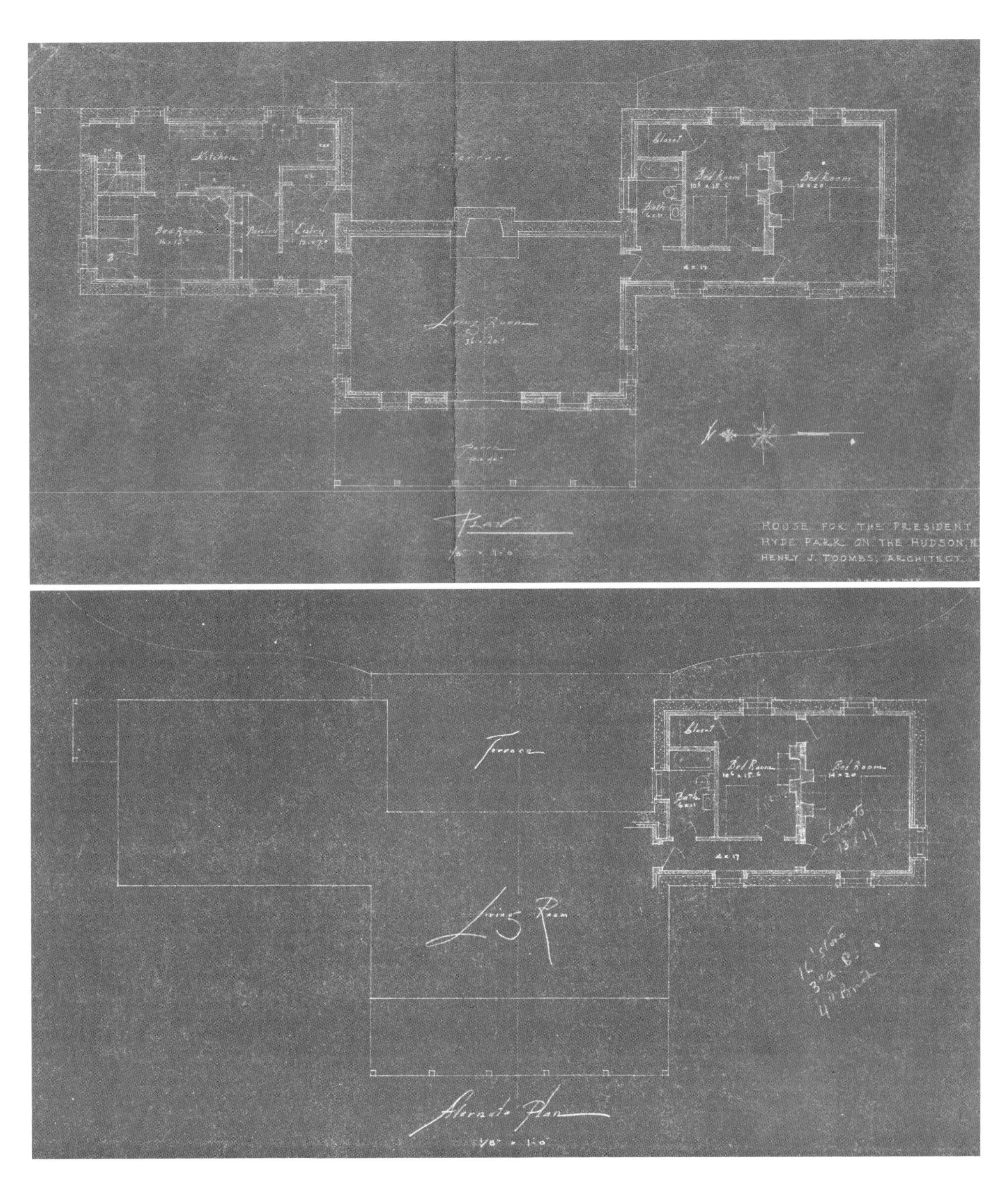

Above: First-floor plan by Henry J. Toombs showing stairs to the basement in the northwest corner of the kitchen (112) and fireplaces in rooms 104, 105, and 109, March 22, 1938. Courtesy of the Georgia Department of Archives and History, Atlanta.

Below: Alternate plan for south wing by Henry J. Toombs, March 22, 1938. Courtesy of the Georgia Department of Archives and History, Atlanta.

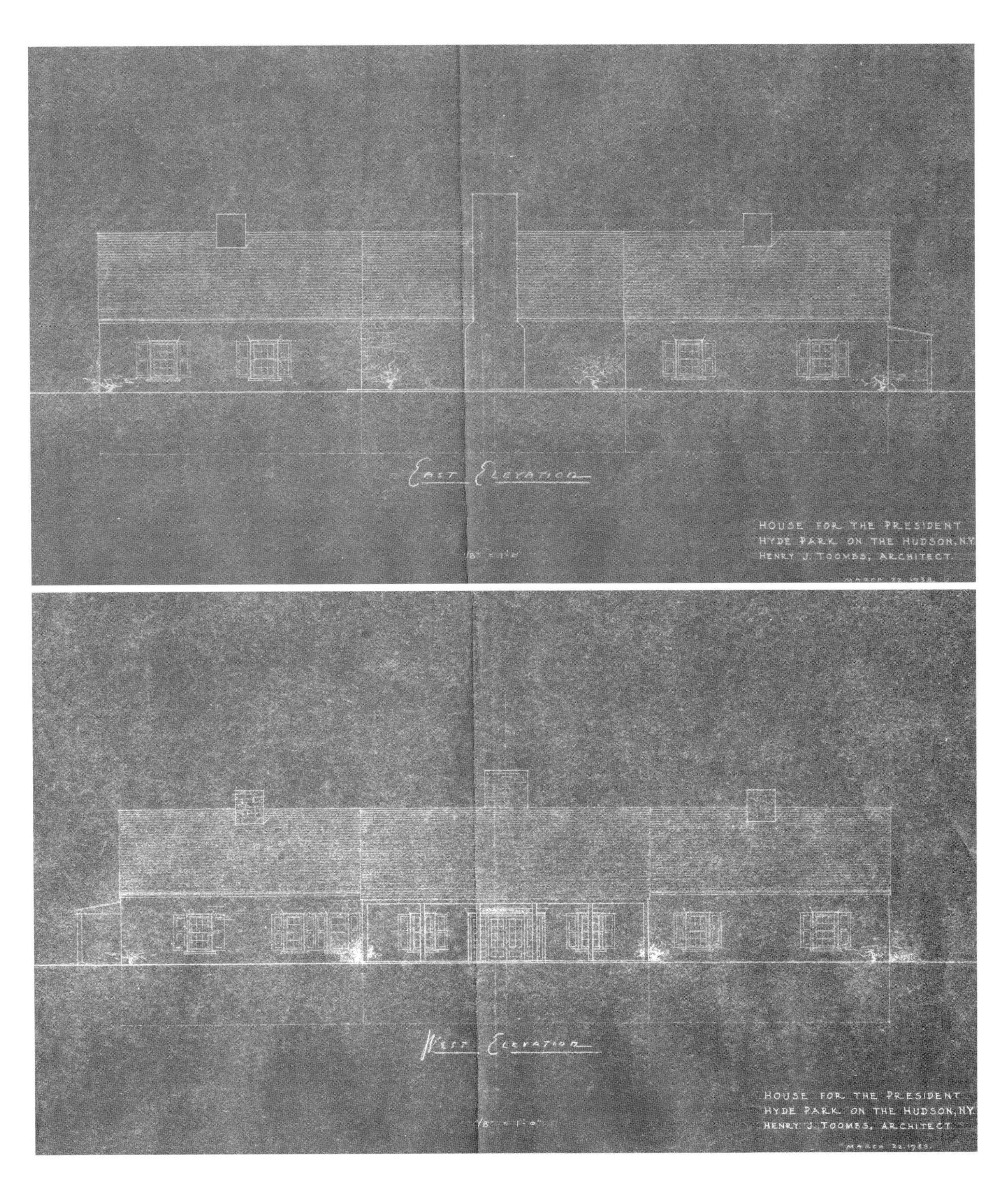

Above: East elevation by Henry J. Toombs, March 22, 1938. Courtesy of the Georgia Department of Archives and History, Atlanta.

Below: West elevation by Henry J. Toombs, March 22, 1938. Courtesy of the Georgia Department of Archives and History, Atlanta.

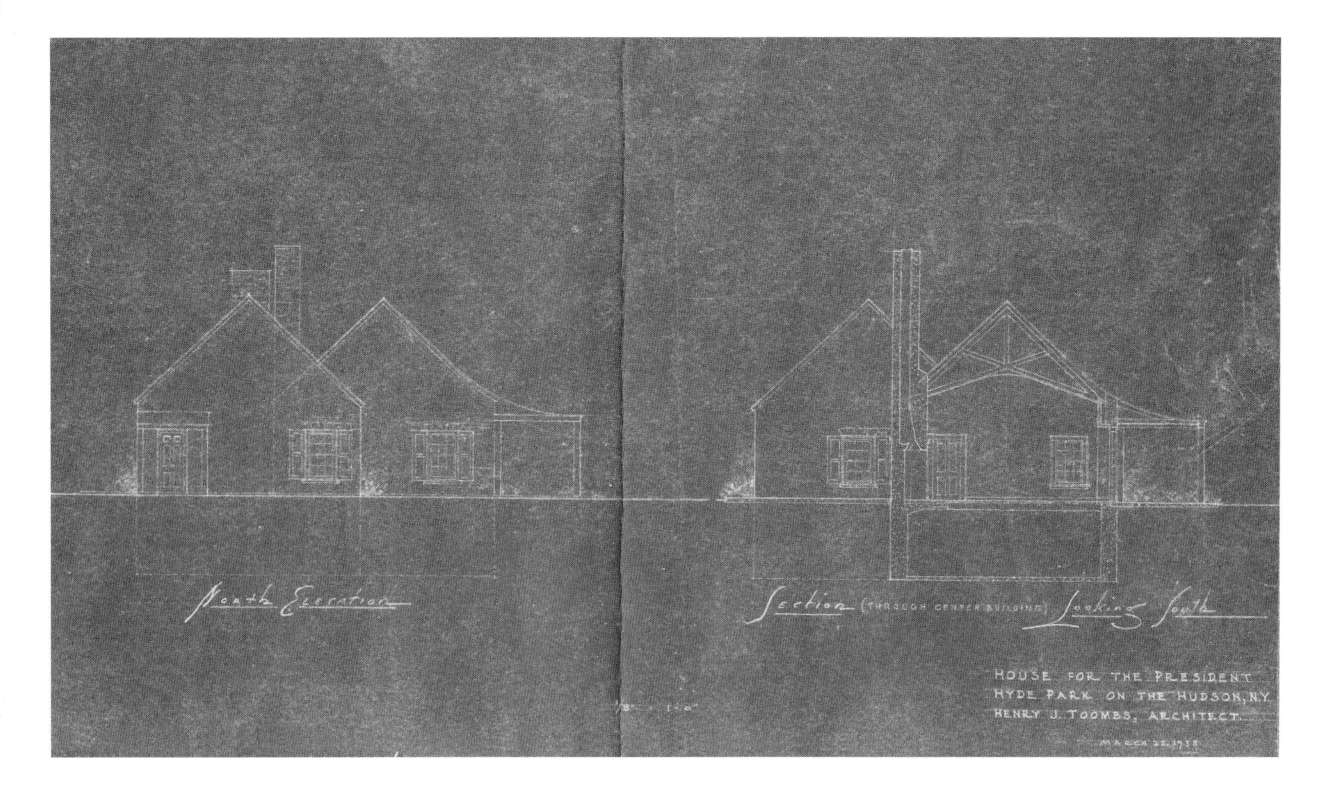

North elevation and section looking south by Henry J. Toombs, March 22, 1938. Courtesy of the Georgia Department of Archives and History, Atlanta.

Toombs had evidently asked about whether the "Stone fireplace" should have a mantel, and the reply was that it should be of stone. All of the electrical wiring was to be "Conduit wiring." There were several notes on the envelope about contractors located in Poughkeepsie and others involved with the Poughkeepsie and Rhinebeck post offices, but no specific names were listed. There was also reference to a stone quarry at Saugerties, located on the west side of the Hudson River above Kingston.[39]

Soon after this consultation with the President, Toombs did more work on the drawings for the cottage. On April 7 he telegraphed Roosevelt, who was then back at the White House, that the plans were being "forwarded by air mail." On April 11 Toombs told Nancy Cook that "The President is apparently going ahead with his house and I am to have the drawings ready in about a month." She, however, warned Toombs that he had not understood the schedule: "The President is killing,—I don't think he can wait a month for the drawings. I think he hopes to get it started in that time."[40]

Toombs's next task was to find contractors who could build the cottage at a reasonable cost and supply the "several bids" that the President had requested. Locating qualified contractors was not an easy task, Toombs explained, since he was "somewhat out of touch with that locality"; furthermore, what he needed was bidders "who are used to doing small work, as a larger contractor would probably not be interested, or would be too expensive." Toombs followed up on leads that the President had provided and called upon friends for suggestions. He explained that he was "designing a small house for the President on his property in Hyde Park," and these letters may be his first public reference of his role in the project.[41]

The President had suggested that the firms that were erecting the post offices at Poughkeepsie and Rhinebeck might be interested in bidding on the cottage. Louis A. Simon, Supervising Architect of the Procurement Division of the U. S. Treasury Department in Washington, was contacted for help in locating these contractors. Simon provided the name of the contractors for the Poughkeepsie building (Silverblatt and Lasker, of New York) but explained that the Rhinebeck post office was not yet under contract. Toombs inquired of Nancy Cook whether John Eylers, of Poughkeepsie, "would be a good person to bid" and also asked her for the names of other local contractors. Cook, in turn, called upon an

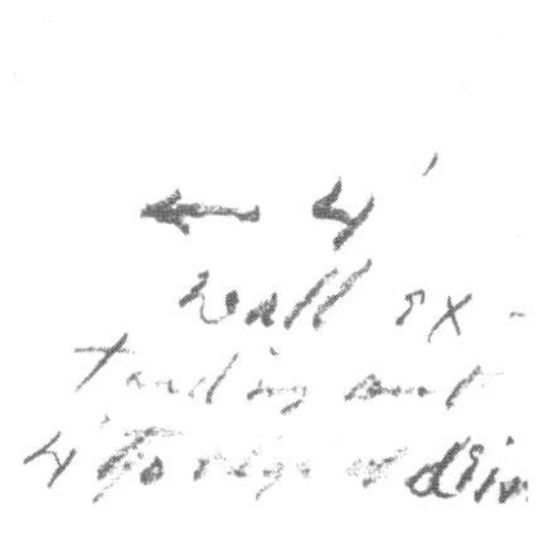

President Roosevelt's sketch of the south elevation of the north wing with its proposed Dutch porch. Courtesy of the Georgia Department of Archives and History, Atlanta.

acquaintance in Poughkeepsie for suggestions, explaining that "Henry is trying to get as many names of contractors in and around Poughkeepsie as possible." Her letter evidently did not turn up any prospects, since she subsequently told Toombs that the only builder she knew was Eylers, whom she liked and trusted and who "always gets a good mason, Mr. Matthews, who is fine." She was "more than pleased with him than any one else we have had." Toombs's letter to Henry T. Hackett, Roosevelt's Poughkeepsie-based attorney, yielded the names of only masons, not general contractors, in Hyde Park.[42]

Once again Toombs decided to combine a trip to see the Backers with a meeting with the President. He asked the White House for an appointment on April 27 and received a reply from Missy LeHand that Roosevelt would be "delighted to see you" then. The President had been working on the drawings that Toombs had sent earlier in the month and now promised to return them "with suggestions in a day or two."[43]

True to his word, Roosevelt dispatched a three-page letter two days later, on April 21. It was filled with specific comments about Toombs's drawings. The President had also drawn two sketches to amplify his text. He was careful to introduce his eight-point list of comments with a positive opening statement: "A careful check-up on the excellent plans for the cottage on top of the hill discloses the following."[44]

Roosevelt's major concerns pertained to the roofs. Toombs's drawing had shown the roofs of the north and south wings and of the central block being the same height. "We all think the two wing roofs should be two feet lower than the top of the roof of the center," Roosevelt wrote. Then he dealt with the implications of this change. Even though the roofs of the wings would be lower, that would "not mean that the eaves of the wings should be greatly lower than the eaves of the center." Instead, he thought that "All eaves should be on the same level as nearly as possible." Roosevelt proposed that Toombs develop the scheme for the eaves; "you can work this out all right," the President wrote, but could not resist adding a word on a possible solution: "One way of doing it would be by putting a hip in the ceilings of the rooms inside the wings, for, of course, the roof angles themselves should be the same in all three places." Someone at the White House had suggested that the alignment of the eaves could be manipulated by reducing the pitch of the roofs of the wings, but Roosevelt disagreed, asking Toombs "frankly, I do not think this would look well—do you?" Roosevelt elaborated on his preferred approach with a sketch showing how a coved ceiling could be tucked into the wings, but he neglected to take into account interior partitions that would create half-coved rooms. It was important to Roosevelt that the bedroom ceilings "be a minimum of ten feet—preferably ten feet six inches." The width of the eaves was important, too; Roosevelt thought that "it looks better on this old type of house to have them project fairly far—say ten or twelve inches beyond the walls."[45]

President Roosevelt's section through one of the wings, showing a coved ceiling, April 21, 1938. Courtesy of the Georgia Department of Archives and History, Atlanta.

One of Roosevelt's sketches illustrated the entrance to the cottage. Where Toombs had shown an unadorned doorway, Roosevelt suggested some protection from the elements that would also allow for an additional historical reference to local vernacular buildings: "How would it do to put outside this door one of those very small covered Dutch porches, such as you have examples of in the books—the covered portion to be about six feet wide and four feet deep, with a very simple design of porch and doorway." In Dutch houses, however, such porches, or stoops, were typically set well above grade level; perhaps it was with this in mind that Roosevelt reminded Toombs that "It is important, of course, that the entrance hall, porch and terrace be on the same level on account of wheelchair."[46]

Roosevelt proposed a second change to the entranceway: "At southeast corner of north wing carry out a stone wall in continuation of the building stone." This wall was to be about four feet high and extend east about four feet to the edge of the drive. Toombs incorporated the porch and the wall into the design, but neither was built, probably because of the additional cost. Concerning the other facade, Roosevelt asked, "Didn't we think that the big West porch should be eleven feet wide instead of ten feet wide?" "Yes," Toombs noted in the margin of the letter.[47] The President also suggested several changes to the interior; some dealt with very practical items, while others returned the layout of the bedroom wing to the design shown in his February 1938 drawing. He added a linen closet in the bathroom and moved the door connecting the bedrooms to the west end of the partition and perhaps made this into a sliding door. He shifted the door from the entry to the pantry eastward so that a sink and drainboard could be installed under the pantry window. Toombs incorporated the President's changes into the plans, except that a hinged door was shown between the bedrooms.[48]

Finally, Roosevelt turned his comments to the lighting. He acknowledged that he had earlier spoken "of having no wall lights and no ceiling lights." He was still opposed to ceiling lights but now agreed that "obviously we must have some side light brackets in the kitchen, the pantry, both bathrooms and the closet off the smaller bedroom in south wing." More specifically, he directed that there be "lights over the pantry and kitchen sinks, one over the range and one on the side wall near the icebox so as to be able to see into the latter." Outside, there was to be "a light on the servants' porch," as well as "a light on each side of the front door on the proposed little Dutch porch."[49]

Roosevelt was very eager to move ahead, as Nancy Cook had warned. He had sent his April 21 letter by airmail, so that Toombs could study it before their meeting. Roosevelt then also set out a schedule for the spring: "If Congress does not get in the way," the President wrote, he planned to spend the weekend of either May 22 or May 29 at Hyde Park. Dorothy Backer would join them on Sunday. He would engage "a well-digger to try to get me some water for the top of the hill" and also ask the well-digger to sink the Backers' well. Roosevelt told Toombs that "If you could be there then with the plans and specifications, we could go over them for final decision and you could at the same time get in touch with the possible contractors." "One or two days," Roosevelt confidently predicted, "would do the whole thing." This schedule, the President felt, would allow the contractors sufficient time to prepare their estimates in time for Roosevelt's next visit to Hyde Park, scheduled for June 19. Then, he told Toombs, "we could let the contracts within a very few days, enabling the contractor to start work by early July," and get the house "under roof before cold weather."[50]

Soon after his meeting with the President at the White House on April 27, Toombs finalized the drawings. Among the adjustments was an important change in the access to the basement. Roosevelt's February 1938 scheme had not shown a basement entrance. Toombs's March 22 drawing originally had a stairway to the basement at the north end of the kitchen. Annotated drawings showed a basement stairway projecting out from behind the east wall of the living room. Roosevelt later explained that the basement was going to be "Only big enough for a heater," and he described the basement stairway as "a trick." "We did not want to have an ugly staircase going down into the cellar," he said, "so we made the staircase going down to the cellar inside of the chimney."[51]

On May 5 Toombs made a proposal for the title block of the architectural drawings that would later provoke considerable controversy within the architectural profession. "It would [be] fun," Toombs wrote to Missy LeHand, "to title the drawings for the President's little house—'Franklin D. Roosevelt, Architect, Henry J. Toombs, Associate.' " "Of course he hasn't a license to practice Architecture in New York State," Toombs continued, "but I don't think we would get in trouble." How they "would split the 'fee' " was "another matter," to be discussed later. Missy LeHand replied that Roosevelt had approved the idea and that her letter "constitutes an assignment of fees from the Architect to the Associate—provided the fees are not exorbitant."[52]

Evidently Congress did not interfere with

the President's spring schedule, for he and Toombs were able to meet at Hyde Park on the weekend of May 28. Roosevelt asked Toombs to "let Mrs. Backer know also so we can complete plans," and he asked Nancy Cook to host both Toombs and Dorothy Backer at Val-Kill.[53]

Roosevelt had requested that Toombs arrive in Hyde Park with not only the drawings in hand but also the specifications. Accordingly, Toombs prepared six contract drawings before the meeting: a foundation and basement plan, a first-floor plan, a roof plan, east and west elevations, north and south elevations and sections, and a sheet of details. He had also had a model of the cottage built. Neither the contract drawings nor the model have been located.[54]

However, the specifications have survived. They are dated May 26, 1938, just two days before the Hyde Park meeting. Toombs developed two sets of specifications, one for the general contractor and the other for the heating contractor. Consistent with the title block of the drawings, Roosevelt was listed on the specifications as the architect, and Toombs as associate, but bidders were to direct "all communications" to Toombs in Warm Springs.[55]

The Construction Specifications

The construction specifications, which included portions of the "Standard Documents of the American Institute of Architects" (Toombs had been a member of the AIA since 1929), had seventeen sections: general conditions, earth work, concrete, masonry, waterproofing of the basement, miscellaneous metal work, rough carpentry, finish carpentry, caulking and weather-stripping, roofing, composition floors, plastering, heat insulation, painting, plumbing, bathroom and closet accessories, and electrical work.[56]

The general contractors were asked to provide a lump-sum bid for the work and also to furnish prices for ten alternates. Three of the alternates—which called for using ponderosa pine panels rather than plaster under the windows, copper rather than galvanized-steel water and heating pipes, and "flat diamond mesh metal lath" rather than Rocklath—would have increased the cost of the project. Other alternates were seen as means for reducing the construction cost: substituting different models for the kitchen and pantry sinks; using an electric rather than oil-burning hot-water heater; omitting storm sashes, thermal insulation, and basement waterproofing; and substituting asbestos shingles ("Williamsburg type, brown-black, 16" long, and 5", 6" & 8" random widths, 3/8" to 1/2" butts, or other approved equal") in place of the slate roofing. The cost of another alternate—applying a "sand finish plaster" for the finish coat in the living room and entry rather than "smooth finish plaster"— may have been requested because Roosevelt had not yet decided which he preferred. Each contractor was required to certify that he had "visited the grounds and understands by this personal observation all requirements for keeping the work in full accordance with the drawings and specifications."

The first section of the specifications stipulated that the owner and architect were to approve the selection of all subcontractors, that the contractor was responsible for furnishing the architect with shop drawings for the architect's approval, that the contractor was to supply all water and electric service needed during construction, and that payments were to be made in accordance with the AIA standard agreement between the contractor and owner.

The earthwork specifications provided for excavation, backfilling, and replacement of topsoil and for pumping to keep the site dry. The concrete specifications detailed the composition of concrete mixtures, the reinforcing steel bars, and the 4-inch concrete slab in the basement.

The stonework was very important to Roosevelt and Toombs. FDR agreed to supply the stone for the walls. He told reporters that "I have a lot of old walls in the woods that were put in there about a hundred and fifty years ago to keep the cattle in and I am just using the field stone out of those walls"; he estimated that the cottage would "take about half a mile of wall."[57]

The facing stone was to "be generally long and flat in character," and "no round large or irregular stone" was to show. "A good stone job is desired," the specifications continued, "and the Architect will insist on its being laid to his approval." To clarify the requisite quality and character of the stonework, the specifications suggested that the contractor study the "walls of the cottage of Miss Nancy Cook on the Roosevelt property at Hyde Park" for "an idea of what is desired." The mortar mix was to consist of one part Magnolia brand slag cement, one part lime putty, and six parts sand, by volume.

The perimeter foundation walls were to be of fieldstone, whereas the interior foundation walls were to be of common brick. The "inside face of all walls coming in contact with the earth" were to be sealed with the "Ironite method of waterproofing, as furnished and applied by the Western Waterproofing Company." The chimneys were to be "built of field stone and faced on exterior with same," and the flues were to have terra-cotta linings and "H. W. Coverts Company's old style dampers." The hearths were to have 4-inch-thick, reinforced-concrete bases. The living-room fireplace lining and hearth were to be finished with fieldstone, and the facing was to be "field stone at least 4" thick and rough cut." The other fireplaces were to be "faced with selected brick and have hearths of same."

Detailed information was also set forth for the paving stones for the west porch and east terrace. They were to be "local blue stone flagstones selected for smooth surface and color as approved by the Architect." All edges were to "be snapped to a straight line," and the stones were to be "at least 2" thick for paving and of sizes shown on drawings."

The lumber for the framing was to be "No. 2 Common Southern Yellow Pine or Douglas Fir," except for the sills and beams, which were to be "No. 1 Common." The "first floor beams, ledgers, joists and sills" were to be "pressure treated with creosote." Trusses were to be used in the roof above the living room. Unless shown differently on the drawings, the roofs were to be "sheathed with ⅞" x 6" and 8" T[ongue] & G[roove] No. 2 Common Southern [pine] laid horizontally." The sheathing was to be covered with "asphalt felt weighing not less than 30 lbs. per square" and "laid with 6" laps in weatherboard fashion and nailed." Like the roof sheathing, the subflooring was to be ⅞-inch-thick boards, 6 inches and 8 inches wide, and number 2 common Southern pine; in the subflooring, however, the boards were to be laid diagonally and covered with "Sisalkraft in the widest widths practicable" with 4-inch laps. The Sisalkraft paper was to be extended up behind the baseboards "to provide a cold air stop."

The finish-carpentry specifications provided that the exterior woodwork was to "be made of B & Better Southern Yellow Pine, B & Better White Pine." "All wood columns" were to be cypress, while the poles of the pergola (evidently the structure at the east entrance) were to be made of birch. The shutters were to be 1⅜ inches thick and were to be made of "B & Better Idaho White Pine, or B & Better Ponderosa Pine treated with 'Permatol "A" or 'Partox.' " The window sashes were to be made of the same wood and treated with Permatol A. The porch ceilings were to be finished with ⅞-inch "beaded ceiling boards" and with quarter-round moldings.

Hardware for the sliding doors was to be purchased from the Coburn Trolley Track Company or an approved equal. All windows were to have "Zip-in Frameless all bronze screens" with an antique finish, manufactured by the Cincinnati Fly Screen Company. The screen doors were to be made of "kiln-dried sugar pine" with antique-finish bronze wire screening and with "copper bronze diamond mesh guards" over the bottom panels. The west porch was to have similar bronze screening, set in removable panels.

Inside, the finish woodwork was to be made of "B & Better Ponderosa Pine," whereas the paneling around windows and doors and the mantels of the fireplaces in the wings were to be "B & Better Ponderosa Pine, or Idaho White Pine." Floors in public areas were to be covered with "quartered clear White Oak 13/16" x 2¼" end matched"; the "best pieces" of this flooring were to be "selected and laid in the Living Room and other prominent places." The subflooring under the linoleum was to be "second grade Flat Grain Shortleaf Southern Yellow Pine, Birch, Beech, or Maple 1 5/16" x 2¼" end matched." Kitchen cabinets were to be selected from the Curtis company catalog or an approved equal, while clothes closets were to have two 12-inch "wood shelves and a wood shoe rack the height of the baseboard along the long end of each closet"; rather than a pole, the closets were to have wooden strips with hooks on the sides. There was a $300 allowance for hardware, which was to be purchased from the Corbin, Yale and Towne, or

Russell Erwin firms or from an approved equal.

Joints around exterior window and door frames were to "be thoroughly caulked with 'Accurate,' Tock Brothers' R. I. W. Elastic, Truscons' and, or C. C. Horn Company's caulking compound, or other approved equal, applied with a gun." The color of the caulking compound was to be a "light gray to match stone." Exterior doors were to have " 'Accurate' One Piece Extruded Bronze Saddles No. 32, 5" wide" or an equal, and all windows in the living areas were to have "storm sash made of fabricated cap and frame construction as manufactured by The Burrowes Corp." or an equal and be manufactured in "electro plated steel."

The original specifications for Top Cottage called for the roofs to be covered with slate quarried in Vermont by the Rising and Nelson Slate Company, of West Pawlet. The slates were to be selected and laid "in special combinations of thicknesses from ¼" to ½" thick, graduated lengths from 12" to 18", random widths, percentages of different thicknesses to be mixed in the same courses" and hung from copper nails. The slate colors were also detailed: they were to be "a carefully selected combination of the Verde Antique green, medium and light shades of Velenheli blend, purple, weathering greens, browns and buffs, and pheasants." The valleys and ridges were to be of slate, while the flashing and counterflashing were to be of "16 oz. soft rolled copper." Gutters and downspouts were to be of "18 oz. lead coated copper."

A separate section of the specifications dealt with linoleum, or "composition," floors. The contractor was to submit for the architect's approval "samples of each pattern of linoleum illustrating the grade, color, texture and material." "Factory formed cove bases of same thickness and pattern as specified for border" were to be installed. Where the linoleum abutted the finished wood flooring, "Bar Edging No. 51 (⅛") with a high luster yellow brass finish, as manufactured by the Wooster Products Company, Wooster, Ohio," was to be installed. The linoleum was to be waxed and polished "to a rich gloss."

Considerable detail was also provided in the plastering specifications. The plaster itself was to be "an approved Gypsum Plaster as manufactured by the U. S. Gypsum Company, National Gypsum Company, or Certainteed Products delivered to the site in the original package." The other ingredients were Portland cement, "finely pulverized quick lime complying with Federal Specification No. SS-Q351," "clean, well graded" sand, water, and clean hair and fiber.

The compositions of the plaster mixes were listed with the parts measured by weight. The scratch coats were to have one part of "Neat Gypsum Plaster, fibered" and two parts of sand. When applied on metal lath and directly on masonry, the brown coats were to have one part neat gypsum plaster, either fibered or unfibered, and three parts of sand. On concrete the brown coat was to be neat gypsum plaster without sand, or "Bond Crete" was to be used. The finish coats were to consist of "about 3 parts of lime to 1 part of Plaster of Paris," mixed "to produce a smooth, hard, white finish." The bathrooms were to have 6-foot-high plaster wainscotings; here the scratch coat and the brown coat were to be mixed of Portland cement and sand, while the finish coat was to be made up of equal parts of Keene's Cement and lime putty, to produce a hard, more water-resistant finish. Behind wood paneling, in the stairwell to the basement, and on the furnace-room ceiling, the finish was to be a cement plaster made of one part cement, two and one-half parts of sand, "gauged with 10% Lime Putty."

Metal lath of "expanded copper bearing steel" was to be used in the bathrooms and on the living room and furnace room ceilings; elsewhere "Rocklath," manufactured by the U. S. Gypsum Company, was to be installed. Cornerite-brand diamond-mesh angles and number 14 expanded corner beads, also made by U. S. Gypsum, were to be used. All ceilings of the cottage were to be insulated with snug-fitting 4-inch batts of "Barrett Company's Rock Wool, Johns Manville's Rock Wool, U. S. Gypsum Company's Insulating Wool," or an equal.

The painters' materials were to include Spencer-Kellogg brand boiled and raw linseed oil, putty made of white lead and whiting, turpentine, a drier, shellac, and wax. The interior and exterior wood primers, which were to be mixed by the painters, were to be composed of soft-paste white lead, raw linseed oil, turpentine, and drier. Other paints evidently were factory mixed, with Pratt and Lambert or Sherwin-Williams generally identified as a desired source; the specifications always provided for the substitution of approved equals. The exterior woodwork was to receive one coat of primer and two coats of exterior paint. The exterior metalwork (including cast-iron ventilators and steel lintels, but not the lead-coated copper gutters and downspouts or the hardware) was to be protected with two coats of exterior paint in addition to the shop coat.

Inside, the plaster walls were to have one coat of pigmented primer and two coats of flat paint. The ceilings were to "be given one coat of Hydraulic Cement Primer and two coats of Casein Paint," and the woodwork and metalwork were to receive eggshell enamel. In the serving pantry, kitchen, and bathrooms, the walls and ceilings were to be finished with an eggshell enamel, while the woodwork in these rooms was to be finished with gloss enamel. The exposed wood floors were to receive the following finish: "one coat of oil stain, one [of] filler, one coat of shellac, two coats of floor varnish, and two coats of wax." Like the floors that would be covered with linoleum, the exposed floors were to be machine sanded first and then scraped.

The plumbing specifications required that the work be done to the standards of the New York City Plumbing Ordinance. The house sewer, made of 6-inch vitrified pipe, was to have a grease trap and be connected to a 6-foot-long septic tank with a leach field. All downspouts were to have cast-iron boots connected to 4-inch vitrified-clay pipes. The hot-water pipes were to be of galvanized steel, insulated with "3-ply K & M Ambler Air Cell Pipe Insulation" or equal. The hot-water heater was to be "Duo-Therm Automatic Oil Burning Heater No. 41-B," insulated with a boiler jacket and asbestos cement. In the basement there was to be a "Penberthy Model 'R' Size 0 Automatic cellar drain." [58]

The preferred plumbing fixtures were also identified: the bathroom in the south wing was to have a Standard 6-foot-long cast-iron enameled tub with shower valves and a shower curtain of white duck. The Standard cast-iron enameled sink was to be hung from the wall, rather than be supported by legs, perhaps to facilitate the President's access from a wheelchair. The water closet was to be a Standard elongated compact porcelain model. The fixtures in the second bathroom were the same, except that the tub was just 5 feet long and did not have a shower. The "double drain board sinks, with four inch backs" in the kitchen and pantry were to be set in steel cabinets; an alternate without the cabinets was also listed. All exposed metal parts of the plumbing fixtures were to have a "Chromard Finish." Model numbers for towel bars, tissue holders, soap holders, and a medicine cabinet, all made by Hall-Mack, were stipulated.

The electrical work was to follow the rules and regulations of the Southeastern Underwriters Association. All wiring was to be in galvanized rigid-metal conduit, with B and X gauge wires; the service was to be "three wire, 110-220 volts, single phase 60 cycle."[59] The service entry switch was to be a "safety type, fused enclosed, type C switch for 100 amps, 3 P.S.T. 250 volts, solid neutral"; the panel box was to be a "Trumbull No. HP1008RC for flush mounting and plug fuses." Switches were to be located 4 feet above the floor. The electrical work was to include Hart and Hegeman radio antenna outlets and a "standard 7/22 copper antenna under roof for same with proper insulators." In addition, a house-bell system was to include call buttons at the front and back doors and in the master bedroom (connected to a white silk cord) and living room; the bells were to ring in the kitchen and in the servants' room. Despite public announcements to the contrary, Roosevelt evidently planned to have some provisions for telephones in the cottage; outlets were to be placed by the bed in the master bedroom and in the living room. There was an allowance of $100 for electrical fixtures.

The heating specifications were based on the installation of a "#650 Holland Oil Fired Air Conditioning Unit." This model was to be of cast-iron with a sectional generator having three expansion chambers, and there was to be a one-thousand-gallon oil tank, which was to be buried underground. Two supply fans were included, and the sheet-metal duct work was to follow national standards. Grilles were to be Hart and Cooley model 90, with a honeycomb pattern. There was also to be a Holland "drip type automatic humidifier."

Awarding the Construction Contract

As Toombs was finalizing the specifications, he dispatched letters to three contractors to ascertain whether they were interested in bidding on the project. Form letters dated May 24, 1938, were addressed to John Eylers, the Poughkeepsie carpenter and contractor whom Nancy Cook had recommended; Frederick Lane, of Hyde Park; and Silverblatt and Lasker, the engineers and builders from Manhattan who had constructed the Poughkeepsie post office. On June 2 Toombs sent a similar inquiry to three more Poughkeepsie contractors (Frank Seaman, the G. D. Campbell Building Company, and the Miller and Gaynor Corporation) and to the Adams-Faber Company, a New Jersey firm. All but Lane expressed interest in bidding on the work. The Adams-Faber Company, which ultimately won the contract, replied that they believed they would give "a price which will be interesting."[60]

As the contractors prepared their bids, the well for Top Cottage was being dug. On May 30 a well-digger and contractor from Red Hook, William Feller, of Feller Brothers, inspected the property and, with Roosevelt's help, decided upon the location of the well. Feller drew up a memorandum of their conversation, which stated that the first 25 feet of the well was to be 8 inches in diameter; a 6-inch pipe was to be inserted into this hole and grouted to prevent seepage of surface water. The drilling was to continue at a 6-inch diameter until a sufficient flow of water was achieved. Roosevelt wrote to Feller from Washington on June 9 that he hoped that the work was underway and agreed to leave the discussion about proper depth to Feller's discretion. He reminded Feller that "there will be little need for water outside of household services," since there would be "no lawn and no garden."[61]

The well was drilled to a depth of 184 feet, at a cost of $2.00 a foot. A log states that the work was completed on June 23, 1938. The contractors had drilled through bluestone and shale at a diameter of 8 inches and to a depth of 22 feet. A 6-inch pipe was then inserted and grouted. The full capacity of the well was 4.75 gallons per minute at 80 feet. The well soon proved troublesome; the builders found that the water supply was inadequate for use with a hand pump, and they had to rent a gasoline pump. Feller later told Toombs that he "would have liked to have gotten a heavier flow of water but the President himself was here and saw the well tested and thought the flow we had would be sufficient."[62]

Meanwhile, subcontractors were approaching Toombs with hopes of winning contracts. J. E. Clay, of Hyde Park, wrote about the painting contract, reminding Toombs that he had done "all of the work Interior & exterior on the Memorial Library" and mentioning that he had done "all the painting for the President's Mother for the past thirty five years." The Lumb Woodworking Company, Poughkeepsie manufacturers of architectural woodwork and dealers in Curtis products, requested a list of all bidders; they also sent Toombs a seventieth-anniversary history, since they assumed that he had "probably never heard of our Company." Lumb's specialty was producing "fine woodwork for country homes near Poughkeepsie," and they pointed out that they had done "quite a bit of work" for Eleanor Roosevelt during a remodeling of Val-Kill. The O'Brien Brothers Slate Company, of Granville, New York, wrote with the hope that they could bid on the project. Once newspapers began carrying stories on the house, many other contractors and vendors asked to have their services and products considered.[63]

The President was very concerned about the cost of construction. Toombs submitted his first invoice for design services on June 6, 1938, basing his fee on a projected total construction cost of $18,000. Roosevelt paid Toombs promptly but sent a warning along with the check. "Perhaps we may have to make some adjustments on this estimate," Roosevelt wrote, "for I cannot possibly afford to build an $18,000 house... and it is even possible that if the bids run anything like as high as that, I may decide to give up both the wings and build only the center at this time." Toombs replied that he had not meant "to scare" the President about the cost and hoped "very much that we may juggle it so that we may get it done considerably below that." On June 15 the *New York Times* reported that if the bids were "not low enough," the work would "not begin for some time."[64]

PRESIDENT ROOSEVELT'S COTTAGE now nearing completion by Adams-Faber Company, New Jersey home builders. Legend on drawings reads, "Franklin D. Roosevelt, Architect; Henry J. Toombs, Associate."

Building a House for F. D. R.

Adams and Faber, New Jersey Residential Builders, Find the President Keenly Interested in Home Building and Construction Details

By JOSEPH B. MASON

PAUL D. ADAMS JOHN H. FABER
Builders of President Roosevelt's Cottage

PAUL D. ADAMS and John H. Faber have been building houses for 15 years and have had some very interesting customers. But on July 2 this year they acquired a new customer who outranked all others in interest—the President of the United States, Franklin D. Roosevelt.

The Adams-Faber Company put a construction crew at work on the President's home early in July and were expected to finish it by November 1. They were low bidders out of a total of six contractors who were invited to submit bids on the detailed plans drawn by Henry J. Toombs, architect of the Warm Springs Foundation at Warm Springs, Ga.

Final negotiations were made directly with the President and were conducted in the little Ford car he uses to drive around his Hyde Park, N. Y., estate. They found him a practical, well informed customer who checked details and costs carefully and who displayed a considerable knowledge of building methods. According to Adams and Faber, the job has gone smoothly, the checks have come in regularly on time and the job has been one of the most interesting they have ever undertaken. The President took a great deal of interest and personally supervised the work.

The house is a five-room, solid stone, one-story Dutch cottage located on a wooded knoll above the Hudson River on a tract of land recently purchased by the President, adjoining the family home at Hyde Park.

The President himself drew painstaking sketches of the plan which were then reviewed and

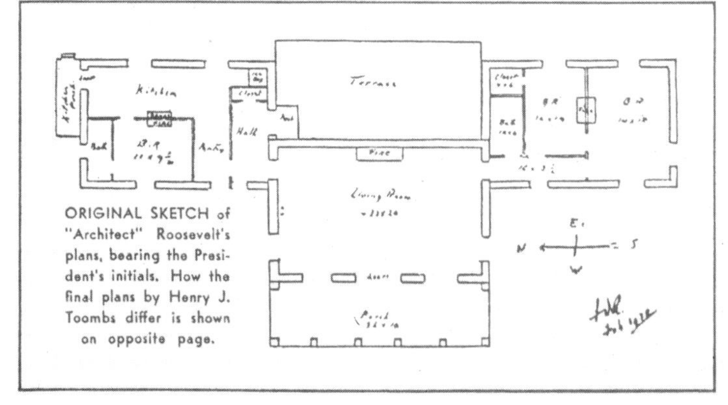

ORIGINAL SKETCH of "Architect" Roosevelt's plans, bearing the President's initials. How the final plans by Henry J. Toombs differ is shown on opposite page.

"Building a House for FDR," November 1938. Reprinted, by permission, from *American Builder.*

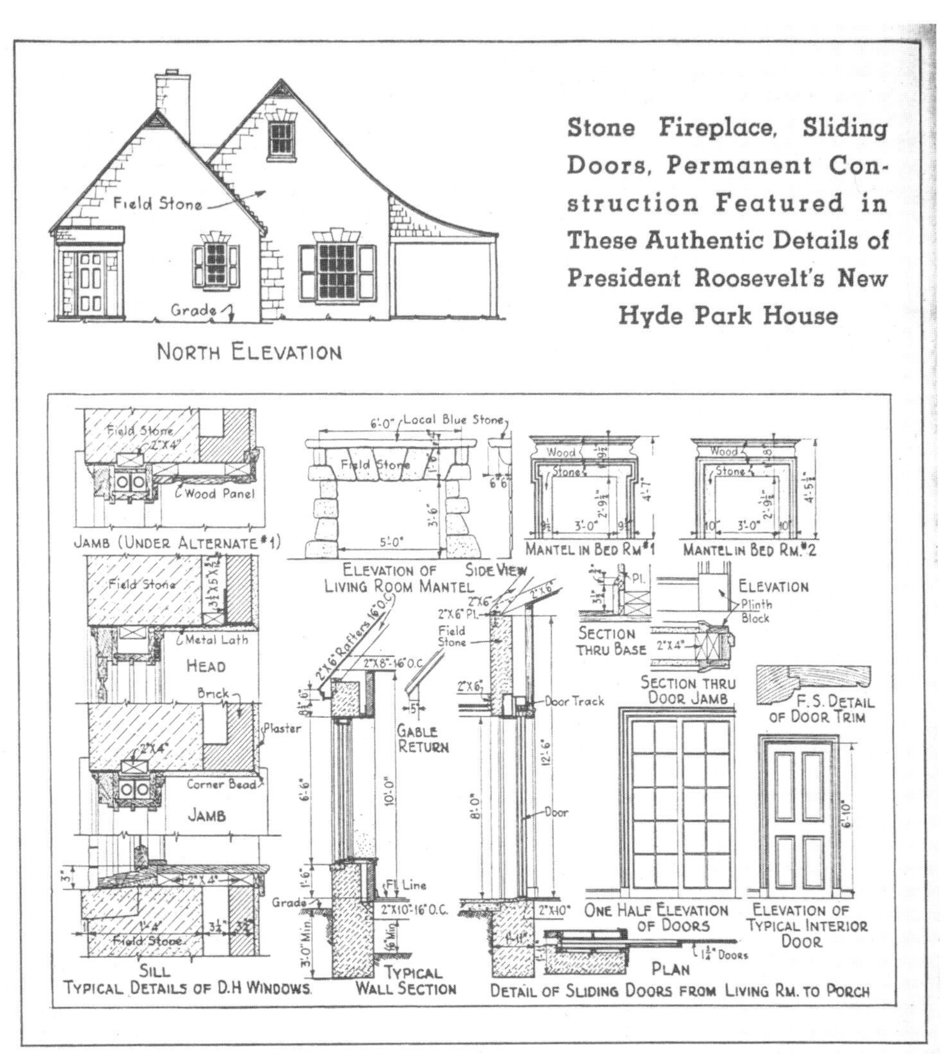

Illustration from "Building a House for FDR," November 1938. Reprinted, by permission, from *American Builder.*

The contractors' bids were due on June 25. Toombs planned to meet with the President at Hyde Park a few days later, and they planned "to make final arrangements" for the contracts for the cottage and for the Backers' residence. Toombs hoped that the extra time he was allowing for the preparation of the bids would "have considerable bearing on lowering the cost."[65]

The successful bidder was the Adams-Faber Company, which was headquartered in Upper Montclair, New Jersey, and had a branch office at White Plains, New York. Both principals of the firm, Paul D. Adams and John H. Faber, had graduated from Princeton University in 1915 with degrees in civil engineering and had been members of the same eating club, Cloister Inn. Adams initially worked as an engineer and construction manager for E. I. du Pont de Nemours and Company, supervising the construction of smokeless-powder plants and carrying out housing, road, and railroad projects. Faber served in the Army in France during World War I and then worked as a cost engineer for a New York City builder.[66]

In 1923 they formed the Adams-Faber Company. An advertising brochure explained that the firm was "devoted to construction of country houses, churches, banks, offices, stores, schools and other buildings of distinction" and that "repeat business," which made up "the large part of our business from year to year," was an indication of "satisfied architects and owners." The flyer assured readers that "The Adams-Faber name has long been associated with efficient building methods, construction and engineering skill, and intelligent co-operation with owners and architects." At the time that they won the contract for Top Cottage, Adams and Faber were in their mid-forties; years later both men still remembered this job as a highlight of their careers.[67]

Exactly how Adams-Faber came to be invited to submit a bid for the project is not clear. One possible link may have been a mutual acquaintance. In 1938 Toombs still maintained an office in Manhattan (an Atlanta reporter wrote that this office was "nothing more than a name on the door these days, which he plans to have erased soon"). Nevertheless, it may be worth noting that this office was at 101 Park Avenue and that three of the Adams-Faber Company's business references also had offices there. Furthermore, Toombs made a passing reference in a letter of January 1939 to "some mutual friends of the Adams." Roosevelt seems to have had no prior acquaintance with the contractors; when he returned the signed construction contract in July 1938, the President told Toombs simply that "I like Mr. Adams and Mr. Faber and I am sure they will do a good job." The selection had certainly not been based on politics, for Adams later wrote that the "President liked to refer to us as his non-political builders and he seemed to relish heartily this situation as well as our Harvard-Princeton relationship." The decision was probably based mostly on cost, and Roosevelt stated that he had awarded the contract to the lowest bidder.[68]

Toombs took the written bids to Hyde Park, and Roosevelt had them in hand during a morning press conference on June 28, when he told reporters that he hoped to "look over the bids for this little cottage on top of the hill." The President must have been dismayed to find that the bids substantially exceeded his budget. The Adams-Faber proposal, the lowest one, totaled more than $20,000, even after making adjustments for cost-cutting alternatives.[69] Intent on moving ahead, the President put in a call to Paul Adams later that day, as Adams later recounted:

> My initial contact started with a telephone call about 11 o'clock one night when the Essex Fells operator informed me that Hyde Park was calling and that the President of the United States wanted to talk to Mr. Paul Adams of the Adams-Faber Co. The next day John Faber and I had a date with the President.[70]

Faber recalled that he had "closed the contract with the President on the front seat of his blue Ford Roadster."[71]

Although apparently no longer proposing to eliminate the kitchen and bedroom wings as he had earlier hinted to the press, Roosevelt must have spent considerable time on June 29 reviewing all possible cost-cutting options with Toombs and the contractors. In the end they agreed on 24 changes, some saving as little as $15 but others amounting to hundreds of dollars, which together would reduce the cost by $4,490. Adams and Faber returned to their New Jersey office and on the next day, June 30, drew up a contract for the house, using a standard AIA contractor-owner construction agreement.[72]

Attached to this contract was an addendum detailing the changes. A major savings was achieved by omitting the "interior brick furring of the masonry walls," reducing the thickness of the foundation walls to 18 inches, substituting concrete blocks for bricks in the foundations, and using "asphalt dampproofing" rather than the "special waterproofing" originally specified. Several design features were eliminated: the two stone walls jutting out from the wings on the east elevation, the porch at the front entry, shutters, storm windows and doors, insulation, the kitchen porch, screens for the west porch, and the bedroom fireplace. Work in a few areas was reduced in scope, perhaps with the thought that those elements could be augmented or finished later: the east terrace was to be reduced to "a flagstone platform approximately six feet square"; the plaster walls and ceilings were not to be painted; and two coats of varnish on the floors were eliminated. Substituting an electric hot-water heater for one that burned oil eliminated a flue. The kitchen cabinets were to be "simplified," and another model of sink was chosen for the kitchen and pantry. Framing of the first-floor beams in the two wings was also altered.[73]

Several changes involved the use of less-costly building materials. The exposed flooring was now to be "#2 red oak 1³⁄₁₆ x 2¼," and the lead coating was eliminated from the copper sheet-metal work. Perhaps most significantly, "210# asphalt strip shingles, 10 x 36, with plain backs" were substituted for the slate that Roosevelt had wanted (Roosevelt termed them "Patent shingle stuff, whatever they call it, fireproof shingles"). Making the stone window arches "generally like the stone arches in the Nancy Cook house" was expected to save $35, and having Roosevelt's estate staff take care of trees and stumps that might interfere with construction would save $100. Only three items in the addendum added to the total cost—asphalt dampproofing ($40), "Ponderosa pine raised wood panels" in the window reveals ($178), and copper pipes for the heating and water-supply pipes. Apparently just two items were left unresolved at the end of the meeting on June 29: whether to spend an extra $168 on diamond-mesh metal lath rather than to use Rocklath and whether or not to use sand-finished plaster as the final coat in the living room and entry (there was no cost difference in the plaster alternates).[74]

The contract drawn up by the Adams-Faber Company restated the amount of their June 21 proposal ($20,796), deducted the $4,490 in savings, and added $293 in new costs, making the revised total of the contract $16,599. The cottage was to be completed in just four months, by November 1, 1938. Toombs sent three copies of the contract to Roosevelt for his signature.[75]

Building the Cottage

Adams-Faber began work on the project even before the signed contracts had been returned to them. By July 1, 1938, the perimeters of the house had been "outlined in the woods with stakes and strings," and Roosevelt showed the layout to the press: "The rooms are awfully small," he explained, "all except the living room, and that is awfully big." Another of the contractors' initial tasks was to establish the grade level for the house. Paul Adams spent part of the Fourth of July writing Toombs about possibly raising the grade by 6 inches to avoid problems with water drainage and about fabricating the 6-inch-by-10-inch girders from 2-inch-by-10-inch lumber, in order to gain better impregnation of the wood preservative. Toombs agreed with both of these recommendations.[76]

During the weekend of July 1, Crown Princess Louise of Sweden visited the Roosevelts at Hyde Park and was the guest of honor at a picnic at Dutchess Hill. The *New York Times* reported that "In his new role of country squire turned architect, the President outlined the floor plans of his woodland retreat to the Royal guests... and told them of his boyhood romps over the same lands." Over her mother-in-law's objections, Eleanor Roosevelt served what the *Times* called "the American road-side dish," hot dogs "dripping with mustard." The guests relaxed "on camp stools and deck chairs" and "seemed to enjoy the occasion as much as did President Roosevelt."[77]

In his July 4 letter Adams told Toombs that Roosevelt had confirmed Toombs' model for the exterior stonework. It was to be "like the sample you picked out on the west gable with all the stones in their natural beds except [Roosevelt] wants the joint smeared up more, not so much stone showing." Then Adams posed other queries to Toombs. What color would the asphalt shingles be? ("Blue Black," Toombs jotted in the margin.) Was the cellar to "be as shown on your drawing or cut down as discussed?" ("As cut down," Toombs noted.) Would the shelf of the chimney still be slate? And what was Adams to tell "these local papers" that wanted "to see the plans"?[78]

As the house was going up during the summer and early fall of 1938, scores of letters between the architect and the builders and with the vendors were written and dispatched. Fortunately, much of the correspondence has been preserved at the Georgia Department of Archives and History in Atlanta and at the Roosevelt Library at Hyde Park. Many of these communications dealt with the shop drawings, which the builders or subcontractors prepared from the architect's contract drawings and then submitted to the architect for review and approval.[79] Early letters dealt with revisions to the framing, changes in the dimensions of the basement and the foundation walls, and the omission of a floor drain in the boiler room that would have required "a great deal of expensive rock excavation to carry it any place where it will function."[80]

The correspondence presents a good chronology of the construction. On July 14 John Faber told Toombs that "the excavation for the President's house is now complete." The contractors planned "to start the foundation work at once." The "treated lumber for the first floor framing" was scheduled for delivery within a few days, "so that the framing can all be cut ready to install as soon as the foundations are ready to receive it." A week later Faber wrote that "The foundations are now being installed and we hope the weather permits us to have some of the first floor framing in place next week."[81]

In his next report, dated July 28, Adams wrote that "The work is progressing nicely now although lack of water from the well hindered us and then too much water from heaven held us back." The foundation walls would be topped out by July 29; the floor beams were "being placed on one wing"; and he expected "to have a force of carpenters on the job Monday," August 1. Horace Noyes was the construction superintendent.[82]

On July 30 Adams-Faber submitted their first requisition, for $1,710, which represented work done to date in the amount of $1,900 less a 10 percent retainage. This work included $200 for excavation of earth, $250 for rock excavation, $1,000 for the foundations, $300 for the rough carpentry, and $150 toward general conditions.[83]

Roosevelt spent much of July and early August in the West, but he was soon back at Hyde Park. On August 19 he inspected the building site with John Faber, who told Toombs that the President had "expressed himself as being quite pleased with both the progress that has been made and the quality of the work." At that time the ceiling joists and the rafters were in place on the south wing. The stone wall on the west side of the living room was as high as the tops of the windows, but the east wall of the living room had not been started. Faber predicted that the stone walls on the kitchen wing would be "plate high" within the next few days; then the rafters would be put in place. The plumber was scheduled to begin work on August 22.[84]

During his August inspection, Roosevelt discussed the possibility of omitting the dampproofing on the inside of the stone walls; he was fearful that it would increase the likelihood of condensation. John Faber had strongly recommended the dampproofing as an added precaution against moisture being driven through the stonework, even though the walls were to be "heavily back plastered with cement mortar." Faber proposed putting an asphalt coating atop the cement backing; then there would be a dead air space, wood furring strips, a layer of Sisalkraft paper, lath, and finally the finish plaster (the Sisalkraft paper consisted of "two sheets of kraft paper with bituminous compound between . . . treated against fungus and rot and . . . reinforced by many threads of Sisal"). Roosevelt told Toombs that he was "a little afraid of it because of (a) deterioration and (b) fire hazard." Toombs wired the President on August 31 that he approved of the asphalt dampproofing and of putting "paper back of plaster to prevent condensation." He thought that it was more important to use the paper on the ceilings than on the walls and agreed with the President that the Sisalkraft paper could be a fire hazard. Toombs recommended using "fifteen pound saturated slaters felt" instead of the Sisalkraft.[85]

Toombs's architectural fee included not only the preparation of plans and specifications but also inspection of the construction work. He had been at the building site at the end of June when the contract was being negotiated, but he did not return again until early September. In June he had explained to the President that since it would be expensive for him "to make more than the obligatory number of trips North," he would have "one of my able friends in New York do the necessary supervision trips to check up on routine of the work as it proceeds." That friend was architect William J. Creighton, who also had an office at 101 Park Avenue. Creighton did a little investigation on the Holland heating proposal for Toombs but evidently did not make many, if any, site visits. Creighton reported to Toombs on August 31, two months after the project began, that he had not "been giving you any help on the President's House.. because there hasn't been anything I knew of that would be helpful." He had telephoned the contractors "from time to time but there never seemed to be any matters troubling them or requiring attention." Adams-Faber had told Creighton that they would notify him "if they needed help, but such time has not come." On December 21 Toombs sent Creighton a check for $100, in partial payment "in connection with all the bother of the house of the President, etc."[86]

On August 31 Adams-Faber had submitted the second requisition for payment, which totaled $6,174.22. This statement included small charges for additional excavation, the remainder of the foundation work, most of the stone walls above grade, most of the rough carpentry, half of the chimney and fireplace, and about 40 percent of the finish carpentry.[87]

During September the builders made good progress. The President told reporters on September 6 that "It has a few more stones added to it."[88] In his month-end report to Toombs, John Faber noted that he had visited the job site on Thursday, September 29:

> All sash are in place in the windows and most of the exterior doors are on the job but not yet fitted.
>
> On the interior the lathing should be complete by tonight and we expect to start plastering Monday morning. The heat ducts are all run and Holland Furnace expects to place the furnace the first of the week. The basement floor is down but the steps down to it have not yet been installed.
>
> The chimney is complete except for the splayed stone shelf on the exterior. As soon as the roof is completed next week, we will take down the scaffolding and then clean up the entire outside of all rubbish and excess building materials.
>
> The porch is complete except for the laying of the flagstone which is on the job and it is going to make a wonderfully fine porch.
>
> I hope you will find it convenient to send your certificate up to Miss LeHand quite promptly since it does take longer than usual to get it through to the President, undoubtedly due to the tremendous pressure of other things that he has to deal with.[89]

The contractors' September 30 requisition for payment confirmed this progress: the stone walls and rough carpentry were finished; the chimney, fireplace and roofing nearly done; the finish carpentry and electrical work half completed; and the plumbing well underway.[90]

For several months Toombs had been planning to visit Hyde Park in September and had arranged to stay at Val-Kill with Nancy Cook. Meanwhile, Dorothy Backer had returned from a trip to Holland (she told Toombs that she now had "many ideas for the

Foundation under construction, July 30, 1938. Courtesy of the Franklin D. Roosevelt Library, Hyde Park.

View from the northwest, showing the newly completed cottage, June 1939. Courtesy of the Franklin D. Roosevelt Library, Hyde Park.

house which I am anxious to discuss with you") and expected to be at Hyde Park at the same time.[91]

During this trip north Toombs stopped at the Lightolier Company's showroom in New York City to select lighting fixtures for the cottage. On September 12 he ordered two wall fixtures with a bronze finish for the west porch, one in black for the kitchen porch, three in chrome for the master bath and one for the servants' bath, two in chrome for the kitchen and one for the pantry, and a fixture for the bedroom hallway. The firm also supplied Toombs with illustrations of proposed brackets for the west porch and a black-finished chimney fixture, perhaps so he could submit them to Roosevelt for approval (these fixtures may never have been ordered). During a meeting with Toombs at Hyde Park, Roosevelt had requested that the ceiling light in the entry hall be omitted; there was to be a wall bracket instead. Toombs asked the contractors to have this light "satisfactorily capped" if it had already been installed.[92]

The plastering was to begin on October 3 and was probably underway when the President paid another visit to the cottage on October 4. At that time he spoke with Paul Adams about the paint colors for the exterior trim and for the interior and about the finish of the hardwood floors. The President also asked that "rough wood battens" be fabricated to protect the windows during the winter. Adams-Faber prepared a proposal for battens that "would be constructed of sheathing with sheathing board battens and would be unpainted."[93]

During this meeting Adams learned that the President "will probably want to use the main room some afternoon around Election Day, probably something in the nature of initiating his new house." Adams told Toombs that it was unlikely that "the entire house" would be "finished by this time," but they would "do our best to have the big room reasonably usable." Toombs replied that he wanted to come up before the building was "actually finished, in order to check over everything, and give you time to make any adjustments which might conceivably be necessary."[94]

By mid-October the plastering was complete except for the patching, and the trim was ready for installation, having been "all primed and finished" off site. It was to be delivered on October 18, and Adams-Faber expected that most of it would be installed by Election Day. If the hardware arrived in time, the doors would be hung, and the floors would be laid by that time, although the floor scraping and the painting would not be complete. They still hoped "to have the living room halfway presentable in case the President wants to have a picnic there at election time."[95]

Adams told Toombs that the final coat of paint would likely be started on November 3. "The job is coming along nicely now," Adams wrote on October 31; "we hope to have it substantially completed by next Tuesday although it is possible that some of the painting will not be done." Adams was "confident," though, "that the large room will be finished and probably the bedroom wing also." The requisition that Adams-Faber submitted at the end of October stated that nearly all of the work on the chimney and fireplace, the finish carpentry, the plumbing and electrical work, and the flooring were complete. The painting was about one-third done, and nothing had yet been charged to the linoleum allowance.[96]

Toombs planned to return to Hyde Park for the final inspection of the house on November 5. He and Roosevelt met with representatives of Adams-Faber, including Paul Adams, and apparently developed a list of work needed to complete the house; G. Hall Roosevelt, Eleanor Roosevelt's brother, also attended.[97]

After Toombs left, the President continued his discussions with the builders. He gave his approval to the fabrication of "the wood battens on all the doors and windows," and they were to be installed during the next week. According to the President, the battens were needed because the cottage was not yet completed and was "going to be boarded up." The President reported to Toombs that the electricians and plumbers would be "out in two weeks and the house, except for the electric light next Spring, will be finished."[98]

The President told Toombs that "I do not need to tell you how very happy I am with the house. Everyone who sees it is as enthusiastic as I am and I think you did a wonderful job." Toombs replied that he was "very happy that you are pleased with the results of our collaboration." "As specialists on Hudson Valley Dutch and Georgia Classic Revival," Toombs continued, "maybe we don't do so badly!"[99]

To settle up the accounts, Adams-Faber submitted a requisition for work beyond the scope of the original contract. The charges were $91.00 for the wood battens, $97.00 for renting the gasoline pump to secure water, and $33.50 for temporary heating to "dry out the building." These charges were approved by the President. Adams-Faber listed six items where the President was given a credit and nine others where additional costs had been incurred; the builders did not request payment, even though the new charges exceeded the credits by $30.10 (Roosevelt nevertheless paid for these charges). The credits included changes to the pantry sink, savings in the allowances for lighting fixtures and linoleum, and the omission of two hydrants, hose bibs, and an electric outlet at the front entrance. The extra charges included additional hardware and bathroom accessories, more closet shelving, an electric rather than a water-operated sump pump and an outlet for it, a switch for two outlets on the west porch, and more "rough flooring in attic wings," as well as two items that may have been related to Roosevelt's physical disabilities: raising the "entrance platform" and a "Special mirror under medicine cabinet in master bathroom."[100]

Christian Bie, who later became the resident caretaker at Top Cottage, submitted a bill to the President on December 7 for cash advanced for work at the cottage. It included seven days of work by a man listed only as Edward, lumber, hardware (including some for a kitchen cabinet), and "2 pcs. Presdwood Counter" measuring 3 linear feet.[101]

The final payment to Adams-Faber, for $3,119.82, was made in January 1939; the total cost of their work was $17,086.25. The furnace was an additional cost for which the

View of the west porch, June 1939. Photograph by Von Knoblauch, courtesy of the Franklin D. Roosevelt Library, Hyde Park.

contract price had been $1,200. On January 9 Toombs submitted his "final statement of the 'bad news'," an invoice for $803.88, which was quickly approved and paid.[102]

When Adams-Faber acknowledged receipt of their final payment in January 1939, they asked Missy LeHand to convey to the President that it had been "a pleasure to build for a client who had a real and personal knowledge and appreciation of the intricacies of construction." They wanted the President to "know that we appreciate his helpful advice and suggestions." Toombs told FDR that he had been "much amused to learn from some mutual friends of the Adams, that in spite of being a stalwart Republican, since doing the President's house, he has become a great admirer."[103]

The contractors had promised to visit the house in the spring of 1939 to check conditions after the winter. Paul Adams made this inspection trip on March 22 and provided Toombs with a list of several items that needed attention. He reported, however, that "In general it seems to be in very good shape considering the fact that it has stood without heat all winter so soon after being completed." The linoleum was in "good shape," but the wood floors were "slightly cupped." Another problem was "stone work at the rear of the fireplace" that had "split away." Adams suggested that a cast-iron fireback rather than new stones should be installed. Toombs agreed that the masonry should not be repaired; "It nearly always splits," Toombs replied, "and probably he can have it fixed at some later time." There were a few hairline cracks in the plaster in the living room, "the only noticeable one being alongside the fireplace," according to Adams.[104]

The well, Adams continued, seemed to be "in the same condition as it was when we left the job last Fall so probably no water is available in the house." He planned to visit the property again after the heat had been on for a couple of weeks and adjust some doors. Soon after Adams's visit, Roosevelt's superintendent, William A. Plog, had the heat turned on. On April 14 Adams reported to Toombs that he had adjusted the doors and hoped that the condition of the floors would improve. "Thus we have done everything we know about to adjust and complete the house," he concluded.[105]

View of the north wing and the chimney, June 2, 1939; note the original paneled doors. Reprinted, by permission, from Corbis Images.

Building Materials and Systems

The documentation in the files of the Roosevelt Library at Hyde Park and at the Georgia Department of Archives and History provides detailed information on the following building materials and systems used at Top Cottage: masonry and plaster, roofing, millwork, plumbing, heating, electrical work, painting, flooring, and hardware.

Masonry and Plaster. Roosevelt had returned the signed construction contracts to Henry Toombs on July 7, 1938. The President had found them in order except for the clause stating that he was to furnish the building stone; that clause, Roosevelt wrote to Toombs, "might mean that I would have to furnish the cut stone above the windows and doors." The contractor, the President explained, would have to supply the cut stone, since he did "not think we can find any that is long enough on the place."[106]

The contractors confirmed this understanding about stone: the President was, according to John Faber, "to furnish us with all the building stone both for foundations and walls and chimneys but it is a part of our obligation to furnish the miscellaneous blue stone for window sills, doors, porch floor, etc." The sills, Faber continued, "are to be generally like the sills used at the Nancy Cook house which appear to be old stone curbing."[107]

The stone for the walls of the cottage was to come from the Roosevelt estate, specifically "from old fences" of native stone. Roosevelt also told Toombs that if the stone were not being delivered "fast enough," then the contractor should "get after Mr. Plog," the superintendent, "who has instructions to hire an extra truck if necessary."[108]

By the end of July the mason had laid up some samples of stonework, and Paul Adams sent photographs of them to Toombs, asking him to "study these samples, make comments, or mark up the photographs in any way you choose." The photographs showed how the stones had been laid; the desired effect seemed to be "naturalness," or how closely the stones had been laid in relationship to their natural position before they had been quarried. Various types of pointing were also illustrated: some examples showed the joints "more

View of the east entrance, June 1939. Photograph by Von Knoblauch, courtesy of the Franklin D. Roosevelt Library, Hyde Park.

View of the north elevation, June 1939. Photograph by Von Knoblauch, courtesy of the Franklin D. Roosevelt Library, Hyde Park.

marked," and some showed the individual stones being more exposed. The foundation walls were complete by the last week in July, and Adams-Faber needed Toombs's input so that the mason would know how to proceed with the exposed exterior walls.[109]

The final decisions on the stonework evidently had to be made without a Presidential inspection, since Roosevelt was then out West. In his reply to the contractors, Toombs agreed that the pointing in one of the samples was "excellent and what the President wants" and that another sample was "also very good." "I think you have the right idea," he continued. He predicted that the President would be "pleased."[110]

On September 30 John Faber reported that "the exterior stone walls are complete, fully parged on the inside and the asphalt dampproofing applied." The chimney was also "complete except for the splayed stone shelf on the exterior." He told Toombs that the only work remaining on the porch was "the laying of the flagstone which is on the job and it is going to make a wonderfully fine porch."[111]

When the President, Toombs, and the contractors inspected the house on November 5, there was some discussion about a "bolt which appears on the face of the chimney in the east elevation." The Adams-Faber representatives checked the architectural drawings and told Toombs that it was a tie rod that had been shown on the drawings; the painter was "to paint the head of this bolt to match the stone work."[112]

The specifications for the house had asked for bids for both hard-finish white plaster and sand-finished plaster. Adams-Faber's bid quoted both at the same price. At the end of August Toombs recommended that the living room and perhaps the entryway, bedrooms, and the bedroom hallway would be best with the sand finish. Earlier the President had personally decided to use Rocklath. The house was built with Rocklath and sand-finished plaster.[113]

Roofing. On July 14, 1938, Adams-Faber submitted "a sample of the #210 blue-black asphalt shingles" for Henry Toombs's approval; the cost was $7.00 a square. Toombs approved the sample, which was a Carey 10-by-36-inch #210 shingle. However, the roofing contractor, Henry A. Olsen, of Poughkeepsie, recommended an alternate that he felt was of a better quality. It was also a #210 shingle and was blue-black in color, but it measured 12 by 36 inches and was made by the Cooper Company, of Elizabeth, New Jersey. Olsen felt that the greater width of the Cooper shingle would provide more protection. Because it was a " 'Slam Test' shingle," he explained, "the slate particles used on this shingle are impressed more firmly on the asphalt, and felt," thus making this shingle "harder to dislodge than ordinary asphalt shingles." Furthermore, since the back of the shingle had an asphalt finish rather than talc or sand, it would "stick to the shingle underneath, and in this way, prevent the tabs from blowing off to a great extent." Toombs agreed to the use of this shingle, provided the contractors agreed. There was to be a gutter at the east side of the house but not on the porch.[114]

By September 30 the wings of the cottage had been shingled, and the roof sheathing and the roofing paper were in place over the center section. The standing-seam copper roof on the porch was also complete, and the center section of the house was to be shingled during the first week in October.[115]

Millwork. The millwork contract was awarded by Adams-Faber to the Sandford Woodworking Company, which was located in Mount Vernon, New York, and specialized in "trim, sash, doors, stairs" and "all kinds of interior work." Their work at Top Cottage included the double-hung windows, frames for the exterior doors, a sliding door between the living room and the porch, and the exterior wood cornices. Toombs was responsible for providing details of the millwork; on July 29, for example, he submitted 3-inch-scale details of the sliding doors. The millwork firm further refined the drawings supplied by Toombs; in a letter dated August 2, for example, Sandford asked about a wider bottom rail for the interior doors, the thicknesses of the exterior doors, and the relative placement of plaster and trim.[116]

The millwork was also to include paneled reveals for all windows except those in the kitchen, the pantry, and the servants' bedroom and bathroom. Toombs was to "detail the kitchen and pantry dressers," as well as the weatherstripping for the sliding doors. To reduce costs Toombs "simplified the construction of the cabinets" and omitted doors on the wall cabinets and cabinets under the sink. Toombs was to select the hardware from the Tull Metal and Supply Company.[117]

By September 30 the window sashes had been installed in the cottage, and many of the exterior doors had been manufactured. Two weeks later all the millwork was "primed and finished"; this work had been done off site and was to be delivered on October 18.[118]

Plumbing. The plumber selected for the cottage was Joseph Fimble, a Poughkeepsie man who had been recommended by Nancy Cook ("he is the most reliable plumber we have ever had," she had written to Toombs).[119]

The plumber was to begin work during the first week of August. A question that needed Toombs's response was the location of the leach field for the septic tank. Toombs left the decision to the discretion of the builders but alerted them to the possibility that the President might someday build a garage on the east side of the house. On August 22 John Faber told Toombs that the plumber was scheduled to start work that day. Evidently he had not started earlier in the month, perhaps because of the delayed decision on the heating system (similarly, the electrical work had not yet been started).[120]

The plumber's prior relationship with the Roosevelt family caused some difficulties in the customary chain-of-command at the building site. On September 20 Toombs received a telegram directly from Eleanor Roosevelt stating that the plumber had told her that "your grease trap . . . is 75 feet from house instead of right near opening" and directing Toombs to "wire him immediately." Toombs responded with a telegram to Adams-Faber acknowledging his error (having the grease trap so far from the house was "obviously incorrect") but directing the builders in the future to tell the plumber "to take up such matters with you and you alone."[121]

Some additional trouble arose in October, when Fimble discovered that the 6-foot-long Standard bathtub specified for the south wing had been discontinued. Fimble at first suggested substituting a very similar 6-foot tub from Kohler but then spoke directly to Roosevelt, apparently when the President visited

View of the north entrance, June 1939. Courtesy of the Franklin D. Roosevelt Library, Hyde Park.

the cottage on October 4. The President told Fimble "to get a 5'6" Master Pembroke Tub." Adams-Faber found themselves caught in a predicament between the President and his plumber on the one hand and architect Toombs on the other. Adams-Faber wrote Toombs that "We lectured Fimble about taking these matters up direct with the President but he is incorrigible and seems to consider himself the confid[a]nt of the whole family on plumbing matters." The builders threw the decision to Toombs: "If you have any objection to this 5'6" tub," they wrote, "please let us know." They were eager to have a decision so that they could "set the tub before plastering the bathroom," but they soon had second thoughts because there were too many "complications of furring and replastering" and because "the finished result will not be as good." Finally, Paul Adams directed Fimble to install the 6-foot Kohler tub and pointedly told him that "both the architect and ourselves resent your taking these matters up directly with the owner before consulting with us." In a separate letter Adams asked Toombs to "back us up in the position we have taken" with Fimble. Toombs did so, telling Paul Adams "I think by all means I would request that the Kohler 6' tub be installed."[122]

Heating. Correspondence about the heating system began with an Atlanta branch manager of the Holland Furnace Company who apparently had worked with Toombs before and now asked a colleague in Poughkeepsie to extend "courtesies" to Toombs. The Atlanta representative noted that the cottage "is of unusual construction, with concrete and brick for the outside walls."[123]

As late as July 11 there were still many unresolved questions about the heating system and even about whether there would be central heating. Adams-Faber wrote on that date to Toombs that "if there is any thought of putting a heating system in the building the furnace probably should be placed in the basement before the first floor beams are framed and sheathed." Toombs responded that he was then "investigating heating," but that "In any case" Roosevelt "must have a furnace and we have got to provide for the access to put in the furnace." Toombs anticipated that "this might best be done through the floor joists" and expected "to have the matter settled before you get to that point."[124]

On July 15 Toombs wrote to his colleague in New York, architect William J. Creighton, asking him to help with the heating plans, evidently meaning that he should secure a better price. In the letter Toombs gave some background on the project: "The President said that he wanted to do a very simple system and cut down on this if possible. As you will note, the system included is for oil with a 1000-gallon tank, acceptable registers and fan.... It is to be remembered that this house is a sort of weekend place which is not likely to be used a great deal in the winter time, and this is in no sense to be a gold-plated job."[125]

The Holland Furnace Company, which advertised that it was the "world's largest installers of home heating and air conditioning systems," insisted that the best system for the house was one using "baseboard registers as originally planned" and an oil-fired furnace. The firm described it as "a simple, forced air heating system using good controls, properly sized and designed furnace, quietly operating oil burner and blower, backed by thirty-two years of heating experience."[126]

Despite Toombs's entreaties the Holland Company would not reduce its price further; part of the cost was attributed to the extensive length of the ductwork. Toombs needed Roosevelt's agreement before authorizing the heating work to begin: "I can't make that a decision until he gives me the word," Toombs stated.[127]

Toombs wrote to Missy LeHand on July 31, explaining that "the lowest price... for a satisfactory job" was the Holland Company's $1,200 proposal and that "this is my recommendation for heating which will not give trouble." A coal-fired "gravity installation can be done," Toombs continued, "but this would be most unsatisfactory." He asked her to "get an OK,...as it is urgently necessary to install ducts as the house is being built, and progress soon will be delayed." If the President were "unwilling to authorize the complete plant," Toombs asked, would "he authorize the installation of the duct work." Toombs did not receive the President's approval until August 11. One savings was accomplished by reducing the size of the oil tank to 500 gallons.[128]

Once the contract was awarded, the heating company's Poughkeepsie representative told Toombs that the "original layout" with "baseboard warm and cold air directional flow type registers will be installed" and promised that "we are going to give you the finest type of installation that it is possible for the Holland Furnace Company to install." The Holland Company provided shop drawings, dated August 15, 1938, to show the layout of the ductwork and registers. These plans were probably traced from Toombs's original contract drawings, which have not been located.[129]

By September 30 the ductwork had been installed, the basement floor was completed, and the heating company expected to "place the furnace" during the first week in October, before the basement steps were built.[130]

Roosevelt's decision to use an oil heater caused some political ripples. In October the president of the Vulcan Anthracite Stoker Company, of Wilkes-Barre, Pennsylvania, wrote to the head of the United Mine Workers of America about a story that had appeared in a local Republican publication about the oil burner. The "sinister purpose" of the story had been "to prove Our President was not in sympathy with the interests of the anthracite miners, numbering 100,000, in the hard coal field of Pennsylvania." The United Mine Workers thought that the rumor about the oil burner "is hurting the cause of the Democratic Party and its candidates in the vast anthracite region in northeastern Pennslvania."[131]

Roosevelt defended his choice of oil as "the simplest fuel to 'turn on' for a few hours or a day." He would be occupying the cottage only "for a few hours or a day or for a Saturday-Sunday at the most." Consequently there was only a small tank for oil, and, Roosevelt continued, "if I had been putting in a furnace to be used through the winter, I would most certainly have used some form of Anthracite Stoker." Evidently FDR was not too concerned: he did not reply to the miners until after "the pre-election rush" and called the issue "the very small matter of the heating of my very small cottage."[132]

Electrical Work. Roosevelt had expected that electrical service would be installed at the building site during the summer of 1938. Power was especially needed by the masons, since they planned to use an electric pump to draw water from the new well. The lack of electricity meant that a gasoline pump was required and that water had to be trucked to the site. Since the furnace could not be operated without electricity, temporary heating was required to dry out the house.

Part of the delay in installing the electrical service was the cost of the poles to run the overhead wires to the cottage from Cream Street. At this time property owners, through their electrical contractors, were responsible for supplying the poles, as well as the wiring. Because Central Hudson Gas and Electric charged customers per pole, the President wrote he had "got the specifications" and "cut and skinned eighteen poles from my own woods—hemlock thirty to thirty-five feet long." This would reduce the cost "by seven or eight dollars a pole," since this was "the stumpage value of oak trees suitable for poles on the stump." Another problem was that Central Hudson wanted to provide duplicate service to rural customers wherever possible (duplicate service to the cottage would have required running poles through what Roosevelt called "the very rough woods that lie between the new cottage and the Val-Kill Cottage"). Roosevelt did not want this duplicate service.[133]

The electrician for the work inside the cottage was Joseph D. Quinn, of Poughkeepsie, who was also the electrical subcontractor at the Rhinebeck post office. He told Roosevelt that "you may rest assured that I am giving you the highest class electrical installation that is humanly possible." By the end of January 1939 the "small amount of clearing" necessary to install the poles from Cream Street was completed. The power company ultimately decided to use Roosevelt's hemlock poles for experimental purposes and therefore assumed the cost of the installation; they refunded to the President the sum of $59.50, his cost of securing 17 poles at $3.50 each. The President asked the head of the power company, "for my own protection," to send a confirmation that "the running of this new line from Cream Street is in accordance with the general practice of Central Hudson." "I cannot," Roosevelt continued, "of course, afford to be given any 'special treatment' in view of my position." The power company completed work and established service at Top Cottage on January 28.[134] The wiring inside the house was to all be run in "rigid metal conduit." Toombs explained that the President had specifically requested rigid metal conduit.[135]

The stories about Top Cottage that appeared in the popular press had explained that Top Cottage was to be a retreat for the President "to which he can withdraw on his visits to Hyde Park when he wants to avoid the interruptions that sometimes occur at the small study in his mother's home there." More specifically, it was to be "a home without a telephone where Mr. Roosevelt can relax and 'get away from it all.' " The *New York Times* editorialized that "Americans are always building themselves little cabins where they can get away from the hurly-burly of this complicated life" but then "equip the cabin with two telephones and a radio." At Top Cottage the electricians made installations for exactly those purposes: one telephone outlet was to go in a bedroom, and the other telephone outlet and the radio outlet were to be placed to the right of the fireplace. However, a phone was not installed, at least not at first: the President told a reporter for *The New Yorker* magazine that "There isn't any telephone in the place . . . because, you know, if there's a telephone, somebody is sure to use it." A Poughkeepsie furniture dealer proposed in 1939 that the President might want to have a television set installed, but Roosevelt replied that he wanted "to be entirely free from both telephones and radio."[136]

During construction in 1938 a problem arose over an electric exhaust fan in the kitchen. Toombs had decided to eliminate it, but it still appeared on the drawings. Joseph Quinn, the electrician, complained to Adams-Faber that the fan was not part of his contract. Paul Adams wrote to Toombs to resolve the dilemma: "Mr. Quinn, you may remember, was the electrician who mentioned to the President that he was the only Democrat figuring the electric work. In spite of this virtue, he is somewhat difficult to get along with so we told him we had to put the matter up to you and if you said the fan was part of the electrical work, we would expect him to supply it." Toombs replied that it would be best to "relieve" Quinn "of that responsibility."[137]

The New York Fire Insurance Rating Organization issued a certificate for the electrical work on November 21. The approved equipment, which was located in the basement and first floor, included 18 switch outlets, 37 receptacle outlets, 15 fixture outlets, 16 "Inc. Lamps," and "one 2 K.W. Water Heater." *Life* magazine reported in 1938 that in place of security guards at the cottage, there would be "an electric eye for firing a gun at the approach of intruders," but no evidence of such an installation was located.[138]

Painting. The paint colors for the cottage were decided upon in general terms by the President, and specific colors were then selected by the architect and the contractors. Pratt and Lambert materials were to be used.[139]

Adams-Faber took care in conveying the President's thoughts on the paint colors to Toombs. Roosevelt had visited the cottage on October 4, 1938, and told Paul Adams that the exterior paint "should be about the same color as the priming," which was white. "Should this be cream white," Adams subsequently asked Toombs, "or a true white?" Roosevelt had also requested that the interior be painted white, and Adams asked Toombs for "your instruction on this."[140] Toombs replied that "The exterior white should be, not a true white, but something between a cream white and an oyster white. It is difficult to say exactly. It should go with the joints of the masonry. If there is any question in your mind about this, I suggest you ask Mr. Creighton to go up with you. I think in order to get it, a true white should be greyed slightly so that the wood work is not too conspicuous."[141]

For the interior trim Toombs suggested "what is called an oyster white." On October 31 Adams-Faber told Toombs that they expected to start the final coat of interior paint on November 3 and noted that they needed more definition of Toombs's request of oyster white; the painter, Paul Adams telegraphed Toombs, "says there are many different colored Oysters."[142]

Flooring. On October 4, 1938, during a visit to the cottage, the President told a representative of Adams-Faber that the wood "floors should be medium, not light or dark." Adams-Faber sent "two samples of a floor finish" for Toombs's approval on October 24.[143] From these Toombs selected the following finish but added that it seemed "a little light" and asked the builders to "darken it somewhat." The finish was to be "1 Coat of Pratt & Lambert Golden Oak Paste Filler, wiped off. 2 coats of Pratt & Lambert '61' Quick Drying Floor Varnish, Clear Gloss. 1 coat of Pratt & Lambert '61' Quick Drying Floor Varnish Satin Finish."[144]

The flooring contractor was Larson Brothers of Mount Vernon, New York, who advertised as being "Famous for Finer Floors." The wood flooring contract work was completed on November 2.[145]

Toombs assumed the responsibility of specifying the linoleum. On October 17 he sent blueprints of the first-floor plan that he had revised to show the linoleum details and patterns. The linoleum was installed by mid-November. The builders were concerned that it might "pull away in places," because the house was to be closed up for the winter very shortly after construction had been finished.[146]

During the inspection of the house made with the President on November 5, Hall Roosevelt had expressed concern "about floors buckling because there did not seem to be much ventilation beneath them and the heating ducts were not covered." The contractors agreed that there could be a problem with the wood floors warping but not for those reasons; instead, they were concerned "because no heat will be in the house during a long period."[147]

In fact it was not long before problems appeared. The Poughkeepsie branch manager of the Holland Furnace Company, J. C. Hutchinson, wrote the President that he had visited the house and that "one of the men working there called my attention to the condition of your floors which are beginning to warp." He attributed the warping "to extreme cold and dampness in the house which, of course, can only be corrected by some means of heating." Hutchinson recommended that since it did not seem "practical to erect a permanent power line at this time... it would be vastly worth while to lay a temporary line on the ground." The President however, decided to proceed with "putting in the poles from Cream Street to the new cottage" and gave strict instructions that he did "not want the furnace lighted unless there is somebody in the house while it is going."[148]

Hardware. The hardware schedule was prepared by the J. M. Tull Metal and Supply Company, of Atlanta, and then submitted by the architect's office to the builder in August 1938. Many of the items listed on the schedule came from the catalog of P. and F. Corbin; other items were sold by the Stanley Works of New Britain, Connecticut.[149]

The schedule for the cottage listed hinges, bolts, locks, stops, glass plates, hooks, window fasts and lifts, latches, and checks for the screen doors, as well as hinges, catches, pulls, and knobs for the kitchen and pantry cabinets and drawers. However, no hardware had been listed for the "scuttles-screen windows" or the ironing board; there was also a note that 14 pairs of blinds had been omitted. Adams-Faber found the schedule acceptable except that there was nothing listed for the attic door, which the President had said might be used "to haul trunks through." Toombs added a cylinder lock to the schedule before returning the list to the Atlanta supplier; the supplier confirmed that he was ordering additional hinges, a night latch, and a pull. The hardware was to be billed to Adams-Faber and shipped to their White Plains office, for delivery to the cottage.[150]

Press Coverage of Top Cottage

From the time that Top Cottage was being planned, it had caught the attention of the press and the public. Architect Henry Toombs and builders Adams-Faber immediately recognized the professional value of a commission from the President of the United States.

The *Architectural Forum* contacted Toombs in July 1938 about publishing a story on the house. Since he had not prepared any perspectives or presentation drawings, Toombs suggested that the cottage be illustrated through a photograph of the model that he had constructed. Alternatively "a rendered perspective could be made," Toombs told the editor, but "I would expect you to pay for it."[151]

Meanwhile, Toombs asked the President for permission to have the project published in the architectural press. The White House had received inquiries from newspapers and

Rendering of east elevation by Schell Lewis, 1938. Courtesy of the Georgia Department of Archives and History, Atlanta.

magazines. Roosevelt approved the requests through his staff, but with a stipulation that the material should be released simultaneously to all media. The magazines protested, since the newspapers could publish the material much more quickly. Finally, it was decided to give the magazines a three-week lead.[152]

In the interim Toombs had decided to finance the cost of the renderings himself and engaged Schell Lewis, one of the country's best architectural delineators, to prepare "a couple of your good perspectives." Toombs sent Lewis a set of plans and asked the contractors to supply him with "some photographs of the trees and house so far as it is built." Toombs wanted the house to "sit close to the ground" in the renderings and hoped that Lewis would capture "the character of a house in woods." Toombs rarely complained about the project, but his next statement to the artist revealed his frustration. "I'd like these to be swell, Schell, as they'll probably get published all over the country, but for God's sake don't spend too much time on them so that you'll have to charge me a lot, as I'll have to pay for them myself, and this house is already costing me plenty."[153]

On September 27 Toombs released a media kit consisting of the President's plans and elevation, the "Final Plan," photographs of the model, Lewis's perspectives, and a brief description. This material initially went to two architectural magazines and to the *New York Times*, two Atlanta newspapers, and three wire services.[154]

Toombs had forecast the public interest in the house correctly. The renderings were immediately published by the *Los Angeles Times*, the *New York Herald Tribune*, the *Pittsburgh Press*, and the Washington, D.C., *Sunday Star*. The publicity brought the President a flood of critiques on the layout of the cottage from architects and lay people alike. Several people commented on the inadvisability of locating the bathroom window so that it opened onto the entrance terrace, while many others faulted the President for not providing sufficient closet space. The closets became an issue during one of Eleanor Roosevelt's press conferences, and even Aunt Het, a cartoon character in an Atlanta newspaper, offered an opinion on the closets: "That new dream house of Roosevelt's has cooked his goose, as far as I'm concerned. Any man that would

Rendering of west elevation by Schell Lewis, 1938. Courtesy of the Georgia Department of Archives and History, Atlanta.

design bedrooms without closets will make a mess of anythin'!" Once the editors of a Montclair, New Jersey, newspaper learned from the *New York Times* that a hometown firm was building the President's cottage, they too wanted to do a story. Editors of national publications were similarly captivated, and stories soon appeared in *Life, Time, Progressive Farmer,* and *American Builder,* many with reproductions of Roosevelt's original plan and sections.[155]

In May 1938 Toombs had proposed the idea of listing Roosevelt as the architect of the cottage and himself as the associate; his media release, as well as Schell Lewis's renderings, prominently carried those attributions. Comments from architects across the country soon appeared in the press and in Roosevelt's mailbox. John Lloyd Wright, a son of architect Frank Lloyd Wright, complained in a letter to *Life* that the architects of Indiana "with the help of State law, have been trying to confine the title Architect to only those qualified as Architects. That's bad enough—but after seeing the title Architect after F. D. Roosevelt in your magazine, I give up.... The moral breakdown of the integrity and dignity of the Architectural profession seems now complete."[156]

In another letter to the editor, an architect from Middletown, New York, asked sarcastically, "May I hope that in the near future you will give us, your readers, pictures of 'Doctor' Roosevelt performing an appendectomy?"[157]

Henry Toombs prepared a rebuttal that recited his role in proposing the attribution and asked rhetorically, "Does our professional dignity clothe us so tightly that we cannot squeeze out a smile of welcome to a visiting amateur?" The President liked Toombs's letter but suggested adding a postscript: "By the way, did Thomas Jefferson have a license when he drew the sketches for Monticello, the University of Virginia and a number of other rather satisfactory architectural productions?" The journal *Pencil Points* urged the profession to look at "the practical side of the question" and avoid becoming agitated, for "it seems clear that (1) the President has no intention of practising architecture in competition with existing talent and (2) invoking the law against him would make the profession appear ridiculous."[158]

While the President may have enjoyed observing this wrangling within the architectural profession, he was irked when journalists insisted upon calling Top Cottage his "dream house." A reporter for the *New York Times* had written in October 1938 that the cottage "will be the realization of a dream that has been

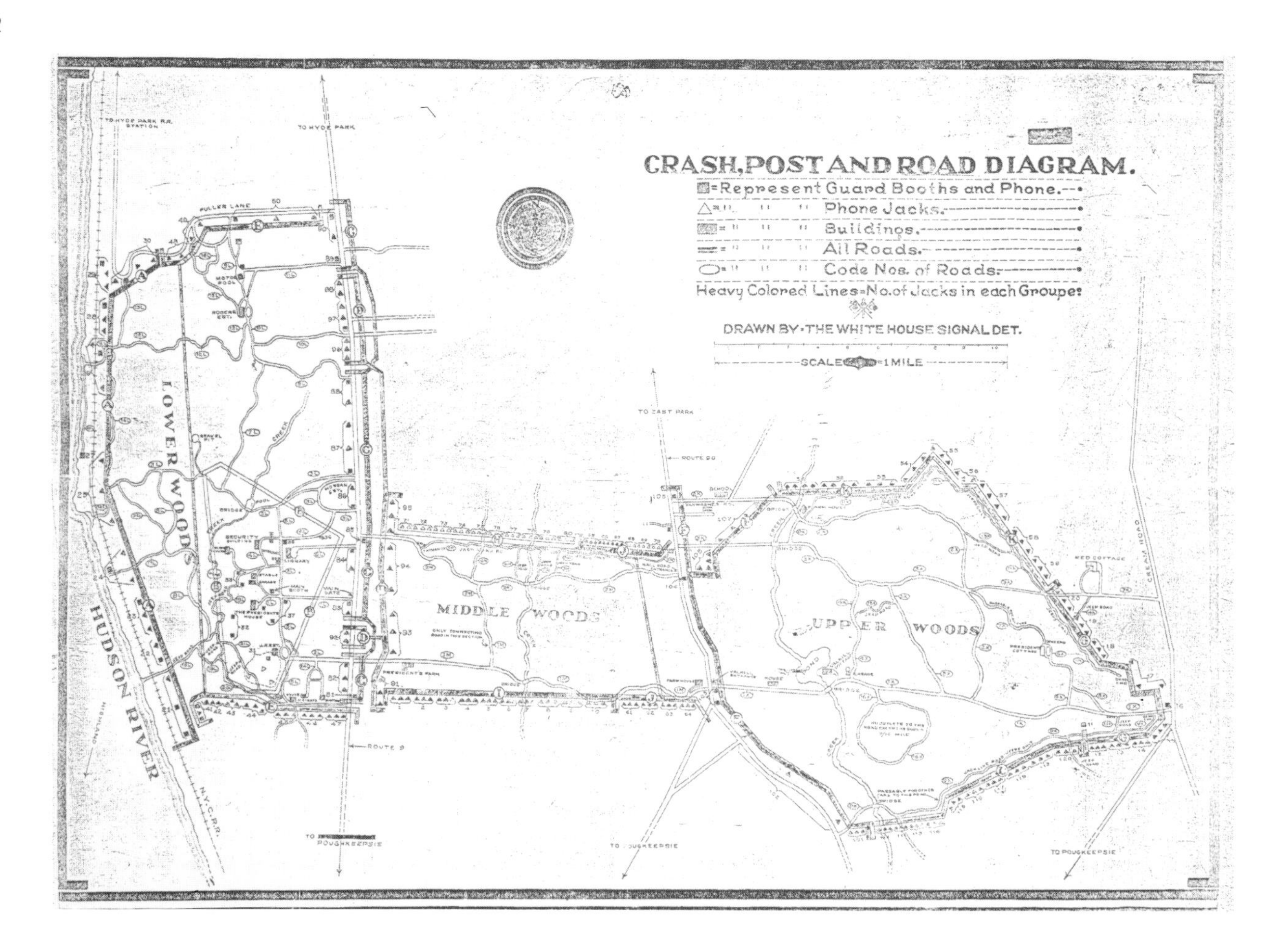

Crash, Post and Road Diagram, prepared by the White House Signal Department to protect President Roosevelt's travel from Springwood to Top Cottage, c. 1940.

with him for twenty years," and other publications also adopted the term.[159] The President's annoyance over this name appeared in the 1942 memorandum that he wrote about the history of the design and construction of the cottage:

> About the time the house was being built, the newspaper men heard of the operation and asked for a story on it. The story was outlined as above written, emphasis being placed on the fact that it was intended solely to get away from official business during the daytime while at Hyde Park.
>
> One or two of the newspaper men, out of a total of about ten, deliberately and without any intimation that it was accurate, invented the name "Dream House," giving the impression that I had regarded it as such and that I had always longed for such a place.
>
> The story was copied in most papers, in spite of the fact that the name was definitely repudiated the following day.
>
> In other words, an untruth was never caught up with.[160]

Earlier in 1938 Roosevelt told reporters that "We will call it after the hill, this old hill along here, from two miles south to a mile north. It has always been known as Dutchess Hill." He replied to a question from the press about the name of the house:

> Just "The Cottage on Dutchess Hill." It is the "Roosevelt Cottage on Dutchess Hill." That is the only name it has and of course the boys that go up to Hyde Park with me understand very thoroughly that it never has been a "Dream Cottage" and they are living up to my request that it should not be called that because it does not happen to be true and never was, so I saw no particular reason for perpetuating the forgery by calling it that.[161]

Holiday magazine reported in 1949 that Top Cottage had been "at one time probably the most publicized bit of private construction in the country, perhaps in the world" and remarked that "A still vivid recollection, for newspaper readers of the period, is the frequently published picture of the late President at the wheel of his little blue Ford, watching the work in progress."[162]

Enjoying the New Cottage

On April 14, 1939, contractor Paul Adams told architect Henry Toombs that "we have done everything we know about to adjust and complete the house." Ten days later Missy LeHand wired the superintendent of the Roosevelt estate, William A. Plog, to "please have truck at station Thursday morning to take large size desk to the new cottage." Even though this telegram is marked "canceled," it indicates that the President's attention was turning to furnishing the cottage. The President was in Hyde Park on May 27, and according to the *New York Times* his purpose was to check on arrangements for the forthcoming visit of King George VI and Queen Elizabeth of Great Britain, who were to enjoy a picnic at Top Cottage in June.[163]

One task that needed attention was the purchase of kitchen appliances. On June 2 Ruth Bie purchased a General Electric electric range and a General Electric refrigerator "equipped with evaporator door, light, quick trays and crisper" from the Wallace Company in Poughkeepsie. General Electric had begun lobbying for the use of its products at the cottage in 1938. At that time a G. E. representative told the President's staff that "the President because of his interest in General Electric has given his approval to putting G. E. equipment in his homes" and wondered "how he should go about getting the President's approval on putting similar equipment in the new home which is now being built at Hyde Park." Ruth Bie also purchased a "Bendix Laundry," probably for the use of her family, who would soon be moving into the house as resident caretakers.[164]

The Sunday afternoon picnic that the Roosevelts arranged for King George and Queen Elizabeth on June 11 was a great success. The President drove the royal couple from Hyde Park to the cottage. The press was not allowed to attend; the *New York Times* reported that "regular photographers were barred from the party but every one present had a camera." The king, in turn, made a movie with his hand-held camera of the amateur photographers taking pictures of him. One hundred fifty people attended; several tables for dignitaries were set up on the porch, while the other guests were accommodated on folding chairs on the lawn. The menu featured hot dogs and draft beer, as well as regional hams, turkey, and salad. Snapshots of the festivities, as well as professional photographs made of last-minute preparations of

View of the west porch during a lunch for the Crown Prince and Princess of Denmark, May 1, 1939. Photograph by Margaret Suckley, courtesy of the Franklin D. Roosevelt Library, Hyde Park.

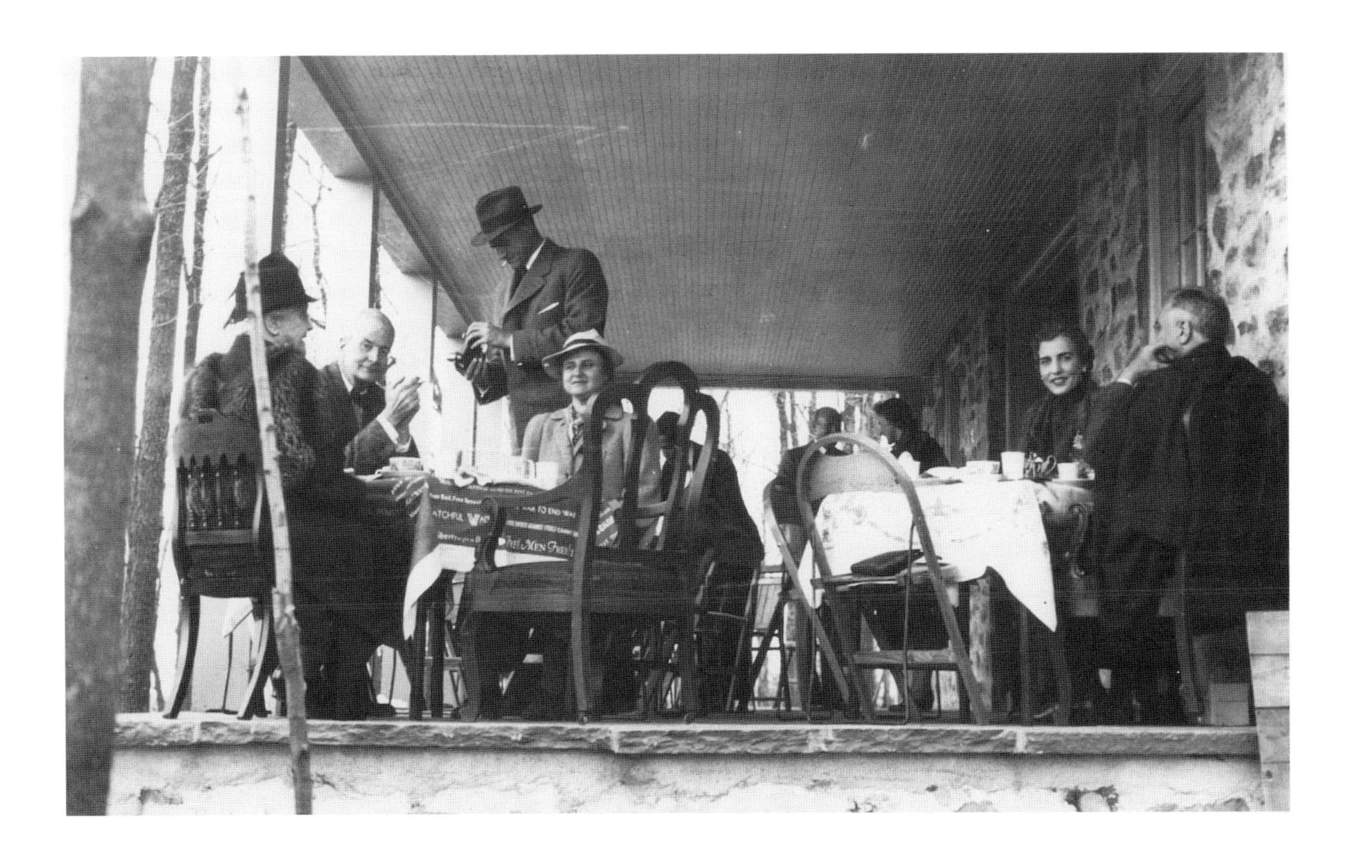

Guests on the west lawn for the June 11, 1939, luncheon in honor of King George VI and Queen Elizabeth. Courtesy of the Franklin D. Roosevelt Library, Hyde Park.

the grounds, provide excellent documentation of the newly completed cottage.[165]

Except for the porch, the house was sparsely furnished. On May 30 Roosevelt had told reporters that "there are now three pieces of furniture in it" and that "Probably by this time next year there should be about eight." "It will probably get furnished over—I do not know what—ten or twelve years." A Bigelow Sanford carpet, which measured 30 feet by 14 feet 5 inches and was purchased through S. S. Spivack of New York, was not delivered until early October, and the Kirch curtain rods, which the President himself was to choose, did not arrive until at least the end of September. The curtains proved troublesome. Missy LeHand had ordered sample rods from Hammacher Schlemmer, but 21 traverse rods were purchased instead from Luckey, Platt and Company, of Poughkeepsie. This firm also made the draperies, which had to be altered to be made wider.[166]

Betsey Cushing Roosevelt, the wife of the President's son James, wrote to FDR in September that she and the President's mother had "found a very nice double walnut bed which used to be in the chintz room" and wondered whether "you want it moved to your house now." The President replied that it was "grand about the double walnut bed" and asked that the estate superintendent deliver it to the cottage.[167]

Christian Bie made other furniture for the cottage. In December 1939 he submitted a bill for $168 for 280 hours that he had spent making a "Center bookcase," two "End bookcases," a table, a bed, and a dresser. Roosevelt described Bie as a "skilled cabinet maker" who had emigrated from Norway and was "sober and conscientious."[168]

As construction work at the cottage was underway, many firms and individuals from across the country wrote to the President to offer furnishings and accessories for his new home. For example, Harry G. Barker, of Carmel, Indiana, offered to make a "hand wrought lead" lantern. His offer was accepted, and the lantern is still in place at the cottage. Roosevelt had selected the design from photographs that Barker had sent and had told him that "it would be my thought to hang it from a bracket in the little courtyard of my new house—and I think it would be best to have opaque, white glass."[169]

"A deeply cushioned lounge chair upholstered in smooth brown fabric, with the initials FDR appliqued in white down the back" was a gift from an upholsterers' union. A "Desk lamp patterned after an old-fashioned pump" made by WPA workers was forwarded from Boston. A furniture company in New York City offered to "furnish with our compliments" the sitting room, but Missy LeHand replied that "The President says it would be grand if Chairs, Inc. would like to give him either a very nice sofa or a comfortable chair or both for his new cottage. But, he thinks that is enough. (Dark wood)." Other people, including Myron S. Teller, an architect who also owned a business in Kingston, New York, that made wrought-iron colonial-style hardware, received very polite but noncommittal responses to their inquiries. Some letters were passed on to Henry Toombs or Adams-Faber for reply.[170]

Daisy Suckley, the President's cousin and friend, recorded in her diaries many occasions on which the President and his companions enjoyed the cottage. On March 28, 1942, she noted how the President had driven Harry Hopkins, Hopkins's daughter Diana, Grace Tully, and Daisy up to the house for a two-hour respite that day:

Off we go to the Top Cottage where we have a delicious lunch—First I get out the tea cloth & napkins purchased by F.D.R. himself at Panama, I think, on one of his cruises—It is like Italian embroidery. I put it on the card table in front of the fireplace. A low glass top table is in front of the P. who sits on the sofa—Miss T., Diana & I unpack the picnic baskets (2) & out come: clam broth—hot—A large Kentucky ham, tomato salad—cheese—fruit—coffee—bread—Mr. Hopkins slices the ham & the P. shows us how to butter two slices of bread—spread ham on one, cheese on the other, mustard over both, & put them together! Delicious![171]

On another occasion later that year, Daisy Suckley wrote that "We went to the Top Cottage, and took in a pile of books on trees & birds, etc. We sat on the porch & talked for a while in the quiet cool evening sunlight. He talked of his boyhood & school-days—a thing he rarely does." On the Friday after Thanksgiving, 1942, she recorded how the President "was entirely alone" at his mother's house "except for Diana Hopkins & her little friend Susan, so he asked me to go to lunch with him. We took a picnic basket & went to the cottage & had: scrambled eggs, cold turkey, mixed vegetable salad, toast (tended & buttered by F.D.R.)." Geoffrey C. Ward has written how "It was a matter of great pride to FDR that things were arranged at Top Cottage so that he could personally serve his guests without help. A toaster, bread, and butter were set up within easy reach on a card table before the fire, and he buttered each piece of toast with a flourish."[172]

Daisy Suckley enjoyed another occasion at the cottage early in the spring of 1943. "We went to the Cottage," she wrote "made tea & toast in front of the fire, & talked. The P. was relaxed & peaceful, & talked mostly about his hopes for future peace. He has it all worked out in his mind already." On a winter afternoon early in 1944, she recalled, "after tea we took some books to the Top Cottage [and] stayed there for a while, talking, the setting sun streaming in through the wide door onto the porch. The living-room looks so attractive—The P.'s things getting gradually arranged as he likes them best."[173] They had done some decorating a few weeks earlier:

Seated around the table on the west porch during the June 11, 1939, luncheon are Mrs. Henry Morgenthau, King George VI, Sara Delano Roosevelt, and Herbert Lehman. Courtesy of the Franklin D. Roosevelt Library, Hyde Park.

Jan. 30th Sunday. . . . On Thursday afternoon, he took GGT, D. Brady & me to Top Cottage to hang pictures. Mr. Plain & Steve took over a stepladder, wire, hooks, etc. Pictures were hung in all the first floor rooms & the Chinese porcelain screen fastened to the wall. That little house is a little museum in itself. The P. is going to have everything in it catalogued.

Friday, the P. & I went up again to see how it all was; then he drove me home, & came in to tea.[174]

Above: Eleanor Roosevelt in the furnished living room, 1942. Courtesy of the Franklin D. Roosevelt Library, Hyde Park.

Below: President Roosevelt and Fala, June 1942. The entry (101) and pantry (108) appear through the north doorway. Photograph by Margaret Suckley, courtesy of the Franklin D. Roosevelt Library, Hyde Park.

Above: President Roosevelt in the living room (102), October 1942. Photograph by Margaret Suckley, courtesy of the Franklin D. Roosevelt Library, Hyde Park.

Below: President Roosevelt on the west porch with Margaret Hambley, King George II of Greece, and the Crown Princess Martha of Norway, June 27, 1942. Photograph by Margaret Suckley, courtesy of the Franklin D. Roosevelt Library, Hyde Park.

In the spring of 1944, as D-Day approached, she and FDR returned to the cottage: "We put a couple of chairs in the sun, north of the porch, & just talked, quietly, about the view, the dogwood, a little about the coming invasion in Europe." A few days later she wrote: "At 5 we went to Hilltop with some books & pictures and I made some tea & he toasted some of the Mickleham bread."[175] They spent afternoons in the late summer of 1944 sitting on the porch working or talking. A visit with friends was part of the agenda for the afternoon of Election Day in 1944: "At 4 P.M. he came for me, & we all piled in to go for tea to the Top Cottage: Anna & John, Admirals McIntire & Leahy, Fala & I. We lighted a welcome fire & spent a couple of hours up there, very peaceful and restful— Then back to the big house where we washed up & gradually collected in the library."[176]

Early Repairs and Alterations

During the summer of 1940 three leaks were discovered in the house; one was described by Hall Roosevelt, Eleanor Roosevelt's brother, as "rather important since it is in the big main room near the fireplace." He attributed the problem to the failure of the roofers to "set the tins into the stonework." Missy LeHand wrote to contractor Paul Adams that the largest leak "near the fireplace had actually developed before the workmen left the building, and the President was told that the matter had been definitely attended to." Adams immediately contacted the roofing subcontractors and told them "to go up and make the repairs at once."[177]

Early in 1940 some alterations were made to the heating system; the Holland Furnace Company submitted a bill for work done in February that included "automatic draft equipment." There was confusion over who had authorized this work; the Holland Company stated that Christian Bie had contracted for the work. The President had understood that the "new arrangement was to be cheaper" but was very concerned that 1,100 gallons of oil were used in a month. Hall Roosevelt wrote that the "new heating installation . . . is apparently as bad as anything I have ever seen." In March 1941 he confronted the Holland Company with news that he had checked with "New York State Authorities" and that the ducts would have to be removed. The company responded that an error had been made in handling the billing and that no charge would be made. Now, rather than removing the new work, Hall Roosevelt and Russell Linaka, who worked in the Roosevelt estate, would "fix it up ourselves and make it work according to the N.Y. State law."[178]

Hall Roosevelt contacted Missy LeHand about some other problems: the "roof still leaks," he wrote, and the disintegration of the fireplace now had reached a depth of one-and-one half inches. The sliding door was "designed to run off the runners and jam instead of opening," while the "shingles over the west portico are wired so that the wind blows them away." Paul Adams was to return in the spring of 1941 and make repairs.[179]

Top Cottage had been deliberately planned as a one-story structure. In 1938 when reporters asked Roosevelt whether he would "finish the second story," he replied that "That is not for use; that is only for air." However, the President soon began planning alterations to finish the second floor. The initial changes, inserting bedrooms in the attic of the north wing, were probably made in order to accommodate resident caretaker Christian Bie and his family. A stair was inserted into the southeast corner of the kitchen in a space previously used as a pantry. This work was probably completed by February 1941, when Hall Roosevelt mentioned "the new quarters occupied by Bie and Company." An article published in the *New York Times Magazine* in August 1941 stated that "a couple" was "permanently established as staff and caretakers." In March 1943 Roosevelt wrote that the Bies "live as caretakers in my Hill Cottage."[180]

Meanwhile, probably during January 1940, Henry Toombs had met with Missy LeHand and other members of the President's circle, and probably with the President himself, to discuss adding bedrooms in what was then the attic over the south wing. On January 31, 1940, Toombs sent Roosevelt a two-page letter and some sketches to explain two schemes for building stairs to the second floor and adding dormers to the west side.[181]

Toombs described one scheme as "something like what" Roosevelt had suggested. It involved adding a partially enclosed stairway

President Roosevelt, July 1944. Photograph by Margaret Suckley, courtesy of the Franklin D. Roosevelt Library, Hyde Park.

that would break through the exterior walls of the building; in order to accommodate the stair, the first-floor bathroom ceiling would be lowered by 18 inches. However, Toombs thought that the resulting exterior view of the stair was "not very happy"; he found it reminiscent "of the old walled towns like Carcasonne" and left it to Roosevelt to decide "whether you would enjoy this variation from the Hudson Valley Dutch tradition."[182]

Toombs's other scheme called for placing the stairway inside, against the south wall of the living room. Toombs thought that this arrangement would be less expensive since there would be fewer alterations to the stonework. This scheme called for lowering the hall ceiling "for a short distance"; it made the larger of the upstairs rooms "slightly awkward." Toombs offered to detail the drawings to carry out this work, or if the President had further ideas, Toombs would be happy to "work them up." Toombs came north in the spring of 1940, but whether this trip was related to these alterations is not known.[183]

Nothing more seems to have been done on these bedrooms until 1942. By July 3 the Holland Furnace Company had submitted a proposed layout for forced-hot-air heating. These plans showed a stairway being inserted in a closet at the northeast corner of the wing; upstairs there were two rooms (the north room was labeled as a living room rather than as a bedroom) separated by a bathroom; there were to be dormers in the north room and in the bathroom, along with a pair of windows in the gables. The designer of this scheme is not known, and it was not followed; Toombs by then was serving in the military and may not have been available to help.[184]

Work was underway on the second-floor alterations by the fall of 1942, when John Blandino was paid $165.00 for "breaking stone wall & setting window frames at Hill Top Cottage." This work probably involved the creation of the new windows in the north and south gables. On February 9, 1943, Frank Hering was paid $17.75 for a "Plaster job" at the cottage. On the same date W. W. Lumb and Company were paid $497.46 for "Labor & materials for addition" to the cottage; a month later they received a second payment, also for labor and materials, in the amount of $576.03, and on April 1 a third payment for $175.71. At this time several related bills were settled: Fred Kloepfer was paid $91.00 for "Wiring & fixtures for 'Hilltop Cottage,' " and Joseph L.

View of the living room (102), looking northwest, May 1, 1945. Courtesy of the Franklin D. Roosevelt Library, Hyde Park.

Fimbel, the Roosevelts' longtime plumber, received $252.21 for "Installing bathroom" on the house. Some "wardrobe rods" were also part of the improvements.[185]

The Holland Furnace Company was scheduled to complete work after mid-May 1943. The new bedrooms were not furnished until later that summer; evidently Christian Bie had also been involved in the construction work, for Daisy Suckley recorded in her diary that on August 28 the President "came to the Library about 4—chose 4 chairs & 4 tables for his cottage. We took them up there & the S[ecret] S[ervice] moved them, & beds & mattresses to the 2nd floor bedrooms just made by Mr. Bie." In 1944 the President referred to these rooms as guest rooms.[186]

Toombs had suspended his architectural practice when he joined the Army during the war. When he wrote to Roosevelt in mid-1944 to tell him that he had reopened his office, the President replied that he was "delighted you are back at the old stand in Atlanta and I hope if I get to Warm Springs I shall have a chance to see you." Toombs also wrote to congratulate the President on his "glorious" victory in November 1944.[187]

Landscaping

During the weekend of May 28, 1938, Roosevelt and Toombs discussed the landscaping around the house, including the creation of a small lake. To implement that scheme, Toombs once again turned to one of Roosevelt's contacts at the U. S. Treasury's Procurement Division for help in locating contractors who had the proper equipment and could do the job economically. The lake was to be about 4 feet deep and would extend onto the Backers' property. An existing brook would supply the water.[188]

On the east side of the house, according to Toombs, the President intended "to raise the road eventually in front of the house to the level of the Terrace." Toombs had discussed other additions to the site; he reported that "very probably" the President was "apt to build a garage near the servant's wing."[189]

The President had summarized his intentions about the landscaping in 1938 when he wrote to a fertilizer salesman that "I am having no lawn and keeping the woods in their natural state." He told the press that "There will be no garden," but he wanted to secure "from out of

View of the living room (102), looking east, May 1, 1945. Courtesy of the Franklin D. Roosevelt Library, Hyde Park, New York.

the woods and from the Catskills, various flowering shrubs, things of that sort, so that we will get something flowering from the first of May through September." In 1941 a nursery in Michigan (a Republican state, Hall Roosevelt noted) wrote that "some prominent" men from Michigan wished to send a half dozen or so hardy plants to the President's estate. The President thought that this was a "grand" idea and welcomed their suggestion of small flowering crabapple trees. He asked that they "be placed on the high point in the open field about two or three hundred feet east of the road leading to the Hill Cottage—in other words, about eight hundred or one thousand feet southeast of the cottage itself."[190]

The views from the hill were very important to the President, but he wanted to open up vistas "just gradually, only one tree at a time, so it won't take too much." A magazine account published in August 1941 noted that the view to the west was not yet cleared: "when the present thicket of trees has been judiciously cleared, as planned, it will command an excellent view of the Catskills, hazy across the miles." Rhododendrons bordered the porch.[191] Photographs taken during Roosevelt's occupancy show an earthen ramp at the north end of the west porch, probably intended to provide wheelchair access to the surrounding landscape.

Inventorying Top Cottage after FDR's Death

After the President's death at Warm Springs on April 12, 1945, the task of inventorying Top Cottage fell to Daisy Suckley. She was at work at the cottage on May 1, three weeks later, and recorded her thoughts in her diary on that day: "Up at Top Cottage I was mentally saying farewell to just another chapter in F.D.R.'s life for it is probable that when I have finished this inventory, I shall never again see that lovely room *as it is.* Such happy hours have been spent there by F.D.R.—relaxed and peaceful; sometimes with one person, or two, or three, or even 6 or 8—but always people with whom he did not have to make an effort—who did not demand anything of him, & always loved every little joke."[192]

The record copy of the inventory, which

was dated May 5, 1945, and then annotated by Miss Suckley, listed the furnishings and occasionally their provenance. She made special notes about several objects and furnishings that she had given or loaned the President. A separate inventory of the books was compiled at the same time.[193]

Identified as being on the front door of the cottage was an "old brass knocker," which Miss Suckley had given FDR and which had previously belonged to a Rhinebeck resident, Miss E. M. Lynch. In the entrance hall was an oval table, a mirror, one painting, and four prints. Stored in the closet was a wheelchair, a small rug, and two wooden signs carved with the words "Private property, no visitors." The pantry, which opened off of the entry, held serving pieces, glassware, and dishes, many with designs associated with FDR's naval years and service as governor of New York. On the "Side Board," evidently the countertop in the pantry, were three trays and a shaker. Above were three shelves filled with sets of china, barware, decanters, jugs, a coffee maker, and an electric toaster. The inventory included a few remarks about the sources of the gifts, and those that dated from 1938 may have been housewarming presents. The drawers in the pantry held linens and utensils, and in the lower cupboards were pans and small electric appliances. Other contents of the north wing were not included, perhaps because those spaces were occupied by the caretakers. A second inventory, prepared by the P. J. Curry Company for FDR's attorneys, noted that there was a 1939 model, 8-cubic-foot General Electric refrigerator and a 1939 Bendix washing machine in the kitchen.

The living room contained a screen painted with a Hudson River view that was a gift from Eleanor Roosevelt, a Chinese screen from the Roosevelt home at 47 East 65th Street in Manhattan, and three items from the Hall house in Tivoli—a table with a green top, a bookcase, and a cabinet with a broken pediment. Also in the living room were a firewood box and fireplace accessories, a small drop leaf table, a large chintz-covered chair, a Chinese Chippendale stand and table with vitrine, a hanging corner stand, a revolving chair and a revolving-top table that were copies of pieces owned by Thomas Jefferson, and a reproduction of a "desk now in City Hall, New York, said to have been given to George Washington by General Lafayette, in 1789."

Roosevelt's black leather Cabinet chair that he had used from 1933 through 1941 was in the living room, as were flower stands and a mahogany table made by Christian Bie, a ladder-back chair with a blue-upholstered seat, and a set of chairs with pink-upholstered seats. To the left of the fireplace was a large sofa with a chintz slipcover and a "Homespun India rug"; the inventory noted that "FDR usually sat on this folded rug, because the sofa was so low it was difficult for him to get into his wheel chair." There were several pieces of furniture that had been loaned by Daisy Suckley and were now being returned to her: four Sheraton chairs with green seats, an old drop leaf table, and an old wing chair with a green-and-white slipcover. There were several lamps and rugs, as well as numerous prints, paintings, and decorative and souvenir objects on the tops of tables.

The only objects that Daisy Suckley inventoried in the first-floor bedrooms in the south wing were the prints, drawings, and paintings on the walls. Her inventory referred to the "2nd floor bedrooms" and noted that the contents were "not listed." The only piece of furniture in these rooms that a second inventory listed was an "American Chippendale Style" slant-front desk.

A set of record photographs of the cottage was made on May 1, 1945, at the same time that Daisy Suckley was preparing the inventory.

Subsequent Owners

On May 3, 1945, James Roosevelt, the President's eldest son, met with an attorney handling his father's estate. A memorandum of their discussions stated that James Roosevelt had made various arrangements regarding the management of the Hyde Park estate. Included was an agreement in which the Bies were to continue to live rent-free at Top Cottage; Mrs. Bie had agreed "to make breakfast for any guests who may stay at Hill Top Cottage from time to time." The estate was to pay electric and telephone bills at the cottage.[194]

Within about a month, however, Elliott Roosevelt, James's brother, had decided to spend at least the summer of 1945 at Top

Cottage. Germany had surrendered on May 7, and Elliott, according to his mother, was hoping "in a few weeks to be out of the army." In a June 11 letter Eleanor Roosevelt wrote that Elliott and his wife, actress Faye Emerson, her young son Scoop, and "a housekeeper all came up with me" the previous weekend. Elliott and Faye left for a few days, but Faye was to return soon and start "to put her house in order." Eleanor subsequently wrote that "We are getting the top cottage in order & I take my hat off to Faye. She works!" In 1946 a lease certifying Elliott Roosevelt's rent of $75.00 a month was filed with the office of Price Administration in Poughkeepsie.[195]

Faye Emerson and Elliott Roosevelt had been married in December 1944. She held a screen contract with Warner Brothers at the time of her marriage, and she performed in summer stock and on Broadway between 1946 and 1948. She accompanied her husband to Russia as a special correspondent for *Look* magazine and helped interview Premier Joseph Stalin. According to one press account, the couple "entertained swarms of important visitors, including Winston Churchill, 'Ike' Eisenhower, Mme. Chiang Kai-shek," at Top Cottage. "Sometimes," the story continued, "Eleanor Roosevelt came over from her house with a crowd of U.N. delegates in tow." The Roosevelts were divorced in 1950.[196]

Meanwhile, Eleanor Roosevelt planned to purchase about 825 acres of farmland and woods from the President's estate, and Elliott planned to manage it as a large dairy farm. In 1948 *Time* magazine carried a story about how partners Elliott and Eleanor would begin offering meals and lodging at the refashioned Val-Kill Inn; they also hoped "to build a much bigger place modeled after F.D.R.'s stone 'hideaway house' at Hyde Park." The magazine also reported that Elliott had resumed the sale of Christmas trees in 1947 and was raising chickens, Guernsey cows, and steers, as well as feed for the livestock. Elliott's best-selling book, *As He Saw It*, which recounted the summit meetings that his father had with Churchill and Stalin, had been published in 1946.[197]

Elliott had the west porch at Top Cottage enclosed. One of his sons, Elliott (Tony) Roosevelt, Jr., and his sister, Chandler, spent the summers of 1948 through 1950 at the cottage. They remembered the smaller bedroom on the first floor still being used as a bedroom (without the closets) and the bathroom in its original configuration. There were no dormers in the south wing, but there was a window seat in the second-floor north bedroom. A cook and her daughter and son-in-law lived in the north wing. It is possible that architect Henry Toombs may have planned some alterations to the cottage, for he included in a list of his projects a notation of "Res. Alt." for Elliott Roosevelt, probably meaning alterations to a residence. However, no further details were available.[198]

One of Eleanor Roosevelt's biographers has written that she had awakened one morning "to read in the *New York Times* that the top cottage built by the President had been sold by Elliott." This was probably the article published on April 18, 1952, which reported that the sale had taken place on April 12 and that Elliott "needed money for a new business venture in Cuba." The price was estimated at about $150,000 for five hundred acres of the estate. The purchaser was identified as William H. Kay, Jr., whom the *Times* described as "head of a construction firm and a beef cattle raiser of near-by Netherwood, N.Y.," who planned to create a "residential development." The Poughkeepsie *Sunday New Yorker* identified Kay as a "Salt Point farmer and equipment dealer" and predicted that Top Cottage "will be resold." Elliott's "farm stock and equipment" had earlier been sold at auction.[199]

In the fall of 1951 Elliott and Eleanor Roosevelt had consigned a "large collection of Franklin Delano Roosevelt items that adorned and furnished the late President's cottage at Hyde Park" as part of a three-week sale at the Hammer Galleries in New York. At about the same time Elliott also sold the President's private library that had been housed at Top Cottage. A newspaper account stated that the library "reflects some of the late President's interests—his love for the sea and his enthusiasm for fishing, for example."[200]

On December 16, 1952, the *New York Times* reported that the cottage had been purchased by Philip S. Potter, Sr., of Poughkeepsie, who was "an executive of the California Oil Company." Potter told the *Times* that "he and his wife and son, Robert, would occupy the house as soon as it could be

Christopher du P. Roosevelt, Franklin D. Roosevelt's grandson, at a ceremony announcing plans for the restoration of Top Cottage and its future acquisition by the National Park Service, May 19, 1998. Photograph by Kathy McLaughlin. Reprinted, by permission, from the *Poughkeepsie Journal.*

redecorated" and that "he would not change the design of the one-story structure." The property included 118 acres. When the deed was executed, on December 23, 1952, the property was actually conveyed to Agnes F. Potter, Philip's wife.[201]

In a recent interview, Owen Potter, Philip Sr.'s grandson, recalled how the house was used by his family and what changes were made. The Potters used the former servants' room on the first floor of the north wing as a dining room and utilized an end of the kitchen as a breakfast nook. The second-story bedrooms in the north wing became guest bedrooms but were seldom used. Owen Potter recalled that the closets in the smaller bedroom in the south wing were already in place and that the children used the upstairs bedrooms.[202]

Philip Potter, Sr., put in a new heating system in the early 1960s; it was difficult to install because the new furnace had to be lowered into place through the floor in the living room (more recently, installation of a new hot-water heater required cutting an opening through the foundation). He also built a greenhouse for his wife in the mid-1950s, in which she grew exotic plants and flowers. Potter constructed a concrete barn with a hay loft and two stalls, where he kept two horses for his grandchildren to ride—"Dream," a palomino, and "Star," a Tennessee walking horse. He built three-rail fences, and the elder Potters kept the acreage intact.[203]

Shortly after Philip Potter's death, however, his sons listed the property for sale with Previews, Inc., a national real-estate firm. A December 1963 story in the *New York Times* about the listing noted that the house had three bedrooms, a "formal dining room," and a "servants' suite of two rooms" in the north wing. The property was offered for sale with just ten acres of land. The *Times* illustrated the article with Schell Lewis's 1938 renderings, and Previews produced an elaborate brochure on the house.[204]

The house was taken off the market after Philip Potter, Jr., convinced his wife (Owen's mother), Jean O. Potter, to live in the house. The younger Potters put in a Gunite swimming pool in 1964; in 1972 they installed a fish pond with a fountain. On Christmas Eve in the mid-1970s an electric cord under the rug in the living room caught fire and caused extensive smoke damage; the floor was charred and required refinishing. Philip Potter, Jr., died in 1982, and Jean Potter, who had come to love the house, remained there until her death in 1993. In the mid-1970s Owen Potter and his wife, Ellen, converted the stable into a residence. The three sons of Philip Potter, Sr., had sold the adjoining land for development in the 1960s; a map filed in the Dutchess County Clerk's Office in March 1966 called a portion of the subdivision Val-Kill Heights.[205]

Owen Potter, as his mother's executor, sold the cottage in May 1996 to the Beaverkill

Conservancy, the land-acquisition affiliate of the Open Space Institute. The Institute, which is dedicated to preserving the natural heritage of New York, has worked closely with New York State to expand and to improve the state's network of open space, parkland, and historic sites. The Top Cottage purchase was made possible with a $750,000 grant from the Lila Acheson and DeWitt Wallace Fund for the Hudson Highlands. As part of the agreement with the donor, the Open Space Institute leased the property to the Franklin and Eleanor Roosevelt Institute (FERI), a nonprofit organization founded for the purpose of supporting the legacy of Franklin and Eleanor Roosevelt. FERI agreed to assume responsibility for the future of Top Cottage and to raise funds for its restoration, preservation, and public programming, in cooperation with the Roosevelt Family Committee.

In September 1996, FERI contracted with John G. Waite Associates, Architects, of Albany, New York, for the preparation of a historic structure report for the cottage. Following the completion of this report in 1997, FERI proceeded with plans for the restoration of the building. In May 1998 FERI asked the architects to complete construction documents for the restoration of the house. In that same month, a press conference was held at the house to announce future plans for the restoration of the cottage and the intent of FERI and the Open Space Institute to deed the property to the National Park Service.

In April 1999, bids were received for the restoration work, and a contract was awarded to Magic General Contracting of Salem, New York. The restoration construction began in June 1999 and continued through the late fall of 2000. In the fall of 2000, FERI commissioned John G. Waite Associates, Architects, in collaboration with the landscape architecture firm Elmore Design Collaborative, of Springfield, Massachusetts, to complete a cultural landscape report in preparation for the restoration of the landscape surrounding the house. The property will be opened to the public during the summer of 2001.

First-floor plan of Top Cottage as it existed c. 1939. Casework and sink were located in the pantry; both swinging doors were located in the pantry; sink with flanking cabinets was located against the east wall of the kitchen; built-in shelving was located against the east wall, to the north of the north-east window; stove, casework, and washing machine appear to have been located against the west wall of the kitchen. Drawing by JGWAA.

Second-floor plan of Top Cottage as it existed c. 1939. Attic space in wings probably had rough flooring; attic access was provided by ceiling hatch in south wing; a similar ceiling hatch probably existed in the north wing; and there were no dormers or gable windows. Drawing by JGWAA.

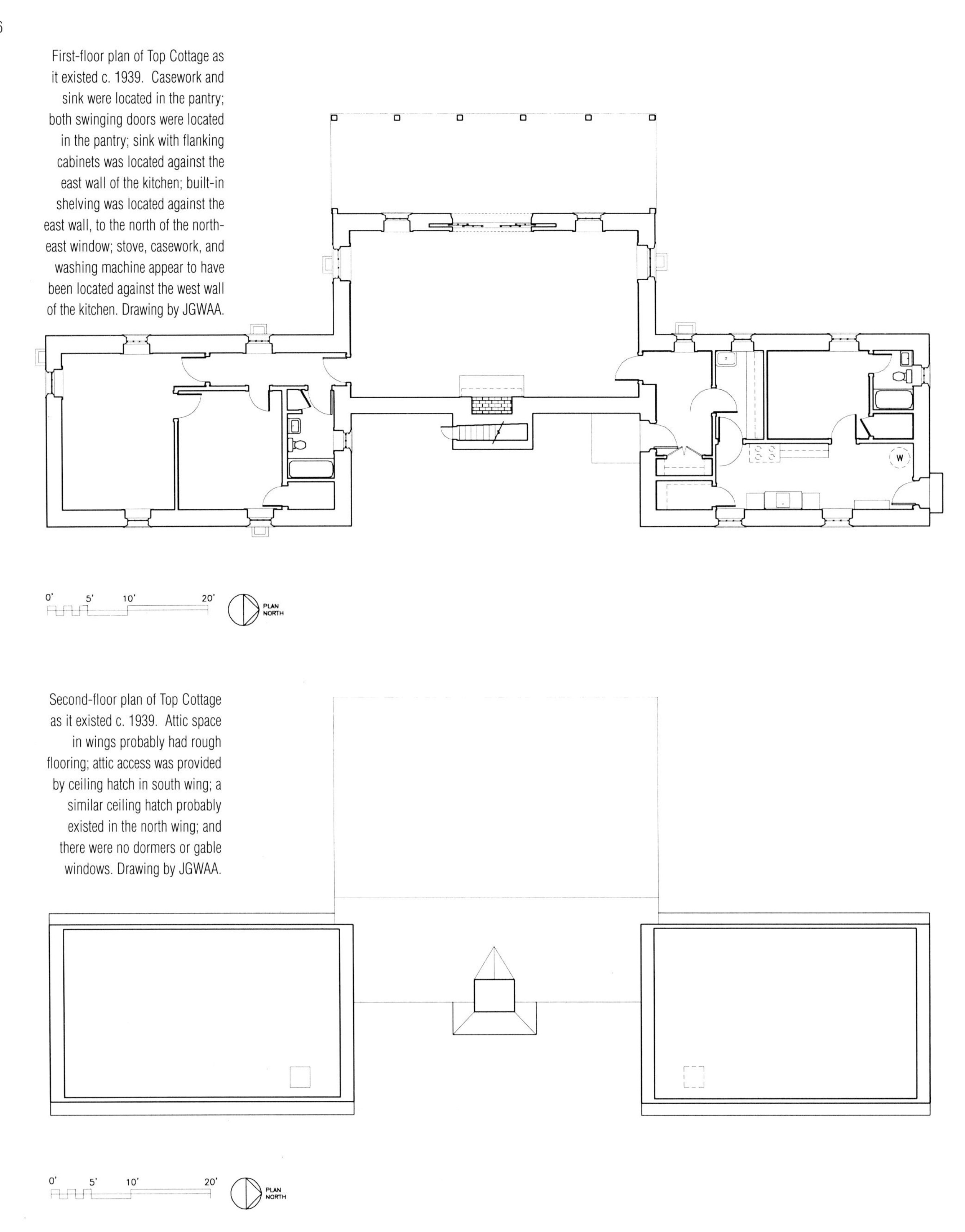

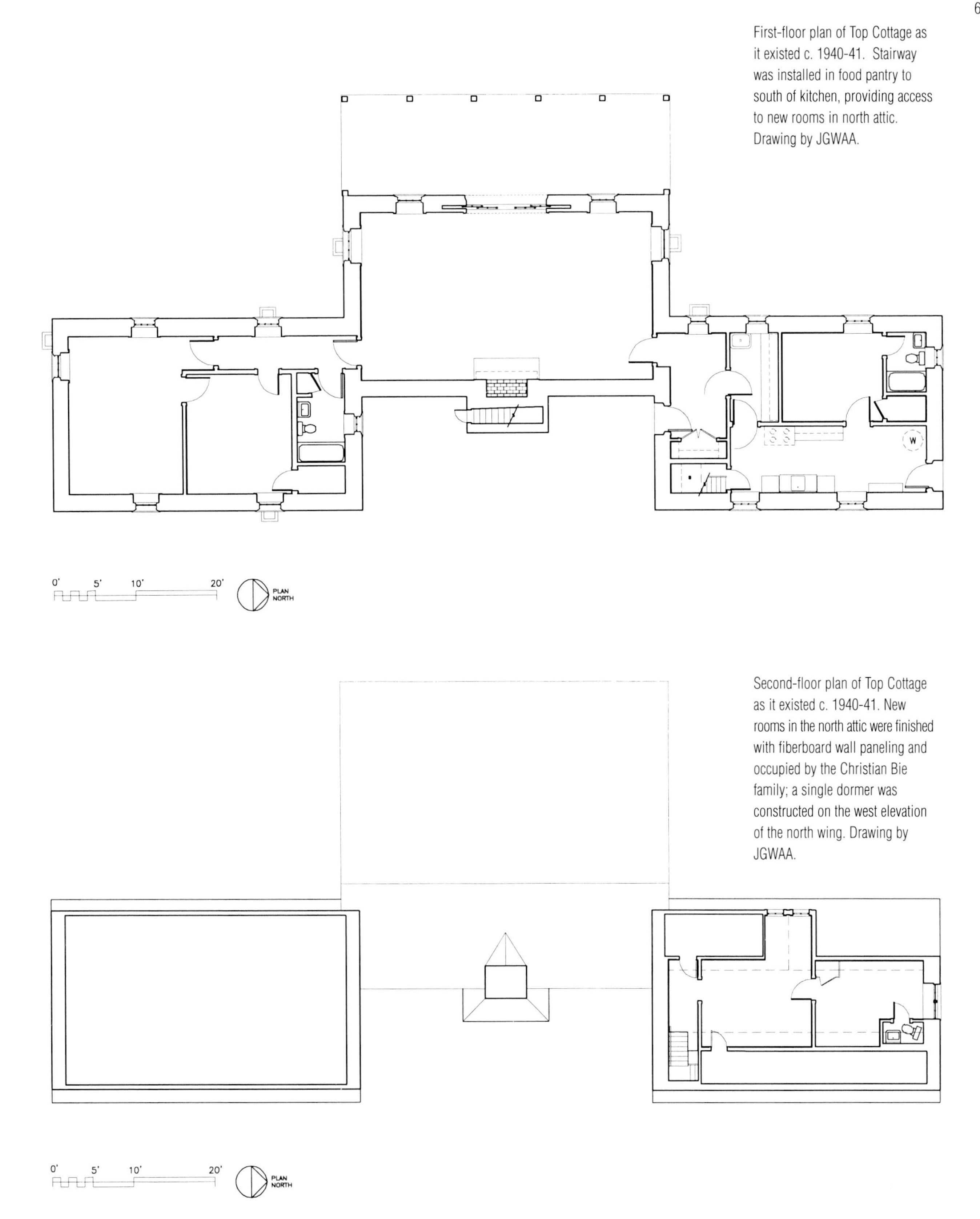

First-floor plan of Top Cottage as it existed c. 1940-41. Stairway was installed in food pantry to south of kitchen, providing access to new rooms in north attic. Drawing by JGWAA.

Second-floor plan of Top Cottage as it existed c. 1940-41. New rooms in the north attic were finished with fiberboard wall paneling and occupied by the Christian Bie family; a single dormer was constructed on the west elevation of the north wing. Drawing by JGWAA.

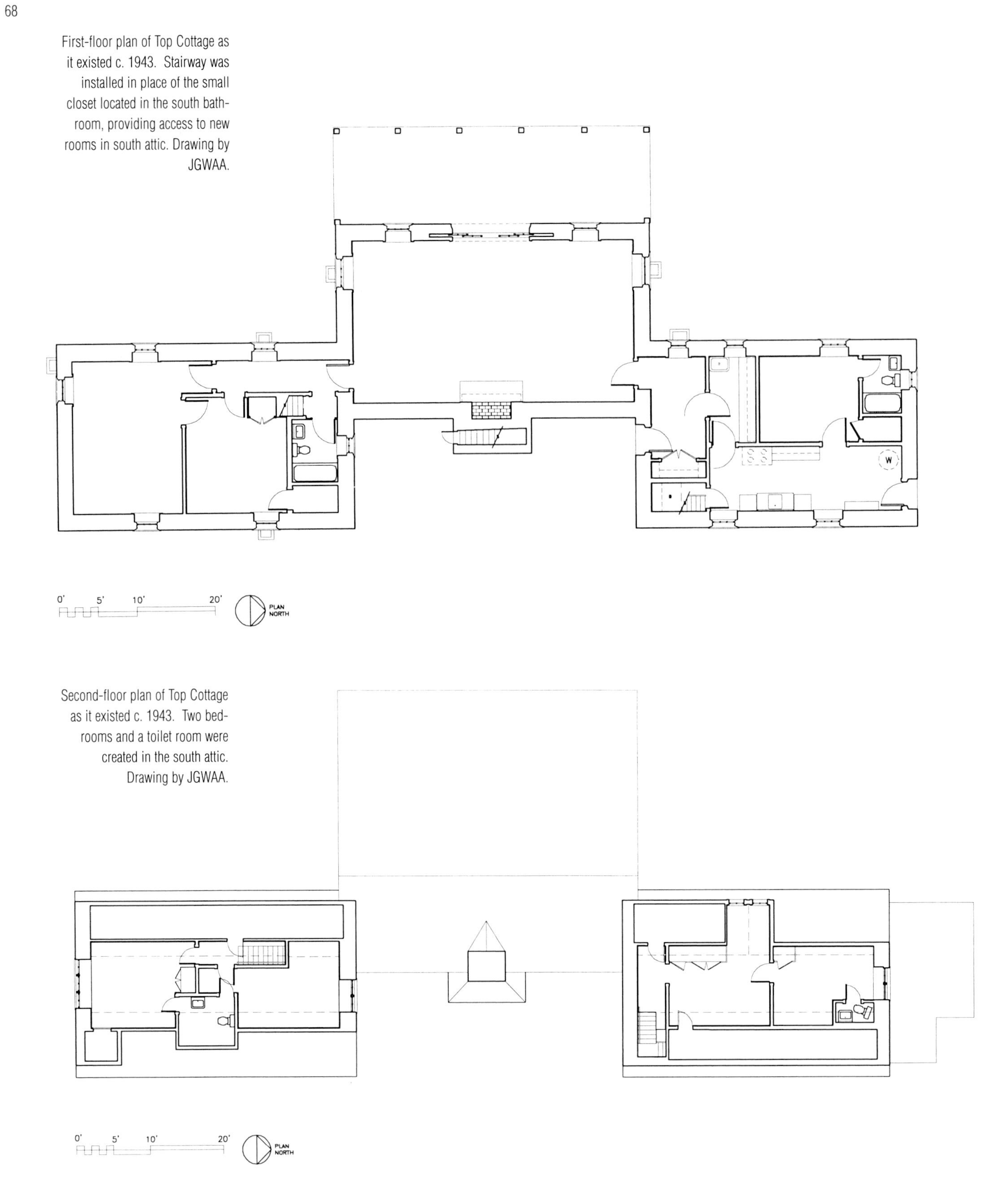

First-floor plan of Top Cottage as it existed c. 1943. Stairway was installed in place of the small closet located in the south bathroom, providing access to new rooms in south attic. Drawing by JGWAA.

Second-floor plan of Top Cottage as it existed c. 1943. Two bedrooms and a toilet room were created in the south attic. Drawing by JGWAA.

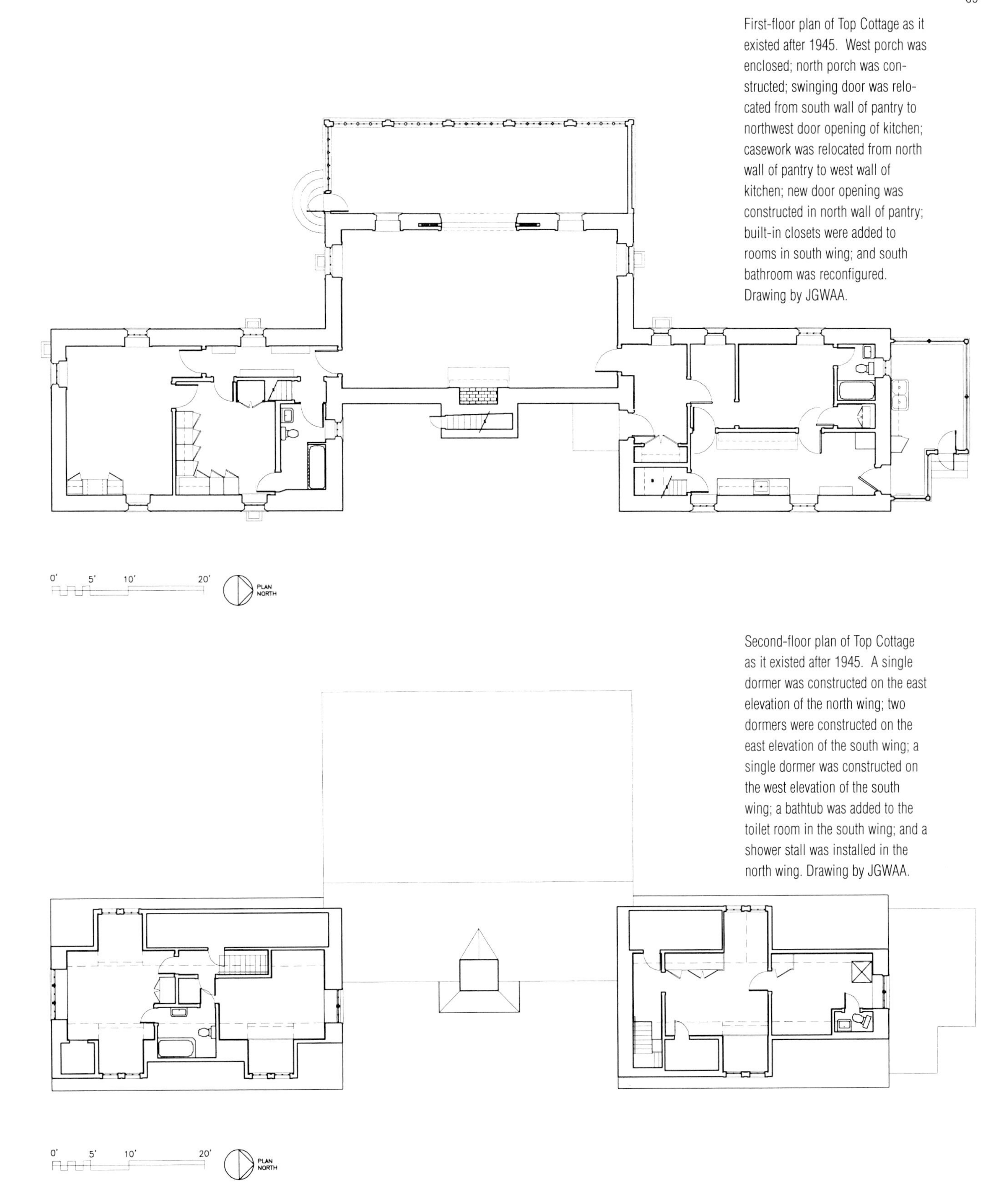

First-floor plan of Top Cottage as it existed after 1945. West porch was enclosed; north porch was constructed; swinging door was relocated from south wall of pantry to northwest door opening of kitchen; casework was relocated from north wall of pantry to west wall of kitchen; new door opening was constructed in north wall of pantry; built-in closets were added to rooms in south wing; and south bathroom was reconfigured. Drawing by JGWAA.

Second-floor plan of Top Cottage as it existed after 1945. A single dormer was constructed on the east elevation of the north wing; two dormers were constructed on the east elevation of the south wing; a single dormer was constructed on the west elevation of the south wing; a bathtub was added to the toilet room in the south wing; and a shower stall was installed in the north wing. Drawing by JGWAA.

Notes

Abbreviations used in notes

A-F	Adams-Faber Co.
CC	Geoffrey C. Ward, *Closest Companion, The Unknown Story of the Intimate Friendship between Franklin Roosevelt and Margaret Suckley* (Boston: Houghton Mifflin, 1995)
CPC	*Complete Presidential Conferences of Franklin D. Roosevelt* (New York: Da Capo Press, 1972)
ER	Eleanor Roosevelt
FDR	Franklin D. Roosevelt
FDRL	Franklin D. Roosevelt Library, Hyde Park, N.Y.
GHR	G. Hall Roosevelt
HE	H. Griffith Edwards
HF	Holland Furnace Co.
HT	Henry Toombs
HTP	Henry Toombs Papers, AC 69-230, Georgia Dept. of Archives and History, Atlanta
HP	Hyde Park
JF	John Faber
ML	Marguerite (Missy) LeHand
MD	Marion Dickerman
NC	Nancy Cook
PA	Paul Adams
PC	Press conference
PPF	President's Personal Files, FDR Papers, FDRL
PPF 1G HTC	President's Personal Files, 1G, Hill Top Cottage File, FDR Papers, FDRL
PPF 119	President's Personal Files, 119, FDR Papers, FDRL
PSF	President's Secretary's Files, FDR Papers, FDRL
PSF 139 TC	President's Secretary's Files, 139, Top Cottage File, FDR Papers, FDRL
RE	R. T. Erickson, of Adams-Faber Co.
WC	William J. Creighton

1. FDR, Memorandum, "Funny or Sad!," Dec. 9, 1942, in FDR, *His Personal Letters*, 1928-1945, Elliott Roosevelt, ed. (New York: Duell, Sloan and Pearce, 1947-50), pp. 1378-79.
2. *PC*, July 1, 1938, CPC 12:1.
3. *CC*, p. 34. The Daisy Suckley materials are quoted with the permission of Wilderstein Preservation, which owns Daisy Suckley's papers.
4. FDR, Memorandum, Dec. 9, 1942, p. 1379.
5. *CC*, pp. 34, 36.
6. *CC*, pp. 44-45.
7. *CC*, p. 44.
8. *CC*, p. 99.
9. Ibid. They had also been discussing the landscape; CC, 99-100.
10. This sketch appears on an endpaper of FDR's copy of *Standard Postage and Stamps Catalog* (New York: Scott Stamp and Coin Co., 1928), copy at FDRL.
11. *CC*, pp. 101-102.
12. *CC*, pp. 102-103.
13. *CC*, pp. 105-106.
14. *CC*, p. 109. Geoffrey Ward points out in *Closest Companion* that Missy LeHand had also hoped to share the cottage with FDR; *CC*, 112-113.
15. *CC*, p. 111.
16. FDR to T. Kennedy, Nov. 12, 1938, PPF 1G HTC.
17. FDR, Memorandum, Dec. 9, 1942, p. 1379.
18. HT, "Doing Architecture with FDR," undated typescript, HTP Box 6, FDR Article File. In this version HT gave the date as 1924. In what appears to be a revised, also undated, version of the typescript, HT dated this meeting to 1925. I thank Elizabeth Knowlton at the Georgia Department of Archives and History for her help in making the Toombs Papers available for this project.
19. Ibid.
20. Ibid.
21. Ibid.
22. Harlan Althea to ML, March 27, 1940, PPF, Box 3449-3485, File 3481, Architecture File.
23. HJT, List of Executed Work, Feb. 25, 1941, PPF 119, HT File.
24. HT, "Doing Architecture with FDR." Nearly all of Toombs's commissions between 1927 and 1938 were for buildings at Warm Springs.
25. Ibid.
26. Ibid.
27. Ibid. See HTP, Presidential Library File, including HT to ML, June 23, 1939. See also William B. Rhoads, "Franklin Delano Roosevelt and Dutch Colonial Architecture," *New York History* 59 (Oct. 1978): 430-464.
28. Tanya Toombs, diary of visit to White House beginning April 7, 1941, HTP, Box 6, White House File.
29. HT to MD and NC, June 1, 1961, MD Papers, Roosevelt Family, Box 5, Folder 5, FDRL. Thanks to Joseph Amisano, former partner of Henry Toombs, for information on Toombs's professional and personal life.
30. HT, "Doing Architecture with FDR."
31. Ibid.
32. NC to HT, telegram, Jan. 31, 1938; HT to NC, telegram, Feb. 1, 1938; HTP, Box 1, 1938 File.
33. HT to NC and MD, Sept. 22, 1937, HTP, Box 1, 1937 File. HT to NC, Feb. 10, 1938; HT to ML, Feb. 10, 1938; HTP, Box 1, 1938 File.
34. John Cutter to FDR, Feb. 18, 1938; FDR to HT, Feb. 24, 1938; HTP, Box 4, HP-1 File. FDR to Cutter, Feb. 24, 1938; FDR to HT, Feb. 24, 1938; Cutter to ML, Feb. 18, 1938; PPF 119.
35. FDR to Cutter, Feb. 24, 1938, PPF 119. PC, June 28, 1938, *CPC*, 11:499.
36. Cutter to FDR, Feb. 18, 1938, HTP, Box 4, HP-1 File.
37. Tanya Toombs to HT, telegram, March 30, 1938; Frank Neely to ER, Feb. 8, 1938; ER to HT, March 5, 1938; HTP, Box 1, 1938 File. ER Papers, FDRL, Speech and Article File, "My Day" Columns, Drafts, Jan.-May, 1938, Box 3071, March 30, 1938.
38. Photostats of these drawings are located in HTP, Tube 10; the originals were not located.
39. Envelope, HTP, Box 4, HP-1 File. Two other notations are difficult to decipher but may relate to water and screens.

40. HT to FDR, telegram, April 7, 1938; HT to NC, April 11, 1938; NC to HT, April 14, 1938; HTP, Box 4, HP-1 File.
41. HT to Henry Hackett, April 16, 1938; HT to L. A. Simon, April 11, 1938; HTP, Box 4, HP-1 File.
42. HT to L. A. Simon, April 11, 1938; Simon to HT, April 13, 1938; HT to NC, April 11, 1938; [NC] to Maurice Finny, April 12, 1938; HTP, Box 4, HP-1 File.
43. HT to ML, April 19, 1938; ML to HT, April 19, 1938; HTP, Box 1, 1938 File.
44. FDR to HT with annotations, April 21, 1938, HTP, Box 10; copy in PSF 139 TC. As with many other documents used in this history, the original letter as well as a copy still survive, one at Atlanta and one at Hyde Park.
45. Ibid. FDR sketches are in HTP, Box 4, HP-4 File.
46. Ibid.
47. Ibid.
48. Ibid.
49. Ibid.
50. Ibid.
51. HT to ML, April 24, 1938, HTP, Box 4, HP-1 File. PC, July 1, 1938, *CPC*, 12:4; PC, Aug. 27, 1938, *CPC*, 12:57.
52. HT to ML, May 5, 1938; FDR, Memorandum for the P. S., May 10, 1938; ML to HT, May 11, 1938; PSF 139 TC.
53. HT to ML, May 16, 1938; HT to ML, May 23, 1938; FDR to HT, telegram, May 16, 1938; PPF 119, HT File. FDR, Memorandum for the P. S., n.d; [ML] to HT, May 20, 1938; PSF 139 TC. HT to NC, May 23, 1938, HTP, Box 4, HP-1 File.
54. A photograph of Toombs holding the model was published in the Atlanta *Constitution*, Oct. 16, 1938. Paul C. Grenier, of Brooklyn, N.Y., built a model of the cottage in 1939, which is in the collection of the museum, FDRL; Wendell A. Parks, memorandum to D. Waite, Dec. 4, 1996. HT also revised drawings 1 and 2 (foundation and basement plans and the first-floor plan); H. G. Edwards to WC, July 19, 1938; HTP, Box 4, HP-3 File.
55. [HT], Specifications of Labor and Materials for the Construction of a House for the President, May 26, 1938; [HT], Specifications of Heating for the Construction of a House for the President, May 26, 1938; HTP, Box 4, HP-1 File.
56. Ibid. All descriptions in this section of the report are quoted from these specifications, with additional information given in notes 57-59.
57. PC, July 1, 1938, *CPC*, 12:1-2.
58. W. H. Carver, Standard Plumbing Fixtures, Specifications for House of the President, n.d., HTP, Box 4, HP-1 File.
59. JF to HT, July 19, 1938, HTP, Box 4, HP-3 File; HT noted on this letter that all wiring was to be run in metal conduit.
60. HT to John Eylers, May 24, 1938; HTP, Box 4, HP-1 File. HT to Frank Seaman, June 2, 1938; similar letters to other contractors were dated June 2-4, 1938; HTP, Box 4, HP-2 File. For contractors' responses, see HTP, Box 4, HP-2 File. For a list of bidders, see HT to Lumb, June 17, 1938; HTP, Box 4, HP-2 File. PA to HT, June 9, 1938, HTP, Box 4, HP-2 File.
61. HT to Henry Ostagen, May 22, 1938; HTP Box 4, HP-1 File. FDR to William C. Feller, June 9, 1938; Feller, Confirmation of Our Conversation of May 30, 1938, June 2, 1938; PSF 139 TC. CPC also contains several references to the well.
62. Feller to FDR, June 13, 1938, PSF 139 TC; Feller Brothers to HT, telegrams, [June 20 and June 21, 1938], HTP, Box 4, HP-1 File. Feller to HT, June 25, 1938, HTP, Box 4, HP-2 File. Feller Brothers, Invoice, July 8, 1938; Feller Brothers, Log of Well, [July 1938]; PSF 139 TC. JF to HT, June 21, 1938, HTP, Box 4, HP-2 File.
63. J. E. Clay to HT, May 31, 1938, HTP, Box 4, HP-1 File. HT to Clay, June 16, 1938, HTP, Box 4, HP-2 File. James L. Lumb to HT, June 14, 1938; see also HT to Lumb Woodworking Co., June 17, 1938; HTP, Box 4, HP-2 File. For other contractors, see PPF IG, Container 20, and HTP, Box 4, HP-3 File.
64. HT to FDR, Invoice, June 6, 1938; HT to FDR, June 6, 1938; FDR to HT, June 9, 1938; HT to FDR, June 16, 1938; PSF 139 TC. *New York Times*, June 15, 1938, p. 23. Nicole Koenig, an intern from Vassar College who assisted with research for this project, located many of the contemporary published accounts about the cottage.
65. FDR to HT, June 9, 1938; HT to FDR, June 16, 1938; PSF 139 TC. HT to John Eylers, June 16, 1938, HTP Box 4, HP-2 File.
66. The staff in the Mudd Manuscript Library at Princeton University, kindly supplied biographical information from the 50-year book of the Class of 1951 (published 1965), obituaries, and biographical data forms on both men.
67. Ibid. Lucy Fitzgerald of the Montclair Historical Society kindly provided a copy of the firm's c. 1940 brochure and city directory listings.
68. HT to ML, Jan. 23, 1939, PPF, Box 119, Toombs File; Atlanta *Constitution*, Oct. 16, 1938. JF to HT, June 20, 1938, with refernce list, HTP, Box 4, HP-2 File. FDR to HT, July 7, 1938, PSF 139 TC. Princeton University, Class of 1915, 50-year book, s. v. Paul Adams. JF to HT, June 27, 1938, Box 4, HP-2 File. PC, July 1, 1938, *CPC*, 12:1.
69. PC, June 28, 1938, CPC, 11:499. JF to FDR, June 27, 1938, HTP, Box 4, HP-2 File.
70. Princeton University, Class of 1915, 50-year book, s. v. Paul Adams.
71. Ibid., s. v. John Faber.
72. Contract, A-F and FDR, July 1, 1939, HTP, Box 4, HP-3 File; the transmittal letter from JF to HT was written on June 30, 1938 (HTP, Box 4, HP-2 File) and listed the cost of the additions and deductions to the contract. A-F also prepared an "Addenda A," which described the changes in more detail; A-F, Addenda "A" to the Specifications," June 30, 1938, HTP, Box 4, HP-3 File.
73. Ibid. A second stone wall had been added at the east front when revisions to Toombs' drawings had been proposed.
74. Ibid. PC, Aug. 27, 1938, *CPC*, 12:59.
75. HT to FDR, n.d., PSF 139 TC. There was also discussion about a discount from the builders if they were to construct the Backers' house at the same time; see HT to FDR, n.d., PPF 119 Toombs File.
76. PC, July 1, 1938, CPC, 12:2-3. JF to HT, June 30, 1938; HTP, Box 4, HP-2 File. PA to HT, July 4, 1938, HTP, Box 4, HP-3 File. *Time*, July 11, 1938, p. 9.
77. *New York Times*, July 3, 1938.
78. PA to HT, July 4, 1938. See also JF to HT, June 30, 1938; HTP, Box 4, HP-2 File.
79. FDR seems to have been little involved in the initial construction, since he left for a trip to the West Coast on July 7 and did not return until August 12; FDR to Moses Smith, July 7, 1938, PSF 139 TC.
80. JF to HT, July 6, 1938; JF to HT, July 11, 1938, HTP, Box 4, HP-3 File. A-F's proposals were approved; HT to JF, July 9, 1938, HTP, Box 4, HP-3 File.
81. JF to HT, July 14, 1938; HTP, Box 4, HP-3 File. JF to HT, [July] 21, 1938, HTP, Box 4, HP-2 File; this letter was erroneously dated June 21, 1938.
82. PA to HT, July 28, 1938, HTP, Box 4, HP-3 File.
83. JF to HT, July 30, 1938, HTP, Box 4, HP-3 File. A-F, Requisition, July 30, 1938, PSF 139 TC.
84. JF to HT, Aug. 22, 1938, HTP, Box 4, HP-4 File. PC, Aug. 23, 1938, *CPC*, 12:41.
85. JF to FDR, Aug. 25, 1938, HTP, Box 4, HP-4 File. FDR to HT, Aug. 27, 1938; HT to FDR, telegram, Aug. 31, 1938; PSF 139 TC.

86. HT to FDR, June 6, 1938, PSF 139 TC. WC to HT, Aug. 31, 1938, HTP, Box 4, HP-4 File. HT to WC, Dec. 21, 1938, HTP, Box 4, HP-6 File.
87. A-F, Requisition, Aug. 31, 1938, PSF 139 TC.
88. PC, Sept. 6, 1938, *CPC*, 12:79. *Life*, Oct. 17, 1938, p. 25.
89. JF to HT, Sept. 30, 1938, HTP, Box 4, HP-4 File.
90. A-F, Requisition, Sept. 30, 1938, HTP, Box 4, HP-4 File.
91. NC to HT, telegram, Aug. 3, 1938; HT to FDR, Aug. 31, 1938, telegram, HTP, Box 4, HP-4 File; Dorothy Backer to HT, Aug. 31, 1938, HTP, Box 1, 1938 File.
92. Lightolier Co. to HT, Sept. 14, 1938; Lightolier Co., Invoice, Sept. 12, 1938; Lightolier Co. to HT, Sept. 15, 1938; HT to A-F, Sept. 15, 1938; HT to A-F, Sept. 29, 1938; HTP, Box 4, HP-4 File.
93. PA to HT, Oct. 5, 1938; HT to A-F, Oct. 8, 1938; PA to HT, Oct. 14, 1938; HTP, Box 4, HP-5 File.
94. PA to HT, Oct. 5, 1938; HT to A-F, Oct. 12, 1938; HTP, Box 4, HP-5 File.
95. PA to HT, Oct. 14, 1938, HTP, Box 4, HP-5 File.
96. PA to HT, Oct. 31, 1938; HTP, Box 4, HP-5 File. A-F, Requisition, Oct. 31, 1938, PSF 139 TC.
97. HT to ML, telegram, Oct. 28, 1938; HT to ML, telegram, Nov. 2, 1938; ML to HT, Nov. 1, 1938; PPF 119, HT File. FDR to Harry G. Barker, Nov. 3, 1938, PPF 1G, HTC. PA to HT, Nov. 10, 1938, HTP, Box 4, HP-6 File.
98. FDR to HT, Nov. 12, 1938; HT to FDR, Oct. 19, 1938, PSF 139, TC. PC, Nov. 4, 1938, *CPC*, 12:212.
99. Ibid. HT to FDR, Nov. 15, 1938, HTP, Box 4, loose in box. At a press conference on July 1, 1938, Roosevelt described the style of the house as "Old Hudson River Dutch."; *CPC*, 12:3.
100. JF to HT, Nov. 29, 1938, HTP, Box 4, HP-6 File. HT to A-F, Dec. 5, 1938, Box 4, HP-6 File. JF to HT, Dec. 8, 1938, and A-F Final Statement, Dec. 8, 1938; HTP, Box 4, HP-6 File.
101. Christian Bie to FDR, with five receipts, Dec. 7, 1938, PSF 139 TC.
102. HT to ML, Dec. 12, 1938; Jan 9, 1939; PSF, Subject Files, Box 167, HT File. HT to ML, Dec. 12, 1938, PSF 139 TC. HT to HF, Dec. 27, 1938, HTP, Box 4, HP-6 File.
103. PA and JF to ML, Jan 16, 1939, PSF Box 140. HL to ML, Jan 23, 1939; ML to HT, Jan 31, 1939; PPF 119, HT File. FDR also wrote to A-F saying how pleased he was with the house, but that letter has not been located.
104. PA to HT, March 23, 1939; HT to PS, March 28, 1939; HTP, Box 4, HP-7 File.
105. PA to HT, April 14, 1939, HTP, Box 4, HP-7 File.
106. FDR to HT, July 7, 1938, PSF 139 TC.
107. JF to HT, [July] 15, 1938, HTP, Box 4, HP-2 File; this letter was erroneously dated June 15, 1938.
108. *Time*, July 11, 1938, p. 9. FDR to HT, July 7, 1938, PSF 139 TC.
109. PA to HT, July 28, 1938, HTP, Box 4, HP-3 File.
110. HT to A-F, July 31, 1938, HTP, Box 4, HP-3 File.
111. JF to HT, Sept. 30, 1938, HTP, Box 4, HP-4 File.
112. RE, Nov. 10, 1938, HTP, Box 4, HP-6 File.
113. HT to A-F, July 30, 1938, HTP, Box 4, HP-4 File.
114. Henry E. Bisordi, Aug. 2, 1938; HT to RE, Aug. 9, 1938; HTP, Box 4, HP-4 File. RE to HT, July 27, 1938; HTP, Box 4, HP-3 File.
115. JF to HT, Sept. 30, 1938; HTP, Box 4, HP-4 File.
116. HE to HT, July 19, 1938; HT to A-F, July 29, 1938; HTP, Box 4, HP-3 File. Henry E. Bisordi to A-F, Aug. 2, 1938, HTP, Box 4, HP-4 File.
117. HT to AF, Aug. 3, 1938; JF to HT, Aug. 30, 1938; HT to A-F, Sept. 19, 1938; RE to HT, Sept. 26, 1938; HTP, Box 4, HP-4 File.
118. PA to HT, Oct. 14, 1938, HTP, Box 4, HP-5 File.
119. NC to HT, May 18, 1938, HTP, Box 4, HP-1 File.
120. RE to HT, July 28, 1938; HT to A-F, Aug. 3, 1938; HTP, Box 4, HP-3 File. JF to HT, Aug. 22, 1938, HTP, Box 4, HP-4 File.
121. ER to HT, telegram, Sept. 20, 1938; HT to A-F, Sept 20, 1938; HTP, Box 4, HP-4 File.
122. RE to HT, Oct. 3, 1938; PA to HT, Oct. 5, 1938; PA to Jos. L. Fimble, Oct. 7, 1938; PA to HT, Oct. 7, 1938; HT to A-F, Oct. 11, 1938; HTP, Box 4, HP-5 File.
123. W. P. Crenshaw to J. C. Hutchinson, May 30, 1938, HTP, Box 4, HP-1 File.
124. JF to HT, July 11, 1938; HT to A-F, July 14, 1938; HTP, Box 4, HP-3 File.
125. HT to WC, July 15, 1938, HTP, Box 4, HP-3 File.
126. HF to HT, July 20, 1938; HTP, Box 4, HP-4 File. HF to HT, July 20, 1938; HTP, Box 4, HP-3 File.
127. HT to WC, July 22, 1938, HTP, Box 4, HP-4 File. HT to WC, Aug. 7, 1938; HTP, Box 1, 1938 File.
128. HT to ML, July 31, 1938, PSF 139 TC; HF to HT, Aug. 13, 1938, HTP, Box 4, HP-4 File. There are many other letters on the heating in HTP.
129. Holland Air Conditioning System, First and Second Floor Plans, Aug. 15, 1938, in FDRL, Maps and Blueprints, Box 15-1-17, Folder BK 83-3/2:1-2.
130. JF to HT, Sept. 30, 1938, HTP, Box 4, HP-4.
131. J. A. Casey to T. Kennedy, Oct. 27, 1938; Kennedy to Marvin McIntyre, Nov. 1, 1938; FDR to Kennedy, Nov. 12, 1938; PPF 1G HTC.
132. Ibid.
133. Moses Smith to FDR, July 4, 1938; FDR to Smith, July 7, 1938; FDR to HT, July 7, 1938; PSF TC. See also PC, Aug. 27, 1938, CPC, 12:61. Ernest A. Acker to FDR, Dec. 7, 1938; FDR to Acker, Dec. 10, 1938, PSF 139 TC. Ibid. PA to HT, Oct. 15, 1938, HTP, Box 4, HP-5 File.
134. Joseph Quinn to FDR, Nov. 1, 1938, PSF 139 TC. Memorandum to Mr. McIntyre, Nov. 8, [1938], PPF, 1G, HTC. Acker to FDR, Jan. 24, 1939; FDR to Acker, Jan. 26, 1939; Acker to FDR, Jan. 30, 1939; PSF, 140, HTC.
135. HT to A-F, Aug. 25, 1938, HTP, Box 4, HP-4 File.
136. *New York Times*, June 7, 1938, p. 20; June 15, 1938, p. 23; Oct. 9, 1938, p. 30. *New Yorker*, April 21, 1945, p. 19. Fred Perlmutter to FDR, June 28. 1939; FDR to Perlmutter, July 1, 1939; PPF 1G HTC. RE to HT, Sept. 26, 1938; HT to A-F, Sept. 29, 1938; HTP, Box 4, HP-6 File. An original telephone outlet is still in place next to the fireplace.
137. PA to HT, Oct. 5, 1938; HT to A-F, Oct. 8, 1938; HTP, Box 4, HP-5 File.
138. N.Y. Fire Insurance Rating Organization, Certificate H81438, Nov. 21, 1938, HTP, Box 4, HP-6 File. *Life*, Oct. 17, 1938, p. 25.
139. Pratt and Lambert to HT, Oct. 11, 1938, HTP, Box 4, HP-5 File.
140. PA to HT, Oct. 5, 1938; HTP, Box 4, HP-5 File.
141. HT to PA, Oct. 8, 1938; HTP, Box 4, HP-5 File.
142. This may have been only painting of the woodwork. HT to A-F, Oct. 8, 1938; PA to HT, Oct. 31, 1938, HTP, Box 4, HP-5 File.
143. PA to HT, Oct. 5, 1938; RE to HT, Oct. 24, 1938, HTP, Box 4, HP-5 File.
144. HT to A-F, Oct. 28, 1938, HTP, Box 4, HP-5 File.
145. Arthur Larson to FDR, Nov. 5, 1938; HTP, Box 4, HP-6 File.
146. HE to A-F, Oct. 17, 1938, HTP, Box 4, HP-5 File. PA to HT, Nov. 10, 1938; HTP, Box 4, HP-6 File.
147. PA to HT, Nov. 10, 1938, HTP, Box 4, HP-6 File.
148. J. C. Hutchinson to FDR, [Jan. 1939]; FDR to Hutchinson, Jan 12, 1939; PPF 1G TC.
149. Hardware Schedule, HTP, Box 4, HP-7 File.
150. HE to A-F, Aug. 16, 1938; John Oatley to HT, Sept. 1, 1938; RE to HT, Aug. 23, 1938; HT to Tull Metal and Supply Co., Sept. 1, 1938; HTP, Box 4, HP-4 File.

151. HT to Nadia Williams, July 13, 1938, HTP, Box 4, HP-3 File.
152. See for instance, HT to FDR, July 13, 1938; SE to HT, Aug. 16, 1938, and Sept. 19, 1938; PPF 119 HT File. There is a considerable amount of additional correspondance in PPF 16, Cont. 20, about this matter.
153. HT to Schell Lewis, Aug. 20, 1938; HTP, Box 4, HP-4 File.
154. HT to United Press, Sept. 27, 1938, HTP, Box 4, HP-4 File.
155. See PPF 1G HTC for press stories. Aunt Het cartoon, Atlanta *Constitution*, 1939, copy in HTP, Box 4, HP-7 File. *Montclair Times*, Dec. 9, 1938; this clipping is part of the historical material that William A. Faber, the son of contractor John Faber, recently made available to the FDRL.
156. *Life*, Oct. 31, 1938, p. 2.
157. Ibid.
158. HT to ML, Nov. 14, 1938; ML to HT, Nov. 17, 19[3]8; HTP, Box 4, Loose. *Pencil Points*, Dec. 1938, p. 4.
159. *New York Times*, Oct. 9, 1938, p. 30; Oct. 21, 1938, p. 25.
160. FDR, Memorandum, Dec. 9, 1942, p. 1379.
161. PC, Aug. 27, 1938, *CPC*, 12:59; PC, June 6, 1939, *CPC*, 13:408.
162. *Holiday*, Sept. 1949, p. 48.
163. PA to HT, April 14, 1939, HTP, Box 4, HP-7 File. ML to William A. Plog, April 24, 1939, PPF 1G HTC. PC, May 30, 1939, *CPC*, 13:394.
164. *New York Times*, May 28, 1939, p. 19. Memorandum to Mr. McIntyre, July 7, 1938; J. Partington to HT, July 14, 1938, PPF 1G Cont. 20. Wallace Co. to FDR, June 6, 1938, PSF, Box 140.
165. *New York Times*, June 12, 1939, pp. 1, 6-8.
166. PC, May 30, 1939; CPC, 13:394-95. ML to S. S. Spivak, Oct. 9, 1939; Spivak to ML, Sept 14, 1939; Sept. 29, 1939; Oct. 24, 1939; Albany-Beacon Express, Invoice, Oct. 6, 1939; ML to Hammacher Schlemmer, Sept. 18, 1939. Luckey, Platt and Co., Invoice, receipted Oct. 16, 1939; Invoice, Hammacher Schlemmer, Oct. 2, 1939; ML to Hammacher Schlemmer, Oct. 15, 1939; PSF, Box 140.
167. Betsey Roosevelt to FDR, Sept. 27, [1939]; FDR to B. Roosevelt, Sept. 28, 1939; PSF, Box 140.
168. Christian Bie, Invoice, Dec. 6, 1939; ML to Bie, Dec. 20, 1939; PSF, Box 140. FDR to Reginald Sturgis, March 16, 1943, PPF 8141, Christian Bie File.
169. H. G. Barker to FDR, Oct. 15, 1938; ML to Barker, Oct. 19, 1938; Barker to FDR, Oct. 26, 1938; FDR to Barker, Nov. 3, 1938; PPF 1G Cont. 20.
170. *New York Times Magazine*, Aug. 24, 1941, p. 23. For letter regarding gifts of furnishings, see PPF 1G Cont. 20.
171. *CC*, p. 155.
172. *CC*, pp. 172, 187.
173. *CC*, pp. 207, 280.
174. *CC*, p. 272.
175. *CC*, pp. 300, 301, 315, 321.
176. *CC*, p. 340.
177. GHR to ML, Sept. 13, 1940; ML to PA, Sept. 19, 1940, PSF, Box 140. PA to ML, Sept. 23, 1940, PPF 1G HTC.
178. HF to ML, Dec. 18, 1940; GHR, n.d.; ML to Russell Linaka, Jan. 3, 1941; GHR to ML, Jan. 11, 1941; GHR to HF, March 3, 1941; P. T. Cheff, March 20, 1941; GHR to ML, March 24, 1941; PSF 140.
179. GAR to ML, Feb. 15, 1941, PPF 1G HTC. ML to GHR, Memorandum, Feb. 28, 1941; PSF 140.
180. PC, Aug. 27, 1938, CPC, 12:57. GHR to ML, Feb. 15, 1941; Feb. 16, 1941; PPF 1G. *New York Times Magazine*, Aug. 24, 1941, p. 23. FDR to Reginald Sturgis, March 16, 1943, PPF 8141, C. Bie File.
181. HT to FDR, Jan. 31, 1940, PSF 140 HTC. Toombs's drawings have been preserved at FDRL.
182. Ibid.
183. Ibid.
184. Holland Air Conditioning System, Plans, July 3, 1942, FDRL.
185. FDR, Guaranty Trust Co., checkbooks, 1938-43, FDR, Family, Business and Personal Papers, Box 54, FDRL.
186. Grace Tully to Christian Bie, May 10, 1943, PPF 1G HTC. *CC*, p. 231.
187. FDR to HT, Nov. 18, 1944; HT to FDR, Nov. 9, 1944; HTP, Box 1, 1944 File.
188. HT to Arthur Knapp, June 2, 1938, HTP, Box 4, HP-2 File.
189. HT to JF, Aug. 3, 1938, HTP, Box 4, HP-4 File. Andrews Hardware Co., Invoice, Aug. 1, 1939; ML to Andrews, Sept. 1, 1939, PSF, Box 140.
190. FDR to Walter Cartwright, Oct. 12, 1938, PPF 1G Cont. 20. Raenk Coryell to GHR, March 19, 1941; GHR to Coryell, March 25, 1941; FDR to GHR,April 7, 1941; PSF, Box 140. PC, Aug. 27, 1938, *CPC*, 12:59.
191. PC, July 1, 1938, *CPC*, 12:2. PC, Aug. 27, 1938, *CPC*, 12:59. *New York Times Magazine*, Aug. 24, 1941, p. 23.
192. *CC*, p. 424.
193. Inventory Taken at Hill-Top Cottage, May 5, 1945, by MLS and [R?] B. N[ichols?]; Margaret L. Suckley Collection, Hill-Top Cottage File, FDRL. The information following is taken from that inventory. Another inventory was prepared by the P. J. Curry Co. of New York City, but is not dated; Hackett Legal Papers, Estate of FDR, Box 19, FDRL. Books in President Roosevelt's Living Room at Top Cottage, Recorded May 4, 1945, Shelf List, FDRL.
194. Memorandum to Files from ERK, O'Connor and Farber, May 3, 1945, Hackett Legal Papers, FDR Estate, Box 19.
195. ER to Lorena Hickok, June 11, 1945, quoted in Joseph P. Lash, *A World of Love: Eleanor Roosevelt and Her Friends* (New York: Doubleday and Co., 1984), p. 196. Agreement, James Roosevelt et al and Elliott Roosevelt, May 1, 1946, Hackett Legal Papers, FDR Estate, Box 19.
196. *New York Times*, Dec. 4, 1944, p. 25; Jan 18, 1950, p. 33. *Look*, Aug. 12, 1950, p. 74. Anna Rothe, ed., *Current Biography* (New York: H. W. Wilson Co., 1951), pp. 184-186.
197. Lash, p. 224. *Time*, April 19, 1948, p. 82.
198. Interview with Elliott Roosevelt, Jr., Jan 20, 1997.
199. Lash, p. 386. *New York Times*, April 18, 1952. Poughkeepsie *Sunday New Yorker*, April 20, 1952.
200. *New York Times*, Oct. 18, 1951, p. 15; Nov. 11, 1951, p. 80; Nov. 13, 1951.
201. *New York Times*, Dec. 16, 1952. Dutchess County Clerk's Office, Deed, Liber 820, p. 451.
202. Interview with Owen Potter, Jan. 15, 1997.
203. Ibid.
204. *New York Times*, Dec. 8, 1963, Sec. 8, p. 1. Owen Potter remembered the brochure and may have a copy in storage.
205. Interview with Owen Potter, Jan. 15, 1997. Deed, May 28, 1996, copy supplied by Van DeWater and Van DeWater, attorneys, Poughkeepsie.

ARCHITECTURAL DESCRIPTION

View of the west porch, looking south, September 1944. Courtesy of the Franklin D. Roosevelt Library, Hyde Park, New York.

THE FOLLOWING ARCHITECTURAL ASSESSMENT OF TOP COTTAGE was made during four visits to the site, between October and November 1996, and thus identifies conditions before restoration began. This information has been supplemented with information gathered in 1998 during the preparation of restoration construction documents and with information uncovered during the restoration construction period from 1999 through 2000.

The goals of the assessment were to produce a permanent record of the cottage as it existed prior to restoration and to establish a chronology for the evolution of the house. Several modifications were made to the house following its initial completion in 1939. In order to plan for the future preservation and restoration of the small structure, it was necessary to differentiate between modifications made for President Roosevelt between 1939 and 1945 and work undertaken by subsequent owners. The Elliott Roosevelt family resided at Top Cottage from June 1945 to 1952, and two generations of the Philip S. Potter family lived in the house from 1952 to 1996.

As part of the investigative process, numerous contemporary journals, catalogs, and books dealing with materials, finishes, and products of the various periods of construction were consulted. As expected, there was little difference in construction materials and related products between the late 1930s and the late 1940s. Therefore great care had to be taken when examining and attempting to date the various conditions that now exist at the cottage.

To understand the original construction of the cottage and how the building evolved, it was necessary to compare the physical clues provided by the structure itself with information obtained from original construction documents, archival photographs, written accounts, and histories from family members. An important tool in the investigative process, the paint and finishes analysis, revealed subtle modifications. To determine the sequence of applied finishes, very small samples were removed from various surfaces and examined under a Bausch and Lomb Stereozoom 7 microscope, and then compared to the *Munsell Book of Color, Matte Finish Collection*.

The chronology of the house, as recorded in this study, has been divided into six periods: the original construction (1938-39); modifications made to the north wing (1940-41); modifications made to the south wing (1942-43); work carried out for the President prior to his death (April 12, 1945); work carried out for Elliott Roosevelt (1945-52); and work carried out for the Potter family (1952-96). Many of the later modifications and additions cannot be specifically dated without additional research of the Elliott Roosevelt and Potter families.

Exterior Description

The exterior of Top Cottage was carefully inspected to gain a thorough understanding of the original 1938-39 structure and its subsequent modifications. Each surface was visually inspected to determine its place within the evolution of the cottage.

A small collection of FDR-era photographs proved to be an important asset in the attempt to understand how the exterior changed over time. Several 1939 photographs recorded the house as it was first completed. Later views show significant additions made for the President, such as the insertion of a window in the south gable of the south wing (one of three similar openings) and the addition of a dormer on the west elevation of the north wing. Information gleaned from these photographs and the original construction specifications helped in the analysis of the exterior conditions.

Selected exterior painted surfaces were analyzed to determine the sequence of applied finishes. The existence of an additional layer of paint on the northwest dormer confirmed the photographic evidence that it predated the other dormers.

The investigation revealed significant additions and modifications undertaken by Elliott Roosevelt and, after 1952, by various members of the Potter family. Included in these projects were the enclosure of the west porch, the construction of four additional dormers, and the addition and later enclosure of the north porch, as well as smaller projects including the addition of shutters and the modification of the front door.

View from the southeast, 1997. Photograph by John G. Waite Associates, Architects.

General

Franklin D. Roosevelt's Top Cottage is located on a wooded site on Dutchess Hill, one of the highest points in Dutchess County, where it originally commanded a magnificent view of the Hudson River and the Catskill Mountains. The design of the house was inspired by Roosevelt's interest in local Dutch colonial buildings and relied on simple forms, scale, steeply pitched roofs, and the texture of the rubble fieldstone walls for architectural interest.

The house is symmetrical in massing, with a large central block facing west and with north and south wings set back toward the east. The central block is three bays wide by two bays deep, and measures approximately 40 feet 4 inches wide by 23 feet 9 inches deep, while the two wings are two bays wide by two bays deep. The north wing is approximately 35 feet 10 inches wide by 23 feet 0 inches deep; the south wing is 3 feet wider. An enclosed porch (originally open) extends fully across the west facade of the central block. A smaller, enclosed porch is attached to the north elevation of the north wing.

Central Block

Walls: The walls are random fieldstone rubble, laid up in cement mortar, generally in wide, irregular joints. The foundation walls are also random fieldstone rubble, supplemented with interior walls of concrete block.

A projecting chimney mass centered on the east elevation is also constructed of stone rubble. Flat stone slabs cap the angled planes of the chimney shoulders. A stairway to the basement is concealed in the chimney mass.

Cornice: The 6-inch-high wood cornice on the east and west elevations is composed of (from bottom to top) a fascia, a fillet, and a cyma recta molding. On the east and west elevations, the raking cornice along the gables is simply a fillet and a cyma recta molding.

Roof: The steeply pitched gabled roof is covered with Potter-era asphalt shingles. An extant wood shingle starter course appears to be original; earlier asphalt shingle roofing remains intact beneath the existing shingles.

Doors: In the central block, the only exterior door opening is located in the south wall of the chimney, and it provides access to the basement stair. The opening has a stone threshold and a flat-arched lintel. The aluminum door has three recessed panels, with a small louvered ventilation panel set in the top panel, and is framed by a plain wood casing. The door and casing are replacements from the Potter era. The original wood frame and wood paneled door are missing.

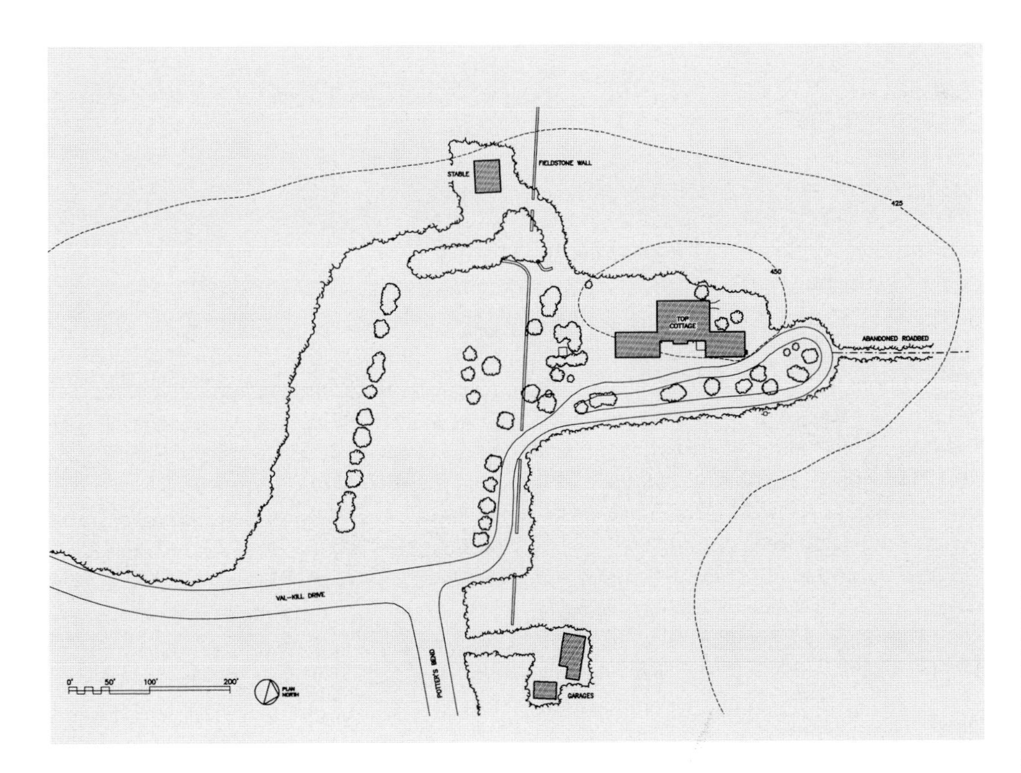

Site plan, c. 1999.
Drawing by JGWAA.

Base of chimney with exterior entrance to basement, 1997.
Photograph by JGWAA.

Windows: There are two original basement ventilation openings in the central block: one in the north elevation and the other in the south elevation. These small, horizontal openings with bluestone sills and concrete wells are located at the west end of the elevations. They are fitted with cast-iron grilles and ventilate the crawl space beneath the living room.

Originally, the central block had four exterior first-story windows: two in the west elevation and one each in the north and south elevations. When the west porch was enclosed for Elliott Roosevelt, the west windows were no longer exterior openings, and eventually the sash were removed. The remaining north and south windows have bluestone sills and flat-arched lintels, and they are framed by 3¾-inch-wide single-fascia architraves composed of a fascia trimmed with a flush bead around the opening and a perimeter filleted quarter-round molding. The openings are fitted with 8-over-8 wood sash.

Apparently, the shutters shown in the original renderings were never included in the original construction; the existing board-and-batten shutters at each window were installed after 1945. The shutters are composed of ¾-inch-thick tongue-and-groove boards with beveled joints fastened to pairs of square-cut horizontal battens. Each leaf is hung on a pair of 2¼-inch-high shutter hinges. Iron "S"-shaped shutter holdbacks are located approximately 7½ inches to 8 inches from the openings.

Original small louvered panels in the north and south verges ventilate the attic space.

A window-sized opening in the north gable has a bluestone sill and a flat-arched stone lintel like the first-story openings; the lintel is directly beneath the louvered verge panel. A flakeboard panel covers the opening and masks its condition. A letter dated August 23, 1938, from the Adams-Faber Company to Henry Toombs refers to an attic door through which trunks were to be hauled for storage; this opening may be the one to which the Adams-Faber Company was referring.

West Porch

The west porch spans the full width of the central block's west elevation. The porch is five bays wide and rests on a stone foundation that supports the flagstone floor of the original terrace. The original 8-inch-square wood posts support a wood fascia and a cornice (fillet and cyma recta). The shed roof, covered with mineral-rolled roofing, curves up to meet the roof of the central block. On the north and south elevations, 6-inch-high tongue-and-groove boards fill in the gable ends.

West elevation of central block of house, 1997. Photograph by JGWAA.

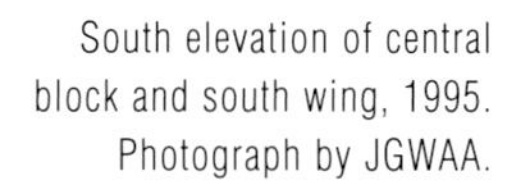

South elevation of central block and south wing, 1995. Photograph by JGWAA.

The porch is now enclosed with wood clapboards (laid 7½ inches to 8 inches to the weather) set above a continuous copper flashing that extends around the full perimeter of the stone foundation. On the west and south elevations, there are banks of casement sash windows. Each of the west bays has four sets of ten-light sash, while the south elevation has five sash and a door. The openings are framed by 2-inch-wide single-fascia architraves. All of these materials were installed by Elliott Roosevelt.

The door opening in the south elevation has two doors: an exterior stile-and-rail storm door with a glazed panel of eight lights set above a raised panel, as well as an interior door with two recessed panels, made up of the same pine paneling used to finish the interior of the porch walls. Three semicircular stone steps descend from the door opening to the southwest patio. The doors and steps were installed by Elliott Roosevelt.

The flagstone patio extends from the south elevation of the central block and porch over to the south end of the south wing, where a stone ramp connects with a walkway from the driveway. A small goldfish pond, installed by Robert Potter, Jr., is built into the southwest corner of the patio.

South Wing

The foundations, walls, cornice, and roof are all similar in finish to the central block.
Doors: There are no exterior door openings in the south wing.
Windows: The south wing has three foundation vents, similar to those in the central block: one at the west end of the south elevation, one at the north end of the east elevation, and one in the north bay of the west elevation.

The first-story windows are similar in finish to the central block windows, but they are smaller. The two east, two west, and single south openings are fitted with original 6-over-6 wood sash; the smaller north opening has a 4-over-4 wood sash.

The second-story window openings in the north and south gables were created in 1942-43 when the south attic was finished. The openings have plain fascia frames and stone sills. The stones forming the voussoirs of the flat-arched lintels are evenly sized, unlike the irregularly sized stones of the first-story's original lintels. The south opening has three 4-over-4 wood sash, separated by plain wood mullions, while the north opening has two 4-over-4 wood sash.

Sometime after the President's death, probably soon after the Potters' acquisition of the cottage in 1952, dormer windows were added to the south wing's gable roof. There are two dormers in the east elevation and one at the south end of the west elevation. The dormers are finished with wood siding and trimmed with a small cornice composed of a cavetto and cyma recta molding. Asphalt shingles cover the gabled roofs. Each dormer has two window openings with 4-over-4 wood sash, framed by a plain wood sill and a fascia trimmed with a fillet at the top edge.

A small, original louvered panel in the south verge ventilates the attic space.
Other Details: A metal letter "P" (for Potter) is mounted to the west elevation between the two windows and survives from that family's ownership.

North Wing

The foundations, walls, wood trim, and roof of the north wing are similar to the finishes used in the central block and the south wing.
Doors: The original main entrance to the house is located in the south elevation of the north wing. The opening has a stone sill and a flat-arched stone lintel. The door frame and single-fascia architrave are set deeply into the opening. The Dutch door is composed of two stile-and-rail leaves: an upper leaf with four raised panels and a lower leaf with two raised panels. The door was originally undivided; it was cut at a later date. A bronze doorknocker mounted to the upper leaf may be the fitting included in the May 5, 1945, inventory and described as formerly belonging to Miss E. M. Lynch of Rhinebeck. It was given to FDR by Margaret Suckley.

A door opening at the east end of the north elevation was originally an exterior opening and has similar finishes to the main entrance. This opening is now enclosed within the north porch.

The doorbell system with push buttons at both doorways is original.
Windows: A single foundation vent at the south end of the west elevation is similar to the basement openings in the south wing and the central block.

At the first-story level, there are two window openings in the east wall and three openings in the west wall. The center and south windows in the west elevation have 4-over-4 sash; the other three openings have 6-over-6 sash. The detailing at these windows is similar to the first-story openings in the south wing and the central block. A small window opening in the north wall with a 4-over-4 sash is now enclosed by the north porch.

A second-story window opening in the north gable has a stone sill and flat-arched lintel and is framed by a plain wood fascia. The two 4-over-4 wood sash are separated by a plain wood mullion. The opening was created in 1940-41 when the north attic was finished to create habitable space.

View from the northeast, 1997.
Photograph by JGWAA.

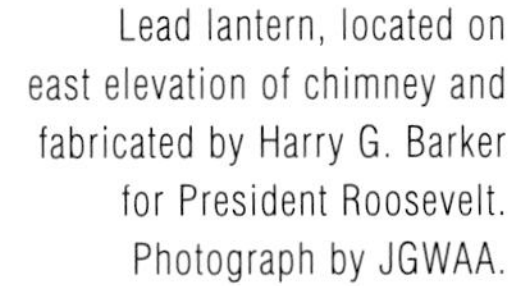

Lead lantern, located on east elevation of chimney and fabricated by Harry G. Barker for President Roosevelt. Photograph by JGWAA.

There is one dormer in the east elevation and another dormer in the west elevation. Each is finished with wood siding, a small wood cornice, and a gabled asphalt shingle roof. Like the dormers in the south wing, each dormer has two window openings with 4-over-4 wood sash, framed by a plain wood sill and a fascia trimmed with a fillet at the top edge. The west dormer varies in detail from the other dormers; it has a gabled ceiling. The west dormer dates to the 1940-41 renovation of the north attic. The east dormer was added after 1952 by the Potters.

A small, original louvered panel in the north verge ventilates the attic space.

North Porch

The porch is constructed of wood-framed walls above a stone foundation. The walls are finished with vertical tongue-and-groove boards with beveled joints, approximately 7 inches to 11 inches wide, with wide banks of horizontal windows above. The windows are installed between wood posts and rest on a 2¾-inch-high wood sill. Above the windows is a wood fascia capped with a 3½-inch-high cornice composed of a fascia, a cavetto, a cyma recta, and a fillet molding. The curved sweep of the shed roof is covered with asphalt shingles. The east and west gables are finished with wood clapboards.

The current appearance of the porch may be the result of more than one period of construction. The vertical siding and windows date to the Potter era, but the roof and foundation may be earlier. The porch may have been added by Elliott Roosevelt, based on a design provided by Henry Toombs.

A plywood cabinet with a shed roof is attached to the west elevation of the porch. The roof is covered with mineral-rolled roofing. The shed dates to the Potters' occupancy.

Systems

Drainage: There are hung gutters with rainwater leaders along the east and west edges of the roof of the central block. On the east facade there are leaders attached to the wall surface on either side of the central chimney mass. Photographs dating to 1939 show similar leaders in the same locations.

Plumbing: There are hose bibs on the north elevation of the central block, the west and east elevations of the south wing, and the east elevation of the north wing.

HVAC: The fuel-oil fill and vent pipes are located near the north elevation of the south wing. Nearby is a Potter-era Lenox air-conditioning condenser on a concrete pad.

Lighting/Electrical: A small electrified lead lantern with opalescent glass is attached to the east face of the chimney breast. The lantern was a gift to the President from Harry G. Barker of Carmel, Indiana, in 1938. The lantern is mounted to the masonry with an original iron bracket and has always remained in this location. Modern, surface-mounted rigid nonmetallic conduit extends from the lantern down to the basement. The base of the lantern is inscribed, "President Franklin D. Roosevelt, A.D. 1938, Harry G. Barker." It appears that Mr. Barker inscribed this, along with the city and state of his residence; however, the later information is obscured.

A small stamped sheet-metal-and-wire lantern with a frosted glass shade is located immediately north of the east exterior door of the north porch. This original Lightolier fixture was purchased in 1938 and was originally positioned on the exterior stone wall next to the service entrance to the kitchen.

Electric service for Top Cottage and for the adjacent caretaker's cottage is provided by overhead wiring. The wiring is attached to the north gable of the north wing; it follows the rake of the roof down to the northeast corner of the house. A General Electric electric meter and a 100-amp electric service disconnect are mounted to the east wall of the north porch. A Westinghouse electric meter is nearby, on the north wall of the north wing.

Electrical cabling extends along the west elevation of the west porch and connects to rigid conduit that is located beneath the projecting ledge of the porch paving.

Lightning Protection: At the southeast corner of the south wing, a copper tag attached to a lightning down conductor reads: "George E. Thompson Co., Minneapolis, Minn, 'Manufacturers of World's Best Lightning Protection Equipment', Installed by Wiley J. Haga, 114 Mansion Street, Poughkeepsie, New York"; it was installed in 1956.

The down conductors from the lightning rods run down the stone walls into the ground and are located at the southwest inside corner between the central block and south wing, at the southeast corner of the south wing, at the southwest inside corner of the chimney, and at the southwest inside corner between the central block and north wing.

Equipment: There are two telephone service networks on the east wall of the north porch. Electric and telephone cabling and television coaxial have been attached to the exterior trim and wall surfaces on nearly every elevation of the house. A Potter-era television-antenna tower is located at the northwest corner of the north wing.

A Potter-era propane gas tank, for a stove on the north porch, is located at the northeast corner of the north wing.

Exterior Fittings

A painted wood eagle and a bent-iron plant bracket attached to the stone surface immediately east of the main entrance are among the most apparent of the exterior fittings. Both of these items probably belonged to the Potters.

Some of the windows retain iron brackets that supported plant boxes at the sill level. These brackets date to sometime after 1945.

An aluminum plant bracket affixed to the south face of the southwest post of the west porch was installed by the Potters.

Finishes Investigation

The original exterior woodwork, including the trim, window sash, and doors, was first covered in a white primer, followed by a finish in yellowish white (2.5Y 9/2-8/2). A letter from Henry Toombs to Paul Adams, dated October 8, 1938, states that the exterior white paint should ". . . not [be] a true white, but something between a cream white and an oyster white. . . . It should go with the joints of the masonry."

This original finish is in turn covered by several more finishes in yellowish white and the more recent whites.

The west dormer on the north wing predates the other dormers (it was constructed in 1940-41), and it retains an additional paint layer not found on the other dormers.

Interior Description

The investigation and analysis of the interior rooms and spaces of Top Cottage involved a careful visual inspection and, in some instances, physical inspection of the various surfaces, finishes, and elements. Extensive probing into the building's fabric was not undertaken at this time, to ensure that significant material would not be damaged.

The primary task was to distinguish between what were the original conditions of the house at the completion of its construction in the years 1938 and 1939 and what were later modifications, additions, and refinements. The post-1939 work was carried out over a long time under the direction of several owners. Since the goal of the restoration of the cottage was to preserve and reconstruct the conditions as they were during the period that the President occupied the structure (1939-45), it was important to distinguish between work carried out before FDR's death in April 1945 and work undertaken after that date.

To understand the original construction of the cottage and how the building evolved, it was necessary to compare information obtained from the physical clues provided by the structure itself with that of original construction documents, archival photographs, written accounts, and histories from family members. An important tool in the investigative process, the paint and finishes analysis, revealed subtle modifications. To determine the sequence of applied finishes, very small samples were removed from various surfaces and examined under a Bausch and Lomb Stereozoom 7 microscope, and then compared to the *Munsell Book of Color, Matte Finish Collection*. The comparisons of finish layers on the architectural elements provided a way to determine their position in the evolution of the cottage.

Along with the paint analysis, the careful study of the small selection of historic interior photographs provided another means to understand the evolution of certain rooms. The available images spanned from 1942 to 1952 and recorded conditions as they existed for Franklin Roosevelt and his son Elliott.

The original building specifications and other construction-related documents provided important information concerning materials, features, and finishes. For example, page S17-3 of the 1938 specifications indicates that the electric switches in the living room were to have mirrored cover plates, a condition that still exists but would otherwise be difficult to date.

Within each space, all surfaces were studied and recorded, including such elements as door and window hardware, light fixtures, electrical fittings, and plumbing fixtures.

All of the information gleaned from archival sources and from the room-by-room investigation revealed that there were several periods of intervention in the original fabric and conditions of the cottage. These periods include the changes made for the President. The first changes were carried out from late 1940 into early 1941 and generally involve the work undertaken to modify the north wing. The second group of changes occurred in the fall of 1942 and into early 1943 in the south wing. It was not until January 1944, according to Margaret Suckley, that pictures were hung in the first-floor rooms. In February she recorded that "The living-room looks so attractive — the P.'s [President's] things getting gradually arranged as he likes them best."

Because there are limited interior photographs of the later modifications, a careful study of exterior photographs, coupled with interior scrutiny and information from Roosevelt and Potter family members, provided the information needed to understand the changes made after the death of the President in April 1945. The two inventories made at that time were invaluable for understanding how the house was used and for interpreting what is shown in the few available interior photographs.

The cottage was modified for Elliott Roosevelt during the period that he occupied and owned the property, 1945-52. Although the exact dates of the work are not yet known, it included such items as the painting of the rooms (photographs indicate that some spaces were painted by 1948), the enclosure of the west porch, and possibly the addition of the north porch. Significant work was carried out by the Potter family, who acquired the cottage in 1952. The work was spread out over many years by several generations of Potters and included the creation of the dining room, modifications in the kitchen and pantry, the installation of closets in the small south bedroom, and the expansion of the south bathroom.

It is now clear what the existing conditions were at Top Cottage before the death of the President.

In this study, the May 1945 date is used as a reference point. Conditions as they existed up to May 1 of that year represent the cottage as it was when occupied by the President, while conditions after that date correspond to other occupants. Modifications made by later owners and

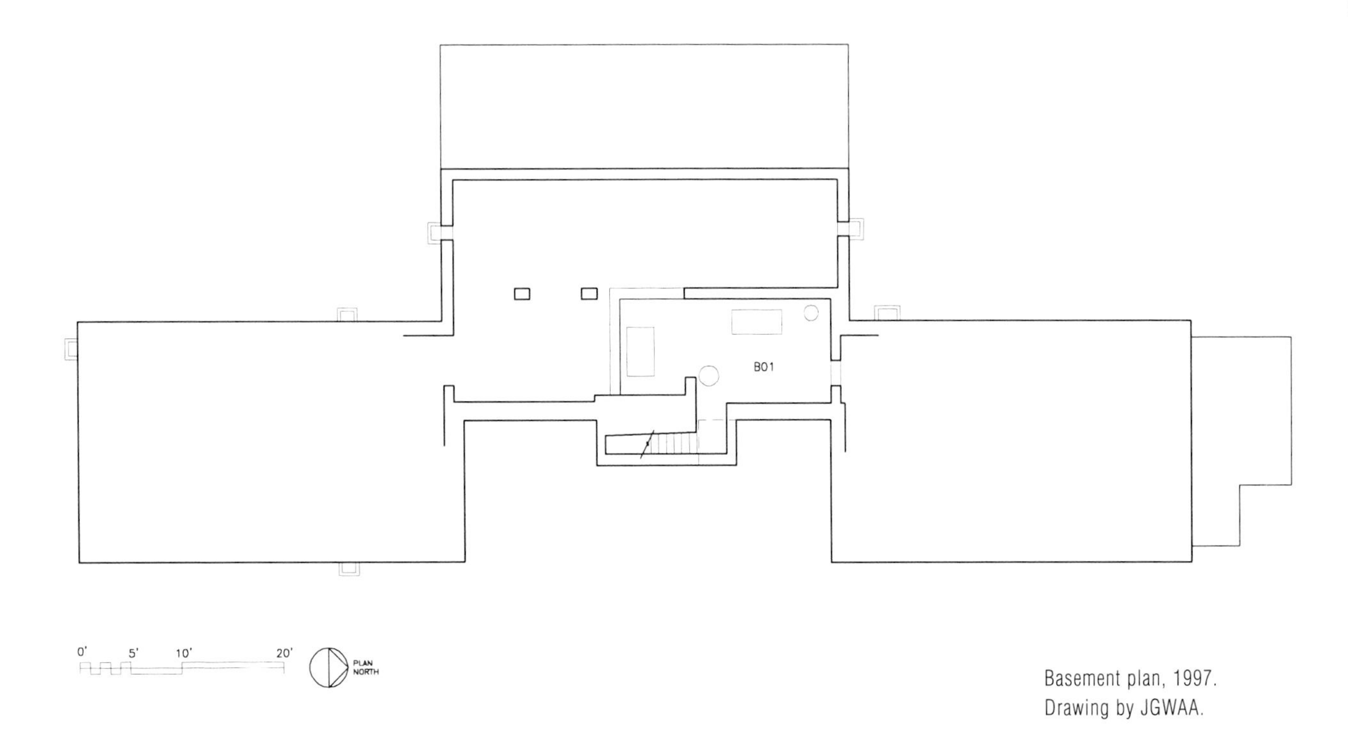

Basement plan, 1997.
Drawing by JGWAA.

occupants of the house (after May 1945) are recognized in a general sense, and additional research may be able to pinpoint exact dates for those changes.

Basement

The space beneath the cottage is composed of four distinct areas: the furnace room (B01) beneath the central block, the crawl space beneath the rest of the central block, the crawl space beneath the north wing, and the crawl space beneath the south wing. The volume and ceiling height of the crawl spaces varies due to the irregular configuration of the ground surface, composed of rock and soil. The main architectural elements in the crawl spaces are the concrete block support piers and the sheet-metal ducts of the forced-air heating system.

Furnace Room (B01)

The primary basement space is the furnace room located in the northeast corner of the central block. This is the only room in the basement. Access to this area is from a very narrow concrete stairway located within the masonry mass of the chimney, which projects from the east elevation of the central block of the cottage. The area at the foot of the stair is actually situated outside of the principal foundation of the cottage; the concrete ceiling of this small vestibule is covered with the soil of the east courtyard.

The small, rectangular furnace room has full-height north, east, and west walls and much lower retaining walls to the south and at the southwest corner. The open area above the retaining walls provides access to the south and west crawl spaces. A small rectangular opening in the north wall provides access to the crawl space beneath the north wing.

The building materials in the furnace room date to the 1938-39 construction of the cottage. A floor plan published in the November 1938 issue of *American Builder* shows this room much as it now exists. On that plan it is labeled "Heater Room."

Floor: Original poured concrete floor surface. A small circular sump pump hole is located near the northwest corner. The ground surface in the crawl space is formed of soil and rock.

Walls: The foundation walls are random-laid fieldstone rubble and are supplemented with interior walls of concrete block.

Ceiling: The roughly finished plaster ceiling is 7 feet 2 inches to 7 feet 3 inches above the floor. A section of concrete ceiling near the base of the stairs is eroded, with exposed steel reinforcing bars. The ceiling surfaces in the crawl spaces consist of the exposed wood framing for the first floor.

Door: The original narrow door opening at the top of the stairs is framed by an aluminum casing set in a pressure-treated wood frame that holds an aluminum door. Originally the opening had a wood architrave and a paneled wood door.

DB011: The aluminum door is 1 foot 7½ inches wide by 6 feet 6¾ inches high and is composed of three recessed panels. A small louvered ventilation panel is set in the top panel. This door was installed by the Potters and replaces a wood door with three panels recorded in FDR-era photographs. The door is hung on the aluminum frame with integral hinges.

Windows: Small, horizontal openings in the basement walls of the crawl spaces are fitted with original cast-iron grilles to permit ventilation. An original wood-framed opening in the north wall provides access to the crawl space beneath the north wing. The opening is covered by a remnant of a wood door hung on a pair of steel strap hinges.

Chimney: The masonry chimney foundation is located at the south end of the east wall of the furnace room (B01). A small cast-iron door provides access to the ash pit.

Furnace room (B01), 1997. View looking southwest. The oil-fired hot-water heater and furnaces are replacements for earlier equipment. Photograph by JGWAA.

Stair: The original concrete stair built into the east end of the chimney foundation ascends in thirteen risers to the exterior grade. The risers are 7 inches high, and the treads are 9 inches deep. The width of the stairwell increases as the stairs descend to the basement.

Plumbing: A Potter-era 32-gallon Bock hot-water heater, model 32E, sits near the center of the room. Domestic water lines run along the east wall. A sump pump and pit are situated in the northwest corner of the furnace room (B01); the electrical outlet for the pump is on the west wall. A PVC drainpipe extends from the sump pump along the west, north, and east walls and up the stairwell to the exterior.

Heating: The heating equipment in this room includes a Chevron warm-air furnace, model #OFL 150 D2, near the west wall, and another furnace (not labeled) with a Hermidifier humidifier near the south wall. Both units were installed by the Potters. According to Owen Potter, the furnaces were lowered into place through the living room floor in the 1960s.

Sheet-metal hot-air ducts extend throughout the basement to the heating grilles in the house; generally, the ductwork dates to the FDR era. The sheet metal flues of the hot-water heater and furnaces are ducted to the masonry chimney.

A remnant of the operational instructions for the original Holland furnace is still posted on a wood board on the west wall.

Lighting/Electrical: The room is lit by incandescent porcelain utility fixtures. An ITE Imperial Corporation electrical panel for the air conditioning and dishwasher is mounted to the west wall.

Furnishings and Fittings: A simple wood shelving unit (5 feet 10 inches long by 3 feet 7 inches high) is situated against the north wall. It is covered in the same blue-green paint used in the south hall (103). This indicates that it dates to the Elliott Roosevelt occupancy, or perhaps earlier.

First Floor

The first floor of the cottage consists of three joined stone structures. The central block, the heart of the house, is flanked by two nearly symmetrical wings; the south wing is slightly greater in length.

The central block has a large living room and a covered, now enclosed, porch that extends along the west side of the block. An impressive stone fireplace, centered on the east wall, is the primary feature of the living room. The north wing houses secondary and service functions such as the entry hall, pantry, kitchen, and caretaker's quarters, including a bathroom. At the north end of the wing, there is an enclosed porch, probably added after 1945. The south wing includes two bedrooms, a bathroom, and a hallway. Access from one wing to the other is through the centrally positioned living room.

In general, the conditions that survive today can be traced to the original construction of the cottage in 1938-39 and to modifications and additions made for the President at a later date. On the first floor, this later work essentially encompassed two campaigns: the work carried out in the north wing during 1940-41, as well as modifications to the south wing in 1942-43. In both

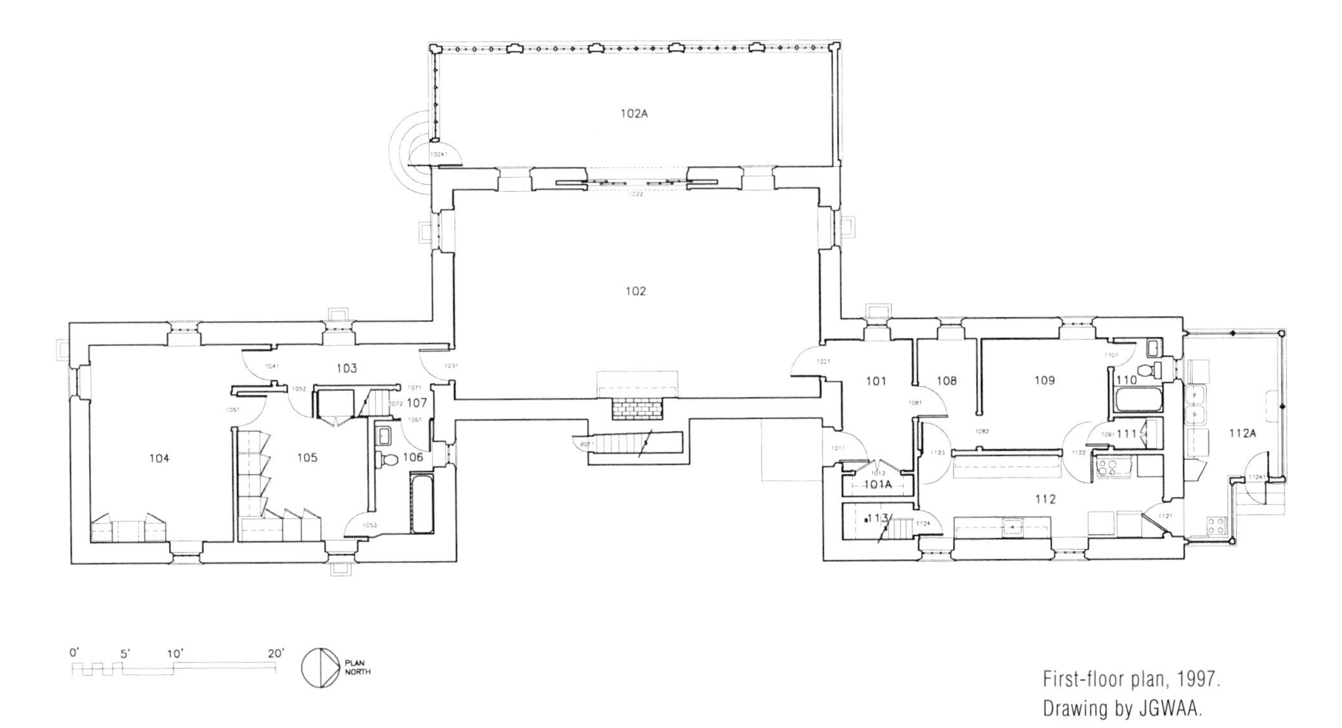

First-floor plan, 1997.
Drawing by JGWAA.

areas, the work involved the creation of additional bedroom space in the attics of the north and south wings for family, guests, and the caretaker. On the first floor, stairways were inserted for access to the new attic rooms. The north stair was placed in the food pantry (113) next to the kitchen. The south stair was positioned in the area that was formerly occupied by the bathroom linen closet and the northwest corner of the small bedroom (105).

Additional modifications to the first floor were made when the President's son Elliott occupied the house with his wife Fay Emerson and their children. Possibly the first project after 1945 was the painting of the wall surfaces in various rooms. The sand-finished and smooth plaster walls had remained unpainted during the FDR era, but apparently Elliott and his family wanted color added to the austere rooms. The entry hall and living room were painted a sunny yellow-gold, while the south hall and adjacent small bedroom were finished in a bright blue-green. The larger bedroom was painted pale pink and had a hand-painted floral motif on the south wall. The cabinets in the pantry and kitchen were covered in a bright grey-blue, and the kitchen walls were painted in a pale yellow-beige.

Significant projects that appear to have been carried out while Elliott and his family occupied the house include the enclosure of the west porch and possibly the addition of the north porch. The closets and vanity were inserted in the large south bedroom (104) at this time. Some or all of these projects may have been carried out with the help of the architect Henry Toombs; in a list of his projects, the architect included an ambiguous reference to "Res. Alt." for Elliott Roosevelt.

Interior photographs taken in 1948 reveal that many of FDR's furnishings and collections remained in the cottage, as if to memorialize the dead President. In 1952, many of these objects were sold through Hammer Galleries in New York City, thereby ending an important aspect of FDR's presence at Top Cottage.

Various generations of the Potter family, who resided at the cottage beginning in 1952, were responsible for additional modifications to the house. On the first floor, the list of work includes the expansion of the south wing bathroom into a bedroom closet, the addition of built-in closets to the small bedroom, the modification of the pantry (108), the creation of a dining room in what was originally a bedroom (109), and the enclosure of the north porch (if not the actual addition of the porch).

Entry (101) The entry hall provides the initial introduction to the cottage. Guests proceeded from this small space directly into the large living room and the west porch beyond. In plan, the entry includes two doorways in the south wall (the entrance from the exterior and the access to the living room); a pair of doors in the east wall, opening to a coat closet; a single door to the pantry beyond the north wall; and a small window in the west wall.

The finishes are simple, as they are throughout the cottage. The most prominent architectural elements are the pair of paneled doors that conceal the closet and the impressive entrance door. The opening to the pantry originally had a swinging door. This door was later moved, by Elliott Roosevelt or the Potters, to the opening between the kitchen and former north bedroom (109).

Originally, the entrance door (D1011) was not divided in the Dutch manner. It is believed that this modification was made for Elliott Roosevelt or for the Potters.

The contents of this room during the FDR era are recorded in two inventories produced in May 1945, but there are no known photographs that show the complete space. The only visual record of the entry is what can be seen through the open doorway between this space and the living room in photographs taken of the latter space in 1945.

Entry (101), 1997.
View looking southeast.
Photograph by JGWAA.

Floor: The floor is finished with Potter-era sheet vinyl on plywood underlayment. This surface is installed over original 2¼-inch-wide oak tongue-and-groove boards running north/south. The original floor surface is continuous into the closet (101A) and the living room (102).

Walls: All four walls are finished with an original skim coat of sand-finished plaster over Rocklath, a gypsum-board lath.

Ceiling: The original plaster on Rocklath (a gypsum-board lath) ceiling is approximately 10 feet above the floor.

Baseboard: The original 5-inch-high baseboard is composed of a plain fascia with a filleted quarter-round cap molding and a post-1945 quarter-round shoe molding.

Doors: There are four original doorways in the entry: the main entrance to the house in the south wall (D1011); another south opening, at the west end of the wall (D1021); a wide opening in the east wall providing access to a closet (D1012); and an opening in the north wall (D1081). All four openings are framed by 4-inch-wide single-fascia architraves. The architrave around the southwest doorway (D1021) has a protruding edge bead, unlike the flush bead found on the architraves of the other openings.

D1011: This Dutch door is composed of two stile-and-rail leaves: an upper leaf (2 feet 11½ inches wide by 4 feet 6¾ inches high by 2¼ inches thick) with four raised panels, and a lower leaf (2 feet 10⅞ inches high) with two raised panels. Originally the door was not divided. The door was probably divided sometime after 1945. Each leaf is hung on a pair of 4½-inch butt hinges. The upper two hinges and bottom hinge are original. The fourth hinge was added when the door was divided. There is also a 7¾-inch-high brass Corbin mortise lockset with brass knobs and a keyed cylinder on the exterior and a turnpiece on the interior; a later brass Dutch door latch; a peephole; and a security chain. A brass doorknocker is mounted to the exterior face of the upper leaf.

D1012: The closet opening has an original pair of 2-foot 2¾-inch-wide by 6-foot 5½-inch-high by 1⅜-inch-thick stile-and-rail doors, each with two raised panels. Each leaf is hung on a pair of 3½-inch-high steel butt hinges. Other original hardware includes a 5¼-inch-high mortise lockset in the south leaf with a brass lever handle and keyhole escutcheon on the exterior face, and a turnpiece on the interior face.

Window: The single original window opening in the west wall is framed by a 4¼-inch single-fascia architrave, similar in profile to the door architraves. The 4-over-4 rope-hung wood window sash are set deeply into the masonry wall with paneled reveals and a plain window shelf. Below the opening is a plain sill and apron. The 9⅞-inch-wide by 11⅛-inch-high panes are separated by ¾-inch-wide muntins. The sash are secured with an original brass thumb latch.

Heating: There is one original supply register set in the baseboard below the window in the west wall, as well as a return-air grille in the baseboard of the north wall. The baseboard molding is carried up to frame the openings. The metal honeycomb screens on the register and grille were supplied by Hart & Cooley.

Lighting/Electrical: Electrical elements include a pair of switches with a decorative plastic Potter-era cover plate near door D1011; it appears that these switches were originally installed to operate the exterior lantern fixture on the chimney and to switch a wall receptacle on the north wall of the entry. There are two duplex receptacles on the north wall (one with a post-1945 mirrored plate, the other with a recent plastic cover plate). This and other mirror cover plates were probably installed after the FDR era to match the original mirrored plates specified for use in the living room in 1938.

Equipment: There is a Magna security panel on the east wall, as well as a red push button near door D1011. The security panel was installed circa 1996. The red push button appears to be a panic switch for an earlier security-alarm system.

Furnishings and Fittings: A sense of the appearance of the entry during the FDR era is provided by two photographs taken in May 1945, the inventory made by Margaret Suckley at the same time, and an inventory made by the P. J. Curry Company. The combined documents indicate that the entry was sparsely furnished. The items located here in 1945 included a rosewood oval table that held a wooden lamp with parchment shade, a mirror, a wicker arm chair, an oil painting (Marine Engagement) by H. G. Garcia, and four framed prints (two on the south wall and two on the west wall).

The two photographs record the living room (102), but the entry is visible through the doorway connecting the two spaces. The oval table is located next to the north wall, between the door to the pantry and the closet. The framed mirror is positioned above the table, while the lamp rests on the table, providing the only artificial light in the entry.

Both photographs show FDR's wheelchair in the entry; in Margaret's inventory it is located in the adjoining closet (101A).

There is no mention or record of a covering on the oak floor or curtains at the single window.

Finishes Investigation: Samples were analyzed from the plaster wall surface and the woodwork to determine the sequence of decorative finishes in the entry.

The sand-finished plaster walls retain five layers of varying paints, which represent four finishes. The first finish is composed of two paint layers: a yellow-gold (2.5Y 8.5/4) with a finish surface of yellow-gold (2.5Y 9/4). This surface in turn is covered in a grey-green, light green, and the current pale yellow-green.

The woodwork is covered in four finishes, including a grey-white (5Y 9/1), two layers of yellowish white, and the current white paint.

The initial decor had woodwork painted in the grey-white (5Y 9/1), while the sand-finished wall surfaces remained unpainted. Apparently all of the walls in the cottage remained unpainted after the completion of the structure in 1939.

At an unrecorded date (after the stairway was added to provide access to the attic of the north wing), the walls in the entry and the adjoining closet were finished in the yellow-gold (2.5Y 9/4), while the trim remained grey-white or was repainted in a yellowish white (2.5Y 9/2). Whether this transformation occurred during FDR's occupancy or when Elliott Roosevelt resided in the house remains unknown, although the latter period is more likely. Physical evidence indicates that the yellowish-white finish on the woodwork was applied during or after the removal of the swinging door from the opening in the north wall (D1081). The doorstop molding now in place at the north door opening does not include the initial grey-white paint finish.

The third decor had walls painted in a grey-green (this finish is still in situ in the closet) and woodwork painted in yellowish-white. The grey-green color was fashionable in the 1940s and early 1950s and dates to the Elliott Roosevelt era or the early Potter ownership.

Closet (101A)

The closet is an original adjunct space to the entry hall. The wide opening with paired doors provides easy access to the closet.

Though now covered with vinyl tiles, the floor was originally a continuation of the oak surface formerly visible in the entry.

This small space was disrupted when the wall and ceiling surfaces were cut to allow for the installation of the stairway to the north attic. This work was possibly carried out as early as 1940 by Christian Bie, the caretaker of Top Cottage.

The May 5, 1945, inventory records that a wheelchair was located here, probably the same chair seen in the entry in two May 1945 photographs.

Floor: The floor is finished with 9-inch-square linoleum tiles, installed by the Potters over the original oak floorboards.
Walls: All four walls are finished with a skim coat of original sand-finished plaster over Rocklath, a gypsum-board lath. At the south end of the closet, the later stairs to the second floor protrude through the east wall and ceiling. The wall and ceiling surfaces were carefully cut to accommodate the stairs.
Ceiling: The original plaster on Rocklath (a gypsum-board lath) ceiling is approximately 10 feet above the floor.
Baseboard: The original 5-inch-high baseboard is composed of a plain fascia with a filleted quarter-round cap molding.
Door: The original opening in the west wall is framed by a plain wood casing.
Lighting/Electrical: The closet is lit by a porcelain utility ceiling fixture with an exposed incandescent bulb. Security-system equipment on the south wall is labeled Magnum Alert and AES Intelliset and was installed c. 1996.
Furnishings and Fittings: The closet is fitted with two tiers of original wood shelves: one on the north, east, and south walls, and another just on the north and south walls. A wood rail with five original clothes hooks is mounted to the east wall. A cavetto molding along the upper edge of the wood rail supports the shelving. There is also a later metal clothes rod (probably dating to the Potter era).

Margaret Suckley's May 5, 1945, inventory records that two carved wood signs ("Private Property" and "No Visitors"), a wheelchair, and a small rug were kept in the closet at that time.
Finishes Investigation: The sand-finished plaster walls were originally unpainted, like the surfaces in the adjoining entry. Paint was introduced after the stair to the north attic was installed. Like the entry (101), the first wall paint was a yellow-gold (2.5Y 9/4) followed by the grey-green that remains as the visible finish.

The wood door trim and baseboard were originally finished in the same grey-white (5Y 9/1) used throughout the cottage.

Living Room (102)

The focus of the entire cottage is the centrally located living room (102) and the adjoining west porch (102A). As the primary room of the cottage, all visitors passed through this space to reach the west porch or rooms in the south wing.

The large rectangular volume of the living room includes a fireplace centered on the east wall, a pair of windows flanking the opening to the west porch in the west wall, and a single window and doorway in the north and south walls. The wide door opening to the west porch contains four divided-light door leaves hung from an overhead track. In the open position, the door leaves are stored in recessed wall pockets. The design of the door and the absence of a raised threshold were intended to accommodate the President's wheelchair. The spatial character of the room is dramatically enhanced by the extension of the ceiling surfaces beneath the gable roof.

Living room (102), 1997.
Fireplace centered on east elevation.
Photograph by JGWAA.

The room as completed in 1939 had contrasting surfaces of white, sand-finished plaster walls; grey-white painted woodwork; a natural grey stone fireplace; and the dark brown, stained finish of the oak floor.

This is the only room that was repeatedly recorded in photographs during FDR's occupancy. The earliest images show portions of the room in 1941 and 1942, well before any objects were placed on the walls. A detailed photographic record was made in May 1945, soon after the death of Franklin Roosevelt. An eclectic accumulation of furnishings, objects, and mementos are shown completely filling the large room. Several of the furnishings were loaned to the President by Margaret Suckley.

Modifications made after the death of the President include the application of paint to the wall surfaces; the removal of the dark, stained floor finish; the removal of the sash from the west window openings; and the permanent fixing of the sliding doors in an open position. The latter projects were carried out sometime after the west porch was enclosed by Elliott Roosevelt. A 1948 photograph shows the sash still in place in the west window next to the President's desk; perhaps the sash were removed by the Potters.

Living room (102), 1997.
View looking north.
Photograph by JGWAA.

Living room (102), 1997.
View looking southwest.
Photograph by JGWAA.

Living room (102), 1997.
View looking west into porch.
Photograph by JGWAA.

Floor: The floor is made up of original 2¼-inch-wide oak floorboards, running north/south, which originally had a dark brown, stained finish. Later the flooring was sanded to remove the dark finish, probably by the Potters. A small electrical fire in the mid-1970s damaged the floor, necessitating another refinishing.
Walls: All four walls are finished with a skim coat of original, sand-finished plaster over Rocklath, a gypsum-board lath. These surfaces were originally unpainted.
Ceiling: The plaster on metal lath ceiling has sloped surfaces beneath the gable roof, with a narrow, curved ridge running north/south down the center of the room; the ceiling planes slope to the east and west. The highest part of the ceiling is approximately 16 feet 4¼ inches above the floor, and the ceiling meets the east and west walls 12 feet 11¼ inches above the floor.
Baseboard: The original 5-inch-high baseboard is composed of a plain fascia with a filleted quarter-round cap molding.
Doors: There are three original door openings in this room: one in the north wall (D1021), one in the south wall (D1031), and a broad opening in the west wall (D1022). All three openings are framed by 4¼-inch-wide single-fascia architraves.

D1021: The 3-foot-wide by 6-foot 9½-inch-high by 1¾-inch-thick stile-and-rail door has four raised panels. One pair of 4-inch steel butt hinges, a 5½-inch-high brass mortise lockset with the strike plate stamped "05"; a pair of plain round brass knobs; and a pair of ovoid keyhole escutcheons with drop covers. The original key, marked "Corbin", remains with the lock.

D1022: The wide door opening contains two pairs of original glazed sliding doors. Each door has ten lights divided by 1-inch muntins, and each slides on a metal track. The doors have flush brass pulls. A steel hasp affixed to the inner north door can be seen in a photograph dated May 1945.
Windows: The four original window openings (two in the west wall, one in the north wall, and one in the south wall) are framed by 4¼-inch-wide single-fascia architraves, similar to those at the doorways. The north and south windows have 8-over-8 rope-hung wood sash with 9½-inch-wide by 1-foot 4-inch-high panes and ¾-inch muntins, and they are secured with brass thumb latches. The metal weather strips appear to be original. The sash in the two openings in the west wall have been removed, and the jambs have been covered with blind panels.
Fireplace: The fireplace hearth, mantel, and firebox are constructed of stone; the floor of the firebox is lined with brick pavers. The fireplace opening is framed at the sides by six roughly cut field stones set in a "rusticated" pattern, with the wider stones extending approximately 6 inches past the narrower stones. At the top of the opening, a series of five fieldstones form a flat arch with a large central keystone. A pair of 6-inch-thick quarter-round stone brackets supports the mantel shelf, which is made up of a single 4-inch-thick stone slab, 1 foot 1½ inches deep and 7 feet 4 inches wide. The stone hearth extends 2 feet 6 inches from the fireplace.
Heating: There is one hot-air-supply register below each window, as well as pairs of return grilles in the northeast and southeast corners of the room. The baseboard molding is carried up to frame these openings. The openings have metal honeycomb screens. The registers and grilles date to the original construction of the cottage and, according to the heating specifications of May 26, 1938, they were supplied by Hart & Cooley.

The 1960s thermostat on the north wall replaces an earlier rectangular model probably like the one in situ in the south hall (103) installed sometime after June 1942. A photograph of that date does not show a thermostat in this location.
Lighting/Electrical: There are no hardwired lighting fixtures in the room; however, there is a switched wall outlet. Electrical elements include single duplex receptacles in the north and south walls, four duplex receptacles in the west wall, and three in the east wall, as well as switches in the west and north walls, all with mirrored cover plates. The 1938 specifications called for mirrored cover plates at the switches and Bakelite plates at the receptacles. The switch plates in place here may be original.

An original outlet with three receptacles is located south of the fireplace and is labeled Bryant; its Bakelite cover plate is labeled "P&S Despard line." Four additional receptacles are located in the floor near the center of the room. Two appear to date to the original construction or just after; the remaining two probably date to the Potter residency.

Equipment: An original service call button, south of the fireplace, is the Edwards Togglepush called out in the specifications as part of the Edwards Annunciette system; the button has been painted over. A telephone outlet, which may be original, is located south of the fireplace; a September 19, 1938, letter from the contractor reports that a telephone outlet was moved to "the right side of the fireplace." A radio antenna outlet was to be located nearby.

Furnishings and Fittings: The living room furnishings are recorded in detail in the two inventories: the more detailed, dated May 5, 1945, was written by Margaret Suckley; the other was produced by the P. J. Curry Company of New York City. The room is also well recorded in several photographs dating from 1941 to May 1945, during FDR's era, and as late as 1948, during Elliott Roosevelt's occupancy.

The large room was amply furnished in an eclectic array of furniture, decorative items, and other objects.

A large (14 feet 5 inch by 30 feet), monochrome, Bigelow-Sanford cut pile rug, supplied by S. S. Spivack of New York City in October 1939, covered most of the dark-stained floor surface.

The four windows and the sliding-door opening all had pairs of straight curtain panels in a chintz fabric suspended from traverse rods; the fabric and rods were supplied in 1939 by Luckey, Platt & Company of Poughkeepsie. Venetian blinds were positioned at each of the windows and can be seen in the early photographs, but the current blinds are not original.

The framed pictures and other objects affixed to the walls were not placed here until January 1944, according to Margaret Suckley.

Artificial lighting was provided by a floor lamp and two table lamps. The lamp located on the President's desk in the May 5, 1945, photograph was a gift to FDR from the National Press Club in November 1941.

The numerous pieces of furniture included a large sofa and chair with matching chintz slipcovers, as well as several additional chairs.

A large, glazed-door, late Victorian bookcase (from the Hall house at Tivoli) dominated the south wall. A much more delicate mahogany Chinese Chippendale-style cabinet (vitrine) was centered on the north wall.

The President's desk, a reproduction of one used by George Washington, was located in the southwest corner. In this same location were two chairs: a reproduction of Jefferson's revolving chair and a black leather upholstered chair that served as the President's Cabinet chair from 1933 to 1941.

Two tall plant stands, made by Mr. Bie, flanked the door opening to the west porch.

An extensive collection of books was housed in a bookcase located south of the fireplace.

The photographs taken in May 1945 record a room whose decor evolved over several years and that appears to be quite comfortable and informal.

A final photographic record, made of portions of the room in 1948, shows many of FDR's furnishings still in place. The formal drapes were replaced by tied-back white organdy ruffled curtains. The deceased President's desk, chair, and personal mementos remain in the southwest corner as a sort of memorial. A large letter "R" is applied to the face of the stone fireplace, and a portrait of the President hangs above the mantel.

Finishes Investigation: Upon completion of the cottage, the sand-finished plaster walls and ceiling were not painted. The woodwork was finished in a grey-white (5Y 9/1) paint provided by Pratt & Lambert. Later this finish was covered in a yellowish white (2.5Y 9/2) paint, followed by an additional yellowish white, white, and the current white finish.

The first paint finish applied to the sand-finished walls was a yellow-gold (2.5Y 9/4). In turn, this was covered in a grey-green, light green, pale yellow-green, and the current pale yellow-green.

Samples taken from the wall adjacent to the current thermostat reveal that the earlier rectangular thermostat was still in place when the walls were painted in the yellow-gold and the grey-green.

The yellow-gold scheme was probably introduced during the occupancy of the cottage by Elliott Roosevelt.

The oak flooring was originally covered in the dark brown, stained finish seen in the FDR-era photographs. The existing light finish is the result of sanding and refinishing by the Potters.

West porch (102A), 1997.
View looking south.
Photograph by JGWAA.

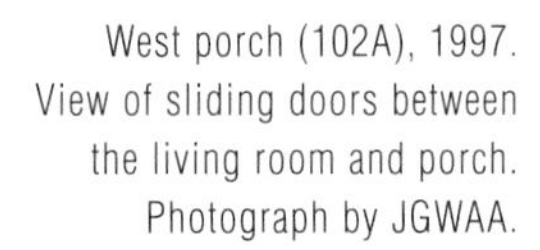

West porch (102A), 1997.
View of sliding doors between
the living room and porch.
Photograph by JGWAA.

West Porch (102A)

The west porch, along with the adjoining living room, are the principal public spaces in the cottage. These were the two areas used by the President to entertain friends and important guests. The broad opening between these areas, fitted with pairs of sliding doors, easily permitted the two spaces to be joined into one grand suite.

As originally constructed, the long rectangular porch extended along the west facade of the central block of the cottage. Six square posts supported the edge of the roof along the west side of the porch; the east side was supported by the stone masonry wall of the living room, with a wide central doorway and two flanking windows. False columns or posts were located at the northeast and southeast corners of the porch, adjacent to the stone wall. Although the flagstone floor of the porch was situated above the level of the surrounding lawn, an earthen ramp at the north end of the porch allowed the President access to the yard while in his wheelchair. Beyond the porch, to the west, was the downward slope of the lawn and the spectacular view through the trees to the Hudson River and the Catskill Mountains.

Several photographs record the west porch as it was frequently used by FDR. An array of furnishings, including a set of painted wicker furniture, was moved as required about the flagstone surface.

During the occupancy of the house by Elliott Roosevelt and his family, the porch was enclosed to create an additional living space. The three open sides were filled in by walls, with casement windows across the south and west elevations. The informal room resulting from this work was in character with the era in which it was created. The amply furnished room is recorded in a newspaper photograph published in 1952, when Elliott Roosevelt was selling the cottage.

Sometime after the creation of this new room, the window sash from the original west windows in the living room were removed and the sliding doors were fixed in an open position. These modifications helped to join the two spaces into a single large living area. Since the sash can be seen in place in a 1948 photograph, it is likely that these modifications were made by the Potters after 1952.

The former porch was further modified when the Potters installed the acoustical tile ceiling.

Floor: The floor is made up of the original bluestone flags, approximately 1 foot 11½ inches wide by 3 feet long, set with ½-inch mortar joints.

Walls: The east wall is the exposed (formerly exterior) stone wall of the house. The other three walls are finished with vertical tongue-and-groove knotty pine boards, ranging from 5¼ inches to 9 inches wide. These wood walls were constructed for Elliott Roosevelt; the original posts that supported the west edge of the porch roof were incorporated in this work.

Ceiling: The ceiling is presently finished with 1-foot by 1-foot acoustical tiles, installed by the Potters after 1952. The tiles are of a fiberboard construction.

The original ceiling consists of narrow tongue-and-groove boards running north/south, approximately 8 feet 4 inches above the floor. A 1952 photograph shows this board ceiling in situ.

Baseboard: A 5½-inch-high pine fascia trims the base of the three wood walls; it is contemporary with the Elliott Roosevelt-era wall surface.

Cornice: A 1½-inch-high crown molding, composed of a cavetto and a quarter-round molding, trims the top of the three wood walls; it is contemporary with the installation of the acoustical ceiling tiles.

Doors: The original wide door opening from the living room (102) is framed by a 1¾-inch-wide molding composed of two fillets and a quarter-round. A doorway in the south wall (D102A1) is set flush in the wood paneling, without trim, and is contemporary with the addition of the wood walls.

D102A1: The interior door is 2 feet 4 inches wide by 6 feet 8¼ inches high by 1½ inches thick. The interior (north) face is finished with vertical pine boards to match those on the walls; the exterior face is of stile-and-rail construction with two recessed panels. This door is contemporary with the doorway. Hardware consists of one pair of 3¾-inch butt hinges with ball finials; a 2¼-inch brass Kwikset mortised passage set with knobs; and a small brass slide bolt near the top of the door.

A storm door at the exterior side of this opening is a 2-foot 3¾-inch-wide by 6-foot 7½-inch-high glazed stile-and-rail door with eight lights set in a frame above a horizontal raised panel. The divided-light frame can be removed for the installation of a screened frame. Hardware consists of one pair of 2½-inch butt hinges, as well as a steel latch and knob.

Windows: The two original window openings in the east wall are framed by single-fascia architraves, similar to those found in the interior of the house, and have stone sills. The sash were probably removed by the Potters.

The south and west walls have banks of windows with pivoting casement sash, installed when Elliott Roosevelt had the west porch enclosed. There are five bays of four windows in the west wall and one bay of five windows in the south wall. Each sash has ten lights, approximately 7½ inches by 11¼ inches, and metal latches. Interior screens cover the openings.

Lighting/Electrical: There are two original electrical junction boxes set in the stone wall surfaces flanking the wide door opening in the east wall. These junction boxes are located at a height appropriate for sconce or lantern fixtures, and they are capped with c. 1938 cover plates. Various FDR-era photographs indicate that light fixtures were never installed in these locations during his lifetime.

There is an electrical junction box set in the stone wall surface beneath each of the window openings in the east wall. These junction boxes have single exterior receptacles. There are duplex receptacles with mirrored cover plates in the three wood-paneled walls.

Equipment: A thermometer, a barometer, and an anemometer are mounted to the north wall. These fittings were installed by the Potters.

A telephone jack is surface-mounted to the west wall.

Furnishings and Fittings: For FDR, the west porch was a very active outdoor room. Many photographs record the use of the porch as a gathering place for personalities of international stature.

The FDR-era photographs reveal that the porch was furnished with a suite of painted wicker furniture, including a settee, armchair, rocker, and table, as well as other assorted chairs and tables. The wicker furniture was situated (probably temporarily stored) in the living room when the P. J. Curry Company inventory was made in 1945. A letter dated September 1, 1939, refers to a Mr. Osthagen in regard to the porch furniture. Perhaps it was he who supplied the wicker items.

A very different decor is revealed for the porch as it existed during Elliott Roosevelt's occupancy. A newspaper photograph of undetermined date, but published in April 1952, shows the porch as it appeared after its conversion to an enclosed room. It was apparently used as an informal living room. An extensive collection of furnishings filled the south end of the space.

The "weather station" positioned on the north wall was placed here by the Potter family.

Finishes Investigation: Original painted elements visible on the west porch include the woodwork of the window and door openings (in the east wall) and the tongue-and-groove board ceiling above the acoustical tile.

The window trim retains six layers of painted finishes plus an additional surface of a white primer. The first finish is a yellowish white (2.5Y 9/2-8/2) paint. This surface was exposed until the porch was enclosed by Elliott Roosevelt, and a visible dirt layer separates this paint from the next layer, another yellowish white. Succeeding finishes include four layers of white paint.

The original porch ceiling surface retains all of its painted finishes, including a white primer and a yellowish white (2.5Y 9/2-8/2), which is the FDR-era finish. This is followed by a bright blue-green (7.5BG 3/4) dating to the Elliott Roosevelt occupancy and visible in the April 1952 newspaper photograph. The next finish is a pale yellow-green that has deteriorated to a deep beige color. This soiled surface is covered with acoustical tile.

A letter from the architect Henry Toombs, dated October 8, 1938, notes that the exterior paint is to be ". . . something between a cream white and an oyster white . . . should go with the joints of the masonry . . . a true white should be greyed slightly. . . ." The first finish layer of yellowish white (2.5Y 9/2-8/2) seems to conform to this specification.

Hall (103)

This hall provides access from the living room to the two bedrooms (104 and 105) and bathroom (106) in the south wing, as well as to the spaces located in the attic of the wing. In plan, the long, narrow space includes single doorways at the north and south ends, a window in the west wall, and two doorways in the east wall. The doorway (D1052) to the small bedroom (105) was moved from near the center of the wall to its current location at the south end of the hall when the stairway to the attic was constructed in 1942-43.

No mention of the hall is made in either of the 1945 inventories, and the only photographic record is a 1948 partial view as seen through the door of the small bedroom (105).

Formerly the space was nearly filled with shelving along the east and west walls; just below the ceiling the shelving extended around all four walls. The latter shelving is still in place. It was installed sometime after the application of the bright blue-green wall and ceiling paint, which appears to date to the Elliott Roosevelt occupancy. The 1948 photograph, looking from the small bedroom (105) into the hall, shows the shelving against the west wall and the blue-green decor.

Floor: The floor is made up of original 2¼-inch-wide oak floorboards, running north/south. Originally, the floor was finished with a dark brown stain; that stain has been removed, and the boards now have a light finish.

Walls: All four walls are finished with a skim coat of sand-finished plaster over Rocklath, a gypsum board lath. A 3-foot-3-inch(±)-wide area near the center of the east wall was plastered in 1942-43 when the door to the small bedroom (105) was moved.
Ceiling: The original plaster on Rocklath (a gypsum-board lath) ceiling is 10 feet ½ inch above the floor.
Baseboard: The original 5-inch-high baseboard is composed of a plain fascia with a filleted quarter-round cap molding. A section of base on the east wall was moved when the position of door D1052 was changed.
Doors: There are four door openings in this hall: one in the north wall (D1031), one in the south wall (D1041), and two in the east wall (D1071, D1052). All four openings are framed by 4¼-inch-wide single-fascia architraves. The north, south, and northeast openings are in their original locations; the southeast opening was moved in 1942-43.

D1031: The original 3-inch-wide by 6-foot 9½-inch-high by 1¾-inch-thick stile-and-rail door has four raised panels. There is one pair of 4-inch butt hinges; a 5½-inch-high brass mortise lock with the strike plate stamped "07"; a pair of plain round brass knobs; and a pair of ovoid keyhole escutcheons with drop covers; all original.
Window: The single original window opening in the west wall is framed by a 4¼-inch single-fascia architrave, similar in profile to the door architrave. The 6-over-6 chain-hung wood window sash are set deeply into the masonry wall with paneled reveals and a plain window shelf. Below the opening is a plain sill and apron. The 9¾-inch-wide by 1-foot 3¾-inch-high panes are separated by ¾-inch-wide muntins. The sash are secured with a brass thumb latch.
Heating: There is an original supply register below the window and a return-air grille in the east wall. The baseboard molding is carried up to frame the openings. The metal honeycomb screens on the register and the grille were supplied by Hart & Cooley.
Lighting/Electrical: The hall is lit by a three-bulb incandescent surface-mounted, ceiling fixture. The fixture has a domed, cut-glass shade and is ornamented with glass pendants. It was placed here sometime after 1945, replacing a simple single-lamp fixture purchased in 1938. The original fixture had a 5¾-inch-diameter base; the sand-finished plaster beneath the original fixture remains unpainted. The plaster ceiling surface beneath the existing 1-foot 3-inch-diameter fixture is painted the same blue-green color as the remainder of the ceiling (this color probably dates to the period of Elliot Roosevelt's occupancy).

Hall (103), 1997. View looking north. Photograph by JGWAA.

Other electrical elements include two switches with mirrored cover plates in the east wall, and an original Minneapolis Honeywell Regulator Company thermostat on the east wall.

The 1938 specifications indicate mirrored cover plates for the living room. The ones here and other matching covers may date to the Elliott Roosevelt era or later.
Furnishings and Fittings: Two tiers of shallow wood perimeter shelves are located near the ceiling. These unusual built-in elements are supported by wood ledgers and steel utility brackets. This shelving appears to have been installed sometime after the walls and ceiling were first painted and currently retains that bright blue-green painted finish.

There is paint-ghost evidence for additional wood shelving on the east and west walls. On the west wall, shelving flanked the window and consisted of five shelves: the lowest at the level of the baseboard and the highest at 3 feet 10½ inches above the floor. Similar shelving was positioned along the east wall. Evidence there indicates that two 3-foot 11-inch-high units flanked the original doorway to the small bedroom (105). This arrangement was modified or removed when door D1052 was moved to its current location.

A 1948 photograph looking from the small bedroom (105) through doorway D1052 shows the shelving on the west wall. In the photo, the walls of both spaces (103 and 105) are covered in the first finish of bright blue-green.

No mention of this hall is found in either of the inventories made after the death of the President, and it is likely that all of the shelving was installed for the Elliott Roosevelt family.
Finishes Investigation: The walls, ceiling, and woodwork were investigated to determine the sequence of finishes. The woodwork, including the doors, was first finished in a grey-white (5Y 9/1) paint. Some of this original surface can be seen on door D1031 where later paint layering has delaminated.

The sand-finished plaster walls and ceiling were originally unpainted. The first applied finish on these surfaces is a bright blue-green (7.5BG 4/4) paint that is also found on the existing shelving near the ceiling. Remarkably, this finish is still exposed on the shelving, the adjoining upper wall surfaces, and the ceiling. It appears that the shelving was installed sometime after the blue-green color was applied to the ceiling and walls; the plaster wall surface behind the ledger strips and furring for the shelf brackets and shelving is painted blue-green. It appears that the shelving was painted by Elliot Roosevelt, or the Potters, to match the existing plaster color. This same rich color was used in the small bedroom (105). A 1948 photograph of the bedroom and the hall records the blue-green finish. Below the shelving, the hall walls were, in turn, painted pale yellow-green, pale grey-green, and the current pale green.

Paint samples taken from the area of the lower wall shelving revealed that the blue-green color covered the wall surface behind the shelves but that the next finish, a pale yellow-green, was applied while the shelves remained in place.

The bright blue-green paint covers the plaster on the east wall where the original door opening to the small bedroom (105) was located. This indicates that the blue-green finish dates to sometime after the door modification. This bold paint was probably placed here for Elliott Roosevelt; deep blues and greens were popular in the 1940s.

Prior to the use of the wall paint, the hall had a rather unfinished appearance due to the relocation of the door and to the replastering of the east wall in 1943. The plaster repairs would have remained very visible in the unpainted, sand-finished surface.

Bedroom (104)

This is the largest of the three original so-called bedrooms in the cottage. The P. J. Curry Company refers to this as the "President's Bedroom," and Margaret Suckley includes it as the "large bedroom" in her inventory. The room has single windows in the east, west, and south walls; a doorway in the north wall; and a second doorway located in a short extension of the room that leads to the south hall (103). A later vanity and flanking built-in closets are located in the southeast corner.

As originally conceived, a fireplace was to be located on the north wall, but this portion of the design was eliminated during construction. Originally there were no closets here; the intent was to use a freestanding wardrobe for clothing.

The probable use of the room as a master bedroom by Elliott Roosevelt and Fay Emerson may have resulted in the addition of the closets and vanity. The transformation of the room after 1945 included the introduction of paint to the walls, as well as the creation of the floral decoration on the south wall, probably positioned to be above the head of the bed.

No known photographs record the room as it appeared during any period of occupancy.

Floor: The original floor is made up of 2¼-inch-wide oak floorboards, running east/west. The flooring originally had a dark brown, stained finish, which can still be seen under the built-in vanity. Wall-to-wall carpet presently covers the floor.

Walls: All four walls are covered with an original skim coat of sand-finished plaster over Rocklath, a gypsum-board lath. A hand-painted mural of a branch of flowering dogwood ornaments the south wall.

Ceiling: The ceiling is finished with plaster on Rocklath, a gypsum-board lath. It is 10 feet ½ inch above the floor.

Baseboard: The original 5-inch-high baseboard is composed of a plain fascia with a filleted quarter-round cap molding.

Doors: There are two original doorways in the north wall (D1041, D1051). Both openings are framed with a 4¼-inch-wide single-fascia architrave.

D1041: The original 3-inch-wide by 6-foot 9½-inch-high by 1¾-inch-thick stile-and-rail door has four raised panels. The original hardware includes one pair of 4-inch butt hinges; a 5½-inch-high brass mortise lockset with the strike plate stamped "06"; a pair of plain round brass knobs; and a pair of ovoid keyhole escutcheons with drop covers.

Windows: There are three original window openings in this room: one in the south wall, one in the east wall, and one in the west wall. All three openings are framed by 4¼-inch-wide single-

Bedroom (104), 1997. East elevation. Photograph by JGWAA.

Bedroom (104), 1997. View looking southwest. Photograph by JGWAA.

fascia architraves, similar to those at the doorways, and are set within paneled reveals. The 6-over-6 wood sash have 9¾-inch-wide by 1-foot 3¾-inch-high panes and ¾-inch-wide muntins. The east sash are rope-hung; the other sash are chain-hung. All three sets of sash are secured with original brass thumb latches. A window air-conditioning unit has been installed in the east window.

Heating: There are supply registers below the south and east windows, and a return-air grille is located near door D1041. The baseboard molding is carried up to frame these openings. The supply registers and return-air grille have metal honeycomb screens supplied by Hart & Cooley.

Lighting/Electrical: Electrical elements include five original duplex receptacles (two in the north wall, one in the south wall, one in the west wall, and one in the east wall behind the built-in vanity) and two switches (one near door D1041 and one in the south wall), as well as the fluorescent fixture lighting the vanity. The light fixture and the south wall switch are contemporary with the built-in closets and vanity. The replacement cover plates at the receptacles and switches are mirrored; the east receptacle, concealed behind the vanity, retains its original plastic cover plate. The 1938 specifications called for Bakelite cover plates in all rooms except the living room and two bathrooms.

Equipment: An original service call button with a replacement mirrored plate on the east wall near door D1041 is the Edwards "Togglepush" called out in the specifications as part of an Edwards Annunciette system; the annunciator panel is found on the south wall of the kitchen (112).

Other equipment includes a Potter-era telephone jack on the south wall. A telephone outlet was specified for this room in 1938. A Potter-era red alarm button is located near the south window. The push-button switch appears to be a panic button for an earlier security alarm system.

Furnishings and Fittings: The various plans refer to this room as a bedroom or, in the case of the P. J. Curry Company inventory, as the "President's Bedroom." The actual function of the room probably varied between 1938 and 1945. The only furniture known to be in the room during that period is an American Chippendale-style slant-front desk included in the Curry Company inventory. Both 1945 inventories list framed prints, watercolors, and an oil painting on the walls of this room. No mention of a bed or other bedroom-type furnishings is made in the documents.

The built-in cabinetry located in the southeast corner was probably installed for Elliott Roosevelt and his wife; this was a much-needed appointment when the room first functioned as a full-time bedroom. The wall surface behind the vanity retains the original unpainted, sand-finished plaster. The original baseboard, with a grey-white painted finish, remains as well. The vanity includes a mirrored vanity flanked by tall wood cabinets. A wood fascia with a shallow arch cutout extends between the two cabinets; the entire composition is topped by a small cornice and an additional wood cabinet with four doors. The cabinets' doors are hung on 2¾-inch-high butt hinges with ball finials, and they are secured with small brass cabinet latches. The lower cabinet doors have three tiers of recessed panels. Within these lower cabinets are wood shoe racks and clothes rods. A fluorescent lighting fixture is recessed into the soffit behind the decorative wood fascia; it is contemporary with the vanity. The rear vanity mirror is original, but the side mirrors are additions, perhaps added by the Potters. The rear mirror is stamped on the reverse side: "Polar Process Mirror; Pittsburgh Plate Glass Company; Ford City, PA.; MAR. 16 1945".

The full-length mirror on door D1051 to the small bedroom (105) was installed when the built-in closets were constructed, or possibly later.

Finishes Investigation: Originally, the sand-finished plaster walls and ceiling were unpainted. The first wall paint, a pale pink (2.5YR 9/2), was probably applied for Elliott Roosevelt. This application included the painted floral motif on the south wall. All subsequent repaintings of the wall surface carefully retained the dogwood decoration. The later repainting includes a bright pink and the current pink.

The original woodwork, including the doors, retains several layers of paint, beginning with the original grey-white (5Y 9/1) finish, followed by a yellowish white, white, pale beige, two whites, a pink-beige, and the current white paint.

The built-in closets, added when the walls were first painted, were finished on the exterior in a yellowish white and on the interior in a light yellow-green (7.5GY 8/4-7/4).

Bedroom (105)

The various floor plans refer to this space as a bedroom, and the 1945 inventories include it as the "small bedroom" or "bedroom # 2," but there is no documentation referring to the actual use of the room or who may have occupied it during the FDR era.

Currently, the room has single doorways in the north, south, and west walls, as well as a window in the east wall. The northwest corner includes the projecting mass of the later attic stairway, as well as a small, built-in closet beneath the slope of the stair. Much of the surface of the east and south walls is covered by large built-in closets that extend from floor to ceiling.

As originally conceived, the room was to include a fireplace on the south wall, but this feature was never constructed. The room as completed did not include the built-in closets or the stair projection. The doorway to the hall was positioned at the north end of the west wall; it was moved to its current position, near the center of the west wall, in 1942-43 when the stair was installed. The north door originally opened to a long, narrow closet; it now gives access to the bathroom.

The arrangement and appearance of the room as it now exists is the result of changes made during all periods of ownership of the house. During the FDR era, the stair projection and related closet were added in the northwest corner. This project included the movement of the door opening in the west wall to its current location and the relocation of the return-air grille from the north wall to the new plywood wall surface beneath the stairway. The enclosed cavity behind the grille cover and beneath the stair preserves important evidence concerning the evolution and finish of the room. The floor surface there retains the original dark brown, stained finish, and the baseboard has the original paint color. The sand-finished plaster walls are unpainted (their original intended condition). The original location of the west doorway can be seen; the opening is carefully filled with sand-finished plaster to match the adjoining wall surface. No baseboard was installed in front of the former door opening, indicating that this area was immediately concealed by the construction of the small closet.

The first significant post-FDR era change involved the painting of the walls in the bright blue-green color. This finish is shown in a photograph taken in 1948 and remains in the closet beneath the stairway.

During the Elliott Roosevelt era the room was occupied by one of his children. Elliott (Tony) Roosevelt, Jr., recalled that the closets in the southeast corner were not in place when he knew the room, and the original closet was still intact.

The next generation of changes included the construction of the two-tiered closets in the southeast portion of the room. Additional work carried out at about the same time may have included the installation of the existing mirrors on the north and south doors (this involved the installation of different door hinges) and the addition of the pressed-glass knobs to the doors.

The intended result of this work was the modification of the space from bedroom to dressing room. This space joined the large bedroom (104) to the bathroom (106), thereby creating a private suite of rooms in the south wing. The incorporation of the original closet into the bathroom space (the tub was relocated against the north wall) occurred as part of this work. This extensive project was probably carried out by the Potters soon after their 1952 purchase of the property. Such changes were almost a necessity for anyone intending to occupy the cottage on a full-time basis.

An additional modification carried out by the Potters in the early 1950s was the installation of the saucer-shaped ceiling-light fixture.

The only period photograph of the room is a partial view of the west wall and doorway looking out into the hall. This view dates to 1948 and records the blue-green wall finish, as well as some of the furnishings.

Floor: The floor is made up of original 2¼-inch-wide light-finished oak floorboards, running east/west. The flooring originally had a dark brown, stained finish that can be seen beneath the area now occupied by the northwest closet. The same dark stain can be seen on the floor surface beneath the casework at the south wall. Wall-to-wall carpet presently covers the floor.

Walls: All four walls are covered with a skim coat of original, sand-finished plaster over Rocklath, a gypsum-board lath. An original small steel access door in the north wall, just above the baseboard, provided access to the plumbing when the bathtub in bathroom (106) was in its original position.

Ceiling: The ceiling is finished with plaster on Rocklath, a gypsum-board lath. It is 10 feet ½ inches above the floor.

Baseboard: The original 4½-inch-high baseboard is composed of a plain fascia (¾ inch by 3¾ inch) with a filleted quarter-round cap molding (¾ inch). A short section of the cap molding is missing from the base next to the doorway in the north wall (D1053).

Doors: There are three door openings in this room: one in the south wall (D1051), one in the west wall (D1052), and one in the north wall (D1053). Each of these openings is framed by a 4¼-inch-wide single-fascia architrave. When the stairway to the attic was inserted in 1942-43, the west opening was moved from its original position at the north end of the wall to a position near the center of the wall.

Bedroom (105), 1997.
View looking northeast.
Photograph by JGWAA.

Bedroom (105), 1997. West elevation. View of casework and stair constructed c. 1943.
Photograph by JGWAA.

D1051: The original 3-foot-wide by 6-foot 9½-inch-high by 1¾-inch-thick stile-and-rail door has four raised panels on the north face; the south face is covered with a full-length mirrored panel. The hardware consists of three 4-inch brass hinges with ball finials replacing the two original hinges to compensate for the added weight of the mirror. Other hardware includes an original 5½-inch-high brass mortise lockset with the strike plate stamped "04"; a pair of pressed-glass knobs; and a pair of original ovoid keyhole escutcheons with drop covers. The addition of the hinges, glass knobs, and mirror was probably made early in the Potter occupancy.

D1052: The 2-foot 6½-inch-wide by 6-foot 9½-inch-high by 1¾-inch-thick stile-and-rail door has four raised panels. The hardware consists of one pair of 4-inch butt hinges; a 5½-inch-high brass mortise lockset with the strike plate stamped "03"; a plain round brass knob on the west (hall) face and a pressed glass knob on the east face; and a pair of ovoid keyhole escutcheons with drop covers. The door, trim, and hardware were moved from their original position when the stair was inserted. The single glass knob is contemporary with the knobs added to door D1051.

D1053: The 2-foot 5¾-inch-wide by 6-foot 9¼-inch-high by 1¾-inch-thick stile-and-rail door has four raised panels on the north face; like door D1051, the south face is covered with a full-length mirrored panel. The hardware consists of three 4-inch brass butt hinges with ball finials; a 5½-inch-high brass mortise lockset with the strike plate stamped "08"; a chrome knob on the north (bathroom) face; a brass knob on the south face; and a brass ovoid keyhole escutcheon with a drop cover on the south face. This original door formerly opened to a closet. The hinges, knobs, and mirror were probably installed by the Potters.

Window: The original window opening in the east wall is framed by a 4¼-inch-wide single-fascia architrave and is set within paneled reveals. The 6-over-6 rope-hung wood sashes have 9¾-inch-wide by 1-foot 3¾-inch-high panes and ¾-inch-wide muntins, and they are secured with an original brass thumb latch.

Closet: A plywood-enclosed closet is built-in beneath the stairs to the attic. The pair of paneled doors was cut and reworked to fit into the angled opening; prior to their installation, each door leaf was rectangular in shape. The south door has three brass butt hinges with ball finials, while the north door, shorter to fit within the angled opening, has just two hinges. The doors are secured with a surface-mounted brass latch. Within the closet are five tiers of shelving.

The rear (west) wall in the closet retains evidence in the plaster for the original position of the door (D1052) to the hall. The doorway was moved and the stairway was constructed in 1942-43. This closet was installed at the same time.

Heating: There is one original supply register in the baseboard below the east window. Like the other registers in the house, the baseboard molding is carried up to frame the opening. The register has a metal honeycomb screen supplied by Hart & Cooley.

An original return-air grille is positioned at the far west end of the north baseboard. When the stairway and closet were inserted in the northwest corner, the grille was reinstalled in the base of the new west plywood wall that enclosed the space beneath the stair.

Lighting/Electrical: The room is lit by a surface-mounted incandescent ceiling fixture with five bulbs and a saucer-shaped, frosted glass shade. The lighting fixture was installed by the Potters. Other electrical elements include duplex receptacles located on the south wall and beneath the east window. There is surface-mounted Wiremold conduit and a duplex receptacle on the north wall. There are also two original switches in the north wall and one later switch in the west wall. The mirror cover plates date to after the FDR era.

Furnishings and Fittings: How this room functioned during the FDR era remains unknown. The 1945 inventories refer to the space as a bedroom, but no furniture is included in the list of contents; only the framed artwork located on the walls is mentioned. An interesting original fitting is the small bathtub plumbing-access door in the north wall, just above the baseboard. The door remains in place, but the plumbing was moved when the bathtub was relocated in the enlarged bathroom (106).

The floor-to-ceiling wood closets in the southeast corner of the room were significant additions. Each has a tall lower cabinet topped by a short upper cabinet and a cornice. The south cabinet is four bays wide, and the east cabinet is three bays wide and extends behind the south cabinet to the south wall. The paneled doors are hung on 3-inch steel butt hinges with ball finials at the top of the hinges and have small brass knobs.

The units on the south wall contain clothes rods. In the east cabinet, there are seven cedar drawers in the north bay; the adjacent bay has wood shoe racks, and the south bay has a clothes rod. The upper cabinets each have one shelf.

These built-in units were installed after the FDR era, probably for the Potters, who may have used this space as a dressing room positioned between the large bedroom (104) and the bathroom (106). Behind the casework on the south wall, the fascia of the original baseboard remains in place; the cap molding was removed so that the fascia could be used as a ledger strip to support the new casework. Where the cap molding was removed the original unpainted sand-finished plaster was exposed.

A 1948 photograph records some of the furnishings positioned against the west wall, including a large framed oil painting and a small drop-leaf gate-leg table that supports a small glazed-door book cabinet. The bookcases along the west wall of the hall (103) can also be seen.

Finishes Investigation: Originally the sand-finished plaster walls and ceiling surfaces were unpainted, and the trim was painted in the typical grey-white (5Y 9/1). Analysis of the paint layers now covering the walls revealed the first painted finish of bright blue-green (7.5BG 4/4). This color remains exposed inside the understair closet in the northwest corner, and it is shown in a 1948 photograph that records the west wall and door to the hall. The blue-green painted finish also remains on the wall plaster behind the plywood casework against the south wall. This bold decor dates to the Elliott Roosevelt era. According to Elliott (Tony) Roosevelt, Jr., the room was occupied by one of Elliott Roosevelt's children. Later colors used on the wall surfaces include a cream, white, pale yellow-green, and the current pink-beige.

Bathroom (106)

The bathroom currently has single doorways in the south and west walls and a single window in the north wall. The toilet and lavatory remain in their original positions against the south wall, but the original tub is now located in a partially enclosed position against the north wall.

More modifications were made in this small room than in any other space in the cottage. As originally conceived and constructed, the bathroom included the space now called the vestibule (107) and extended to a partition formerly located about 3 feet east of the window. The bathroom was entered directly from the south hall (103); immediately inside of the door, to the south, there was a shallow closet, probably for towel and linen storage. The door opening for this closet now provides access to the stair ascending to the finished south attic.

Bathroom (106), 1997. View looking southeast. Photograph by JGWAA.

Finishes included a white ceramic tile wainscot on the walls, white ceramic plumbing fixtures, and various chromium fittings, including light fixtures. All of these elements remain in situ except for the pair of lamps that flanked the medicine cabinet. The floor was covered in linoleum, and a rubber base provided a transition between that surface and the walls.

The first modification was made in 1942-43, when the stairway was inserted to provide access to the south attic. This work involved the relocation of the doorway from the hall opening (D1071) to a newly constructed partition on the east side of the vestibule (107). A small overhead cupboard was constructed above the relocated doorway. The floor linoleum was modified at this time.

After 1945, more changes were made. This work included the expansion of the bathroom into the space originally functioning as a closet off of the small bedroom (105). The original 5-foot 10-inch tub was moved to its current location against the north wall. The former doorway to the closet (D1053) provided private access to the bathroom from the newly created dressing room (105) and the large bedroom (104) beyond. Elliott (Tony) Roosevelt, Jr., maintains that the original closet space was intact when he was familiar with the room, as late as 1950. This suggests that the eastward expansion of the bathroom dates to the early Potter era.

With the removal of the north dormer on the east elevation of the south wing (added sometime after the president's death), the original cased opening and attic hatch in the ceiling of the former first-floor closet (off of bedroom 105) was exposed from above. From below, the hatch was covered with a new ceiling surface when the closet was combined with bathroom 106. The hatch measures 2 feet 7¾ inches in the north-south direction and 2 feet 3 inches in the east-west direction. The wood hatch was cut out in one corner for heating ductwork that would have been located adjacent to the west wall of the former closet. The existing ductwork within the east wall of the enlarged bathroom appears to have resulted from the need to relocate the c. 1943 riser, with the enlargement of the bathroom.

No known photographs record the appearance of the bathroom in its original or later states.

Floor: The floor is currently covered with sheet vinyl on plywood. Below the vinyl is an earlier linoleum floor and pine subfloor.

The current surface and the plywood underlayment date to the Potter occupancy. Although the linoleum preserved beneath the plywood (a marbled cream field with a black inlaid border) is typical of the FDR era and the years immediately following 1945, it appears that an entirely new surface was installed when the room was expanded into the former bedroom closet area at the east end of the space. There are no seams in the linoleum that suggest material was added with the bathroom expansion, and the existing black linoleum border extends along the tub in its relocated position. Beneath the framing of the wing wall, at the west end of the relocated tub, a solid-green-colored linoleum was found; this appears to have been the original flooring material in the bathroom.

Walls: The walls are finished with smooth white plaster; the specifications called for plaster on metal lath. A 4-foot 5¾-inch-high white ceramic tile wainscot extends from the bathtub enclosure on the north wall, along the east and south walls, and over to the door opening in the west wall. Within the bathtub enclosure, the tile covering is approximately 2 feet higher.

The current wall surfaces record the history of change in this room.

The original conditions included tile on the south wall behind the toilet and lavatory, as well as a short expanse of tile on the west wall next to the lavatory and on the wall surfaces enclosing the tub in its original location against the now-removed east wall. Original tile and plaster wall surfaces remain in situ in the first two locations. The other tile currently in place includes some reset original tile (the wall surface east of the toilet) and later similar, but not necessarily matching, white tiles on the east wall and in the tub enclosure. The grout joints of the later tiles are wider than the original condition. The north wall around the window and the wall surfaces now in the vestibule (107) were never tiled.

The portion of the west wall that includes the doorway and the built-in overhead cupboard is faced with plywood and is a later insertion dating to 1942-43, when the attic stair was constructed.

At the east end of the enlarged bathroom the original sand-finished plaster wall of the closet has been concealed behind the existing tile and plaster finishes. The wall appears to have been furred out with the expansion of the bathroom; this was done to conceal the cast-iron soil pipe and water-supply piping that had been installed in the northeast corner of the former closet to serve the second-floor bathroom added c. 1943. Additionally, the cavity between two of the studs in the east wall was utilized as a plenum for heating ductwork serving the second floor. This replaced the c. 1943 ductwork that had been routed along the west wall of the former closet and through the former attic-access hatch.

The expansion of the bathroom eastward into the former closet area was carried out sometime after 1945.

Ceiling: At the west end of the bathroom the original plaster ceiling is 9 feet 11½ inches above the floor. At the east end of the room the original closet ceiling has been covered with wire lath and plaster, and it has been made continuous with the original ceiling surface to the west. The surfaces were carefully joined when the bathroom was expanded.

Baseboard: A vinyl base has been installed where the flooring meets the walls. This replaces the original rubber (probably black) base that was approximately 4 inches high.

Doors: The bathroom has two door openings: one in the south wall (D1053), framed by a plain wood fascia, and one in the west wall (D1061). The south opening was originally the access to the former closet from the small bedroom (105). The frame around the west opening is flush with the wall. Above the west opening is a storage space with two paneled doors that have pairs of brass hinges with ball finials and brass cabinet latches. The partition, opening, and cupboard are contemporary with the installation of the attic stairway in 1942-43.

D1061: The original 3-foot-wide by 6-foot 9½-inch-high by 1¾-inch-thick stile-and-rail door has four raised panels. This door was originally located in doorway D1071, which opened directly into the bathroom until the 1942-43 changes were made. The hardware consists of one pair of 4-inch butt hinges; a 5½-inch-high brass mortise lockset; a plain round brass knob on the west (107) face and a chromium knob on the east face; and a brass keyhole escutcheon on the west (107) face and a chromium escutcheon with a turnpiece on the east face. An original chromium clothes hook is attached to the center stile.

Window: The original small window opening in the north wall is set within a paneled wood reveal. The 4-over-4 rope-hung wood sash have 9¾-inch-wide by 11¼-inch-high panes and ¾-inch-wide muntins and are secured by an original chromium thumb latch.

Plumbing: The original bathroom fittings include a 5-foot 10-inch-long porcelain-enameled cast-iron bathtub against the north wall (moved from its original position against a partition separating the bathroom from a closet to the east), and a Compact vitreous china toilet manufactured by Standard on the south wall. The manufacturing date, "AUG 8 1938," is stamped on the underside of the tank lid. The enameled, cast-iron lavatory on the south wall has the date of 5-27-37, as well as "Standard Sanitary Manufacturing Co., Louisville, P3867, 22x19, 3" cast into the underside of the basin. The toilet and the lavatory are in their original positions. The tub fittings are original, with the exception of the showerhead, which is of recent origin.

Lighting/Electrical: A pair of post-1945 incandescent wall fixtures flanks the medicine cabinet above the lavatory. Each fixture has a chromium wall bracket, a white opal glass shade, and a simplex receptacle. These replace the original fixtures, which had rectangular wall plates. There are also two chromed metal and glass incandescent ceiling fixtures. The larger three-bulb fixture, at the west end of the room, is not original. Paint evidence beneath the base of the fixture establishes the base size of the original fixture at 8¾-inch diameter. The original fixture was a two-bulb chromium fixture purchased from Lightolier in September 1938. The smaller fixture at the east end of the room is in the position of the light for the former closet; this 7-inch-diameter fixture replaced the original closet fixture that had a 3¾-inch-diameter base.

There are two switches in the room, as well as an original duplex receptacle with a chromed plate in the north wall.

Furnishings and Fittings: Most of the bathroom accessories are original chromium fittings and include six towel bars, six glass shelves with brackets, a toothbrush holder, and a garment hook on the west door (D1061). Some of the towel bars were moved when the bathroom was enlarged. A metal, mirrored medicine cabinet (marked Hall & Mack) is recessed into the south wall above the lavatory. A small mirror is positioned between the cabinet and the lavatory. Both of these fittings are original. The small mirror, for which a $15.00 payment was requested, was an addition to the contract in November 1938, presumably so that Roosevelt could look in the mirror while sitting in his wheelchair.

Later additions to the room (post-1945) may include the chromed-metal soap dish and tumbler holder flanking the lavatory, as well as the matching soap dish next to the bathtub. The surviving plastic liners of the soap dishes may indicate an early 1950s date for these fittings; the same design was available in the 1930s, but with a glass liner.

No markings were found on any of these fittings, but ones of similar design were manufactured by the Miami Cabinet Division of the Philip Carey Company of Middletown, Ohio, and were included in a 1938 issue of *Home Owner's Catalogs* published by F. W. Dodge Corporation.

Finishes Investigation: The original conditions here included smooth, unpainted, white plaster walls and ceiling, with woodwork painted in the grey-white (5Y 9/1) color referred to as oyster white in various documents. The lower portion of certain walls had the glazed, white ceramic tiles.

The walls and ceiling at the west end of the space were first painted in a deep grey-green color sometime after the west doorway was moved in 1942-43. This grey-green color can still be seen inside of the cupboard located above the west door and beneath the large ceiling-light fixture at the west end of the room. When the bathroom was expanded into the closet area to the east, the walls were painted a pale yellow.

A visual inspection of the original east wall, formerly a wall in the now-destroyed closet, revealed that the sand-finished surface was painted with a thin beige color that did not obscure the sanded-finish of the plaster. This same paint coating is seen beneath the small ceiling-light fixture at the east end of the room.

Vestibule (107) This small space was formerly part of the adjoining bathroom. Originally the door opening in the west wall was the direct and only access into the bathroom. The original door from the opening is now located in the east doorway; currently it is one of two entries into the bathroom.

The modifications that resulted in the creation of this space were carried out so that a stairway to the south attic could be constructed. Apparently after several design attempts, this location was deemed to be the most straightforward and accessible route to the attic.

Floor: The floor is covered with sheet linoleum bordered by a narrow black linoleum band. This surface continues into the bathroom underneath the more recent vinyl flooring in that space. It dates to the Potters' reconfiguration of the bathroom (106).

Walls: The original north and west walls are finished with a skim coat of smooth plaster. The east partition is faced with plywood. To the south, the vestibule is open to the stair.

Ceiling: The plywood ceiling is 7 feet 2½ inches above the floor.

Baseboard: There is a vinyl base on the west and north walls, as well as evidence for the original 4-inch-high rubber base.

Doors: There are door openings in the east, west, and south walls. The west opening (D1071) and south opening (D1072) are original doorways framed by the typical 4¼-inch-wide single-fascia architrave, cut to fit within the vestibule space. The later east opening (D1061) is framed by a 2-inch-wide single-fascia architrave.

D1071: Currently, there is no door in this opening. Mortises for a pair of 4-inch butt hinges remain in the north jamb, and the mortise for the keeper is visible in the south jamb. The original door is now positioned in opening D1061.

D1072: Currently, there is no door in this opening. Mortises for a pair of 3½-inch butt hinges remain in the west jamb, and the keeper is still in place in the east jamb. Originally this was the access to a shallow closet.

Lighting/Electrical: There are two switches in the west wall. The switch with the chromed brass cover plate is original and activates the bathroom-ceiling fixture. The other switch dates to the construction of the attic stair and activates a utility fixture lighting the stair.

Furnishings and Fittings: Originally, the south side of this space held a shallow closet. The location of the rear wall of the closet can clearly be seen in the west plaster wall of the stairwell. The closet may have included shelving for towel and linen storage. The closet was destroyed when the stairway was inserted in 1942-43.

Pantry (108) The serving pantry functioned as a buffer, separating the kitchen from the public areas (the entry and the living room). In plan the room includes single doors in the north, south, and east walls, as well as a single window in the west wall. With the exception of the north doorway, all of these openings are original.

As completed in 1938-39, the pantry had a built-in counter, cabinet, and cupboard along the full length of the north wall. A porcelain enamel sink, possibly without a cabinet beneath it, was located below or near the window. The two door openings had swinging doors. The original east door remains in situ but the south door is now located in the northwest doorway (D1122) of the kitchen.

A glimpse of the pantry is provided by a May 1945 photograph taken in the living room, looking toward the opened pantry door. The cabinets, drawers, and open shelving can clearly be seen. The two 1945 inventories provide a listing of what was kept here; apparently no food items were stored in the serving pantry.

How this room was used by Elliott Roosevelt and the Potters is not necessarily known. It now appears that it may have served as an informal eating area, with more-formal dining taking place in the adjoining room (109). Owen Potter recalls that a breakfast nook was located at one end of the kitchen; this may actually be the area to which he refers.

This room and the room immediately north (109) were joined by a doorway sometime after 1945, possibly early in the Potter era.

Floor: The floor is finished with sheet vinyl (same pattern as the vinyl in the entry [101]). This surface is installed over a plywood underlayment and the original unfinished 3¼-inch-wide pine boards running east/west. These boards were originally covered in linoleum that was laid without mastic. A small (11-inch by 1-foot 1-inch) area of the wood subfloor beneath the window has been repaired; this may represent the location of plumbing pipes that served the former pantry sink.

Walls: All four walls are finished with a skim coat of smooth white plaster over Rocklath, a gypsum-board lath.

A 1½-inch-high wood picture rail, composed of a filleted quarter-round and a torus, is placed at the height of the door trim. This molding was installed sometime after 1945, probably when the pantry cabinets were removed.

Ceiling: The plaster on Rocklath (a gypsum-board lath) ceiling is approximately 10 feet above the floor.

Baseboard: A vinyl baseboard has been installed along the base of the walls. Originally a rubber base, like that used in the bathrooms, was located here.

Doors: There are three doorways in this room: one in the south wall (D1081), one in the north wall (D1082), and one in the east wall (D1123). The north opening is a post-1945 insertion, added after the pantry cabinets were removed.

D1081: The 3-foot-wide by 6-foot 9½-inch-high by 1¾-inch-thick stile-and-rail door has four raised panels. This original door and its hardware were formerly in the opening between the adjoining room (109) and the kitchen (D1122). The swinging door currently in that opening was originally positioned here. Hardware consists of one pair of 4-inch butt hinges; a 5½-inch-high brass mortise lock; a brass knob and keyhole escutcheon on the north (108) face; and a chromium knob and escutcheon on the south (101) face. When this door was in its original location, the chromium hardware faced into the kitchen.

D1082: There has never been a door in this opening.

Window: The original window opening in the west wall has plain reveals and a bullnosed sill. A cutout at the north end of the sill may relate to the sink or casework originally located on the north wall. The plain fascia apron below the sill was added after the pantry cabinets were removed. The 4-over-4 rope-hung wood sashes are framed with a 4¼-inch-wide single-fascia architrave and are set deeply in the plaster-lined opening. The sashes have 9¾-inch-wide by 11¼-inch-high panes, ¾-inch-muntins, and an original thumb latch.

Heating: There is one supply register in the south wall, next to the floor. The register has a metal honeycomb screen. The original rubber base abutted the west side of the register cover.

Lighting/Electrical: The room is lit by an incandescent hanging fixture with four candelabra lights within a sphere made up of intertwined metal vines. The light fixture dates to the Potter era. A single-lamp chromium ceiling fixture, supplied by Lightolier for $8.50, was originally located here.

Other electrical elements include a duplex receptacle in the north wall (at a level above the original pantry counter) and a double switch in the south wall with a Potter-era painted porcelain cover plate.

A c.1952 Western Electric telephone bell is mounted above the baseboard on the south wall, at the southwest corner of the room.

Pantry (108), 1997.
West elevation.
Photograph by JGWAA.

Furnishings and Fittings: The pantry as originally completed included a built-in cabinet and countertop that extended the full length (10 feet 7 inches) of the north wall. Above this unit, there was a corresponding cupboard with open shelving. A narrow portion of this storage unit can be seen in a May 1945 photograph recording the living room (102) and looking through to the pantry. Fortunately these cabinets and cupboards are still intact in the kitchen (112), where they were moved sometime after 1945. The two 1945 inventories record the items kept on the shelves, in the drawers, and in the cabinets below. The countertop work surface is referred to as the sideboard, and three trays were placed there.

The other important fitting in this room was the pantry sink. It was located along the west wall, below the window or in the southwest corner. A letter dated September 19, 1938, stated that a Standard Plate P-6815 46-inch by 30-inch sink was to be substituted for the sink originally specified. There was to be no cabinet under the sink. Whether this was the model actually installed is unknown.

The existence of these built-in features would not permit the placement of any other furnishings in the pantry, particularly with the constant movement of the two swinging doors.

Finishes Investigation: The original finishes found here included unpainted, smooth-finished, white plaster walls and ceiling. The woodwork, including the built-in cabinetry, was painted in the grey-white (5Y 9/1) color used throughout the cottage. The cabinets are now located against the west wall of the kitchen. Paint evidence on the cabinets indicates that they were painted in a bright grey-blue while still in their original location. This color was probably applied while the cottage was occupied by Elliott Roosevelt and may indicate that the pantry plan was not modified during that period. The cabinets were probably moved after the Potter family acquired the house, at which time they were painted pink.

The floor was covered in linoleum that may have matched the still-extant surface in the former food pantry (113). Prior to the removal of the cabinets, for Elliott Roosevelt or the Potters, the walls were painted pink (10R 8/4). After the cabinets were removed, all of the walls were covered in a pink-beige paint followed by yellow. The current decor, which includes white painted walls and wallpaper below the picture rail, and yellow paint above the rail and on the ceiling, was created by the Potters.

Bedroom (109), 1997.
View looking northwest.
Photograph by JGWAA.

Bedroom (109)

According to original floor plans, this space was to be a bedroom, but its use probably varied even during the FDR era. For many years, beginning sometime after 1945, the room served as a dining room, a room type not included in the original planning of the cottage.

In plan, the room now includes two doors in the north wall, single doors in the east and south walls and a single window in the west wall.

As originally planned, there was to be a fireplace located in the southeast corner, but it was eliminated during construction as a cost-saving measure. The return-air grille was offset in the south wall to accommodate the fireplace.

Originally the room was occupied by the caretaker, Christian Bie. How he and his family used the room is unknown; it may have served as a living room for the Bies. By 1940-41, two simply finished rooms and a toilet room were added in the attic space above for the Bie family.

Sometime after 1945 the function of the room changed. A door opening was placed in the south wall, thereby providing a more direct connection to the more-public areas of the home. Possibly at the same time, the swinging door was relocated from its original position in the former pantry to the opening in the east wall of the room. This work may have been carried out by

Elliott Roosevelt, but it is more likely that these changes were made by the Potters. Certainly a dining room would be desirable in a house occupied by a family.

There are no known photographs of the room as it was during the FDR era, and no mention of the room is made in the two 1945 inventories.

Floor: Wall-to-wall carpet covers a sheet vinyl floor installed above the original 2¼-inch-wide oak floorboards running north/south.

Walls: All four walls are finished with a skim coat of smooth white plaster over Rocklath (a gypsum-board lath). On the east wall, a large plate-glass mirror covers the upper half of the wall south of the door opening. The mirror was installed sometime after 1945 and probably relates to the use of this space as a dining room.

A 1½-inch-high wood picture rail, composed of a filleted quarter-round and a torus, is placed at the height of the door trim. It was installed sometime after 1945.

Ceiling: The plaster on Rocklath (a gypsum-board lath) ceiling is approximately 10 feet above the floor.

Baseboard: The original 5-inch-high baseboard is composed of a plain fascia with a filleted quarter-round cap molding.

Doors: There are four doorways: two in the north wall (D1101, D1091), one in the south wall (D1082), and one in the east wall (D1122). The north and east openings are original, but the south opening was created sometime after 1945. A door was never hung in the south opening; this may indicate that this room was to have a more public function after the insertion of the doorway. All four openings are framed by 4¼-inch-wide single-fascia architraves.

D1091: The original 2-foot 3¾-inch-wide by 6-foot 8¾-inch-high by 1¾-inch-thick stile-and-rail closet door has four raised panels. The hardware consists of one pair of 4-inch butt hinges; a 5½-inch-high brass mortise lockset with the strike plate stamped "09"; a plain round brass knob and a brass ovoid keyhole escutcheon with a drop cover on the south (109) face; and a brass turnpiece on the north (111) face.

Window: The original window opening in the west wall has plain reveals and a bullnosed sill. The 6-over-6 rope-hung wood sashes are framed with a 4¼-inch-wide single-fascia architrave and are set deeply in the opening. The sashes have 9½-inch-wide by 1-foot 3¾-inch-high panes, ¾-inch muntins, and a chromium thumb latch.

Heating: There is one supply register below the window in the west wall, near the floor, and a return-air grille in the south wall. Like the other registers and grilles in the house, the baseboard molding is carried up to frame these openings. The openings have metal honeycomb screens supplied by Hart & Cooley. The return-air grille is not centered on the south wall because the final plan for the room included a fireplace in the southeast corner.

Lighting/Electrical: Electrical elements include original duplex receptacles with post-1945 mirrored cover plates in all four walls and a switch in the east wall. A cutout in the mirror on the east wall allows access to the switch.

A junction box centered in the ceiling may have been installed after 1945. There is no indication that a ceiling fixture was originally purchased for this room.

Equipment: An original buzzer located in the west wall, near the ceiling, is part of the call-bell system. It is called out in the specifications as an Edwards "Buzacall" Type No. 661.

Furnishings and Fittings: Since the room was part of the private living quarters of the cottage caretaker Christian Bie, it is not included in the inventories produced in 1945. How the Bie family used the room is unknown. The various original floor plans of the cottage refer to this space as a bedroom. After the simply finished rooms were created in the attic space of the north wing in 1940-41, it seems likely that they served as bedrooms. This room may have then been used as a living room. In fact, the use of the space probably varied over time.

For the Potters, this was the dining room, and the large plate glass mirror relates to that use. The installation of the ceiling fixture may coincide with the dining function.

Finishes Investigation: Finishes on the smooth white plaster walls, which were originally unpainted, include a pale beige (10YR 9/2), a pink, pale pink, pale beige, and the current white paint used below the line of the picture rail. Above the rail, the wall is now painted pale yellow.

Investigation of the wall surface behind the mirror revealed the pink finish.

The woodwork was first painted grey-white (5Y 9/2), followed by applications of yellow-white, pink, yellow-white, and the current white color.

Bathroom (110)

This small room has always functioned as a bathroom, and the original plumbing fixtures remain in place. In plan, the room includes a doorway in the south wall and a small window in the north wall. The window now looks out onto the enclosed north porch.

The only significant modification made here, aside from the painting of the plaster wall surfaces and the application of plastic tiles around the tub, was the replacement of the original linoleum floor.

There are no known early photographs of the bathroom.

Floor: The floor is finished with 9-inch-square composition tiles, surrounded by a narrow black border. This surface is installed on floor lining paper over original $3\frac{1}{2}$-inch pine boards running north/south, and replaces an earlier, possibly original linoleum floor covering.

Walls: All four walls are finished with smooth white plaster; the specifications called for plaster on metal lath. Around the bathtub, at the east end of the room, there is a later 1-foot $10\frac{3}{4}$-inch-high tub surround made up of 10-inch-square white plastic tiles, installed sometime after 1945 (probably by the Potters after 1952).

Ceiling: The original plaster ceiling is approximately 10 feet above the floor.

Baseboard: A brown vinyl base has been installed along the north, south, and west walls.

Door: The original doorway in the south wall is framed by a $4\frac{1}{4}$-inch-wide single-fascia architrave.

D1101: The original 2-foot 4-inch-wide by 6-foot $8\frac{3}{4}$-inch-high by $1\frac{3}{4}$-inch-thick stile-and-rail door has four raised panels. The hardware consists of one pair of 4-inch butt hinges; a $5\frac{1}{2}$-inch-high brass mortise lockset; a plain round brass knob and a brass ovoid keyhole escutcheon with a drop cover on the south (109) face; with a knob and turnpiece on the north (110) face.

Window: The original window opening in the north wall has deep, plain, plastered reveals and a bullnosed sill. The 4-over-4 rope-hung wood sashes are framed with a 3-inch-wide fascia trimmed with a corner bead, and are set deeply in the opening. The sashes have $9\frac{7}{8}$-inch-wide by $11\frac{1}{4}$-inch-high panes, $\frac{3}{4}$-inch muntins, and a chromium thumb latch.

Plumbing: The original bathroom fittings include a white porcelain-enameled cast-iron bathtub on the east wall and a vitreous china toilet manufactured by Standard on the north wall. The original white, porcelain-enameled, cast-iron lavatory on the north wall has the date of 5-26-37, as well as "Standard Sanitary Manufacturing Co., Louisville, 3867, 22x19, 9, 2" cast into the underside of the basin. All of the chromed brass plumbing fittings appear to be original.

Heating: There is one original supply register in the south wall, near the floor.

Lighting/Electrical: The room is lit by an original incandescent wall fixture on the west wall with a brass bracket and a hand-painted opal glass shade. Other electrical elements include a switch and duplex receptacle on the south wall with a post-1945 hand-painted china cover plate.

Furnishings and Fittings: The most important original fittings consist of the three plumbing fixtures and a circular mirror above the tub. The bathroom is outfitted with two towel bars, one on the west wall and one on the south wall above the tub, a toilet paper holder on the north wall, and the circular mirror on the east wall. A metal, mirrored medicine cabinet is recessed into the west wall. All of these fittings may date to before 1945. The circular mirror measures 30 inches in diameter, and it is identified on the reverse side: "Y.M. & G.(C?), 1937-A, YORK, PA." The painted plaster wall surface behind the mirror has penciled centering marks for the mirror. Brackets for what was probably an original roller shade survive on the window frame.

Finishes Investigation: Originally, the smooth white plaster walls were unpainted, and a visible layer of dirt separates the plaster from the first painted finish, which is a pale pink. This color is followed by finishes of blue-grey, deep yellow, and the current medium yellow. A recent bright yellow paint covers areas of the north, east, and south walls.

Closet (111)

This is one of five closets included in the original planning and construction of the house. The first modification was made here when the piping in the northeast corner was installed to service the small toilet room created in the north attic in 1940-41. Additional piping was added when the shower stall was installed in the attic sometime after 1945. The closet was transformed when the casework was added to the space. The cabinets were set several inches in front of the north wall so that the piping could freely pass through the closet.

Floor: The floor is finished with the original 2¼-inch-wide oak floorboards, running north/south. A 1-foot 6¼-inch-wide area of flooring near the center of the closet has been replaced. It appears that the flooring was cut out to provide access to the crawl space, possibly for the installation of the piping.

Walls: All four walls are finished with an original skim coat of smooth white plaster on Rocklath, a gypsum-board lath.

Ceiling: The original plaster on Rocklath (a gypsum-board lath) ceiling is approximately 10 feet 0 inches above the floor.

Baseboard: The original 4¾-inch-high baseboard is composed of a plain fascia with a filleted quarter-round cap molding. The north section of the baseboard was relocated to the base of the cabinets when they were installed sometime after 1945.

Door: The original doorway in the south wall (D1092) is framed by a plain wood casing.

Plumbing: Water supply and waste piping extend up through the ceiling, behind the closet casework. The piping in the northeast corner dates to the installation of toilet room 208, c. 1940-41. The remaining piping is associated with the Potters' installation of the shower stall in room 207.

Lighting/Electrical: The closet is lit by an incandescent porcelain utility ceiling fixture with pull cord and simplex receptacle. The fixture is probably original.

Furnishings and Fittings: Two built-in wood cabinets on the north wall, one above the other, have pairs of plain wood doors. There is wood shelving inside the cabinets. The doors are hung on 1½-inch hinges with decorative flanges and are secured with chrome pull latches; this hardware is similar to that on the upper cabinets of the east wall of the kitchen.

The construction of these cabinets is crude compared to those on the east wall of the kitchen. The casework in the closet was not fabricated by the same hand that produced the original pantry cabinets or those positioned on the east wall of the kitchen, and it is unlikely that the casework in the closet came from either of these rooms.

Kitchen (112)

The kitchen is located in the northeast corner of the north wing and can be reached from the main entrance by passing through the pantry or from a service entrance that is now enclosed by the north porch.

In plan, the long narrow space includes single-door openings in the north and south walls, two doorways in the west wall, and two window openings in the east wall. The serving pantry is accessible through a swinging door at the south end of the west wall. A small space off the south end of this room was originally a food pantry, an important accessory space for the kitchen.

Of the various pieces of kitchen equipment originally located here (a sink, range, refrigerator, and washing machine) only the location of the sink is known for certain. A much more recent sink occupies the same general position of the original.

Original finishes included unpainted plaster wall and ceiling surfaces, painted woodwork, and a linoleum floor surface that abutted an applied rubber cove base. Two incandescent, single-lamp, chrome and glass light fixtures were attached to the ceiling. A house call-bell system was installed in the south wall.

Built-in cabinetry was apparently minimal, but there is evidence for a cabinet (6 feet wide by 1 foot 8½ inches deep) against the west wall, between the door openings, with a cupboard above. There is also evidence for a shelving unit on the east wall, next to the exterior door. The existence of the food pantry (113) made extensive storage facilities in the kitchen unnecessary.

The first modifications were probably made in the kitchen after the attic stair was installed in the food pantry in 1940-41. The loss of storage space in the pantry may have necessitated the creation of additional shelving or cabinets in the kitchen.

Kitchen (112), 1997.
View looking south.
Photograph by JGWAA.

Kitchen (112), 1997.
View looking north.
Photograph by JGWAA.

At a later date, probably after the Potters purchased the house, the cabinet and cupboard in the service pantry (108) were moved into the kitchen. The installation of additional cabinets and fittings followed.

There are no known photographs that record the kitchen during any of the periods of its use.

Floor: The floor is finished with sheet vinyl, installed over a plywood underlayment and the original flooring of 3¼-inch-wide pine boards running north/south. The original linoleum floor probably matched the surface still in place in the former food pantry (113). The existing vinyl flooring matches the material currently used in toilet room 208 and on the intermediate landing of the north stair.

Walls: All four walls are finished with an original skim coat of smooth white plaster over Rocklath (a gypsum-board lath). A 1½-inch-high wood picture rail, composed of a filleted quarter-round and a torus, was installed after 1945.

Ceiling: The original plaster on Rocklath (a gypsum-board lath) ceiling is approximately 10 feet above the floor.

Baseboard: A vinyl baseboard extends along the base of the walls. Originally, a rubber base was used with the linoleum floor covering.

Doors: There are four original doorways in this space: one in the north wall (D1121), two in the west wall (D1122 and D1123), and one in the south wall (D1124). All four openings are framed by 4¼-inch-wide single-fascia architraves.

D1121: This Dutch door is the original north exterior entrance and is composed of two stile-and-rail leaves: an upper leaf (2 feet 11⅝ inch wide by 4 feet high by 2¼ inches thick) with four raised panels and a lower leaf (3 feet high) with two raised panels. Each leaf is hung on a pair of 4½-inch butt hinges. There is a 7¾-inch-high chromed Corbin mortise lockset with a deadbolt; a brass knob on the exterior face; and a chrome knob on the interior face. A chrome-finished Dutch door bolt is installed on the interior face. All of this hardware is original.

The later modification of the front door (D1011) was based on the original condition here. The mortises for three hinges on the exterior east jamb indicate that a screen door was formerly located here. The hinges are visible in a June 1939 exterior photograph of the door.

D1122/23: Each of these original double-action swing doors is a 2-foot 11¾-inch-wide by 6-foot 9-inch-high by 1¾-inch-thick stile-and-rail door with four raised panels. Each door has a pair of original floor spring hinges and original glass push plates (the painted design is a later addition). Door D1123 is in its original location. Door D1122 was originally located in opening D1081, between the service pantry and the entry.

D1124: The original 2-foot 5¾-inch-wide by 6-foot 9½-inch-high by 1¾-inch-thick stile-and-rail door has four raised panels. Hardware consists of one pair of 4-inch-high butt hinges; a 5½-inch-high chromed mortise lockset stamped "M86" with a chrome knob on the north (kitchen) face; and a turnpiece on the south (stairwell) face. This hardware is original. There is no doorknob on the inside face because this door originally opened to a closet.

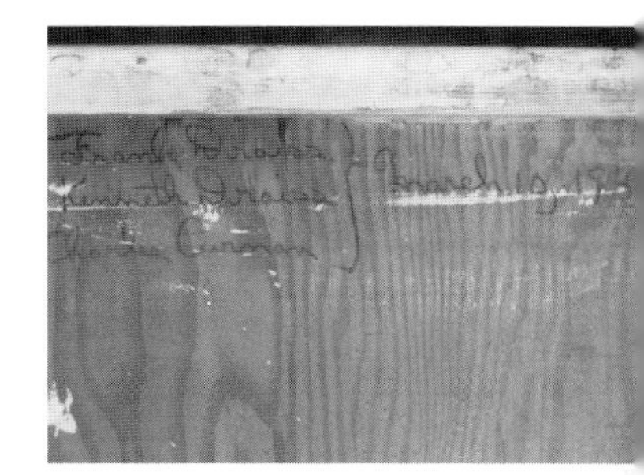

Kitchen (112), 1997. Underside of drawer in casework, with names of fabricators and date of original installation. Photograph by JGWAA.

Windows: The two original window openings in the east wall have plain plastered reveals and a simple bullnosed sill above a plain apron. The 6-over-6 rope-hung wood sashes have 9½-inch-wide by 1-foot 3½-inch-high panes and ¾-inch muntins, and are secured by original chrome-plated thumb latches on the meeting rails.

Plumbing: A single basin, stainless-steel sink is set into the counter located against the east wall. Immediately south of the sink, a dishwasher is positioned beneath the counter. Both of these fittings date to the Potter era.

Heating: There is one original supply register beneath the northeast window. The opening has a metal honeycomb screen supplied by Hart & Cooley. A Honeywell thermostat is mounted to the north wall, adjacent to the electrical panel box.

Lighting/Electrical: The room is lit by two elaborate incandescent pendant fixtures with glass shades. These somewhat formal-style fixtures were placed here early in the Potter era, or by Elliott Roosevelt. The positions for the fixtures date to the FDR era, when two matching single-lamp chrome-finished Lightolier fixtures were installed. At the same time, a matching Lightolier fixture was placed in the pantry (108).

Other electrical fittings include the main electrical panel box in the north wall, which is located behind a plywood door decorated with a hand-painted flower design; the enclosure and panel box date to the Potter era. There are duplex receptacles in all four walls and a pair of switches in the north wall.

Equipment: The original house call-bell system remains in the south wall and appears to have been installed as specified. The specifications called for a junction box with "1 twin convenience receptacle, 1 *Powacall*, 1 *Ringcall*, and one (1) *Buzacall*," covered with a combination gang plate. The annunciator panel above is labeled (on the inside of the face plate) "Edwards Flush Annunciette, Edwards & Co. of NY, Cat # 680, 8-12 v. AC 60 cycle." When a call button is pushed, the name of the room, "Rear Door" (112), "Master Bedroom" (104), or "Living Room" (102) drops down to appear in the glass panel of the annunciator and a buzzer sounds.

The kitchen is presently outfitted with a General Electric P7 range, a Nutone ventilation hood, a General Electric refrigerator-freezer, a General Electric Potscrubber 940 dishwasher, and a wall-mounted food scale, all of which dates to the Potter era.

Furnishings and Fittings: All of the FDR-era floor plans of the cottage place the kitchen sink in the position that it now occupies. A plan dated March 22, 1938, places the cooking range against the west wall between the two doorways (D1122 and D1123), while the refrigerator is shown against the south wall of what actually became a separate space, the food pantry (113). The actual location for the refrigerator is not known. However, the physical evidence for the location of the kitchen sink and range seems to confirm the information on the drawings. The range appears to have been located immediately north of the southwest door opening with a cabinet and cupboard to the north of the range. A washing machine may have been located in the northwest corner, against the west wall. Evidence of plumbing was found in this area.

Specifications dated May 24, 1938, for Standard plumbing fixtures included two choices for the kitchen sink: Standard Plate P-6535 25-inch by 60-inch Hostess Acid-Resisting double chain board sink fitted with a "#20 white duco steel cabinet" or as an alternate the Standard Plate P-6620 2-inch by 60-inch Norton Acid-Resisting cast-iron enamelware double chain board sink (apparently with no cabinet). It is not known which sink was installed; however, ghosting on the painted wall surface behind the existing sink and casework seems to indicate that the original sink was housed in a steel cabinet with diagonal strap bracing. The current stainless-steel sink and wood cabinet dates to the Potter era.

The original kitchen equipment was purchased by Ruth Bie in June 1938 from the Wallace Company in Poughkeepsie. The items purchased included a General Electric range, a General Electric refrigerator, and a Bendix laundry (washing machine). The P. J. Curry Company inventory mentions only two items in the kitchen: "one *General Electric* Electric Refrigerator 1939 - 8 cubic feet, and one *Bendix* Washing Machine 1939."

The built-in wood cabinets currently located in the kitchen date to several periods of occupancy.

A long cabinet dating to the Potter era extends between the two windows on the east wall. The 9-foot 8-inch-wide by 3-foot 1-inch-high by 2-foot 1¼-inch-deep cabinet is four bays wide and has a plastic laminate countertop and splash with an aluminum edging. Each of the two outer bays is composed of a pair of drawers above a pair of doors; hardware includes 1¾-inch-high butt hinges and chrome-finished pulls. There is a dishwasher in the bay south of center and a stainless-steel sink in the bay north of center.

Above this cabinet, a wood cupboard is mounted on the east wall. Investigation of the painted finishes on the casework and on the wall surface behind it indicates that the cupboard probably dates to the Elliott Roosevelt era. The cabinet measures 9 feet wide by 3 feet high by 1 foot 1 inch deep and is three bays wide with a pair of doors in each bay. Hardware includes 1½-inch-high butt hinges with decorative flanges and chrome-finished pull latches.

On the west wall, there is a cabinet extending between the two doorways and a cupboard mounted to the wall above. Both of these long units were originally located against the north wall in the service pantry (108). The wood cabinet is eight bays wide and measures 10 feet 8 inches wide by 3 feet ½ inch high by 2 feet deep with a bullnosed wood countertop. Each bay has a drawer with a chrome-finished pull and a door with 2½-inch-high butt hinges and a chrome-finished knob. On the bottom face of the third drawer from the north is written "Frank Draiss, Kenneth Draiss, Charles Curnan, March 10, 1939." These were probably the names of the cabinetmakers who constructed the casework.

The cupboard above is 10 feet 4½ inches wide by 3 feet high by 1 foot 1 inch deep and is four bays wide. Each bay has a pair of sliding glass doors with recessed pulls. Originally there were no sliding glass doors in the upper cupboard. There are eighteen spring-type cup hooks in the two south bays of the cupboard; these may be original FDR-era fittings.

The cupboard and cabinet were moved to this location sometime after 1945. The repositioning of the units included the addition of plywood end panels to both units, as well as small end extensions to the hardwood counter top.

The small cabinet at the north end of the west wall is original to the kitchen. It was located to one side of the kitchen sink on the east wall. A matching cabinet, located on the opposite side of the sink, was found in the Potters' greenhouse. The exact locations of these cabinets are known because cutouts were made in the sub-flooring of the kitchen to accommodate them. The cabinet remaining in the kitchen measures 2 feet 7 inches wide by 3 feet high by 2 feet deep and has a drawer and door with hardware similar to that used on the other casework along the west wall. The plastic-laminate countertop with its aluminum edge and the extension of the cabinet to the south are recent modifications.

Another cabinet, on the east wall, is located immediately north of the northeast window and dates to the Potter occupancy. This cabinet is 2 feet 6 inches wide by 3 feet high by 2 feet deep and has a marble top over a wood base. The base has a drawer and a pair of doors, with chrome-finished hinges and pulls (similar to the cabinet between the windows).

There is evidence on the painted wall surface north of the northeast window for the location of early, or possibly original, built-in shelving that included at least six shelves to a height of 7 feet 1 inch or more.

Both windows retain brackets for roller shades; these may be the original fittings.

Finishes Investigation: The original finishes in the kitchen included unpainted smooth white plaster walls and ceiling, as well as woodwork painted in the grey-white (5Y 9/1) used throughout the cottage.

The first paint applied to the plaster walls was a pale yellow-beige (10YR 9/4). This color can still be seen, in a soiled condition, on the wall surface concealed by the sink cabinet. The walls were covered with additional layers of paint, including pale yellow, pink, bright pink, and the current white finish.

Paint layers on the cabinets against the west wall (formerly located in the pantry) include the original grey-white color followed by a bright grey-blue, pink, bright pink, and the current pink surface. The side panels, added after the cabinet was moved, were first painted in the pink color over a white primer. This would appear to indicate that the cabinet was covered in the earlier bright grey-blue while still in the pantry location. This bright grey-blue is also found on the cupboard unit located above the kitchen sink. The color relates to the blue-green paint used in the south hall (103), the small south bedroom (105), and on the ceiling of the west porch (102A). They all date to the Elliott Roosevelt era.

North Porch (112A)

All of the preconstruction floor plans and illustrations of the cottage include a porch of some type attached to the north end of the building; the porch defines the service entrance to the kitchen. A photograph of the north end of the cottage, taken in June 1939, shows no porch in this location but does show a fieldstone step in front of the door recess. A portion of this step remains beneath the existing porch construction.

The existing "L"-shaped enclosed porch abuts the north masonry wall of the north wing. That wall includes a small window and the door that opens to the kitchen. The outer walls that enclose the porch are of frame construction, with two tiers of fixed horizontal glazing above a low, vertical-board wall surface. A doorway in the east wall opens to the exterior.

The construction history of this addition remains unknown, but a visual inspection of the detailing indicates that at least two periods of construction are represented. It appears that the porch, as originally completed, was not enclosed.

None of the later FDR-era photographs clearly show the north end of the house or what conditions might have existed there. The subtle curve of the roof duplicates the appearance of the original west porch, suggesting that the addition of the north porch may be part of the work that Henry Toombs may have undertaken for Elliott Roosevelt at an unspecified date.

Floor: The floor is finished with 9-inch-square red composition tiles and bordered by 9-inch-square black composition tiles.

Walls: The south wall is the original exterior stone wall of the house. The other walls are finished with broad bands of horizontal windows and vertical tongue-and-groove boards with beveled joints. The windows and walls inserted between the posts may be later additions, constructed for the enclosure of the porch.

Ceiling: The ceiling is constructed of wide tongue-and-groove boards with beveled joints, 7 feet 11½ inches above the floor.

Baseboard: A quarter-round shoe molding covers the base of the board walls.

Cornice: An 8-inch-high cornice, composed of a fascia with a cavetto and cyma recta crown molding, extends the full length of the north, east, and west elevations.

Doors: The doorway in the south wall is the original service entrance into the kitchen (D1121). The opening is framed by a 4-inch-wide single-fascia architrave. The mortises for three hinges on the east jamb indicate that a screen door was located here. The hinges are visible in a June

1939 photograph of the door. The porch doorway in the east wall (D112A1) is framed by a plain wood casing.

D112A1: The 3-foot-wide by 6-foot 11½-inch-high stile-and-rail glazed door is composed of two horizontal glazed panels above a recessed panel. The panel field is made up of vertical tongue-and-groove boards with beveled joints, like those of the walls and ceiling. There are three 4-inch-high steel butt hinges; a 5½-inch-high mortise lockset; a pair of small chrome-finished knobs; an oval escutcheon on the interior face; a rectangular keyhole escutcheon plate on the exterior face; and a surface-mounted steel night latch and a brass slide bolt on the interior face.

A wood screen door in this opening has three screened panels and a simple brass latch.

Windows: Two tiers of long, horizontal, windows with single-pane fixed sash, separated by intermediate vertical muntins, extend between the porch's corner posts. An original window opening in the south masonry wall, looking into bathroom 110, is framed by a 4-inch-wide single-fascia architrave and has a stone sill.

Plumbing: A metal cabinet on the south wall supports a two-basin, porcelain-enameled cast-iron sink. "10 14 40, R, 203887" is cast into the bottom surface of one of the basins.

Heating: The bases for two electric resistance heaters remain attached to the north wall, and a complete electric resistance heater, with an emergency cut-off switch, is mounted on the east wall. A thermostat is mounted to the west face of the floor-to-ceiling cabinet against the south wall.

North porch (112A), 1997.
View looking southwest.
Photograph by JGWAA.

Lighting/Electrical: The porch is lit by a single-lamp incandescent ceiling fixture of metal and glass. The switch for this fixture is located in a surface-mounted junction box to the west of the exterior door (D1121). Rigid metal conduit extends from the junction box into the ceiling; armored cable is routed from the junction box, over the doorway, and across the surface of the masonry wall to the electric resistance heater on the east wall.

There is a junction box in the location of the original exterior incandescent lantern, immediately west of the masonry door opening in the south wall. The original fixture, purchased from the Lightolier Company in 1938, is now located on the exterior of the porch, to the north of doorway D112A1.

The original electric push button for the doorbell remains in place on the west jamb of the exterior door (D1121).

Miscellaneous wiring devices and conductors are attached to the wall surfaces of the porch. Wiring, conduit, and a junction box are located within the floor-to-ceiling cabinet against the south wall; this wiring includes the electric service wiring that is routed from the crawl space, through the masonry wall, to the panel box in the kitchen (112).

On the south wall there is a junction box with three receptacles. Rigid conduit extends from this box into the crawl space. A duplex receptacle is mounted in the north wall. A surface-mounted switch and duplex receptacle on the west wall are interconnected with surface-mounted Wiremold conduit.

Equipment: The porch is currently furnished with a General Electric washer and dryer against the south wall. A Progress ventilator with metal hood is positioned in one of the north windows; and a Robertshaw Hardwick gas range is located in the northeast corner of the space.

Furnishings and Fittings: The wood cabinets along the south stone wall are constructed of ¾-inch-thick boards. The southeast cabinet is a floor-to-ceiling unit, 2 feet 2 inches wide by 1 foot 5 inches deep, with a tall closet door and a smaller door above. The plain wood doors are hung on small "HL" hinges and are secured with drop latches.

A second cabinet, abutting the floor-to-ceiling cabinet and extending to the window opening in the south wall, is 6 feet 11 inches wide by 2 feet 4½ inches high by 1 foot 2 inches deep. The cabinet is four bays wide and has plain wood doors with hardware similar to that on the first cabinet. Both cabinets are trimmed by a simple cavetto molding at the ceiling.

Finishes Investigation: The paint layering on the frame of the south window includes a white primer followed by a yellowish white (2.5Y 9/2-8/2) finish. In turn, there is another layer of yellowish white paint and the current white finish. The initial paint layers on the service door to the kitchen match those on the window.

The board ceiling of the porch was initially painted in a yellowish white. This was followed by the same bright blue-green (7.5BG 3/4) paint used on the west porch ceiling and dating to the Elliott Roosevelt era. This surface was later covered in the red paint now visible; the red paint was probably applied by the Potters.

Stair (113)

As the plan for the cottage evolved, this area became a closet or, probably more specifically, a pantry for the storage of kitchen supplies and food.

Currently the small, narrow room includes a doorway in the north wall, a simply constructed closed stringer stair along the east and south walls, and original built-in shelving beneath the stair. An exposed sheet-metal duct extends vertically from the first floor to the attic-floor level, against the west wall.

Originally, the room had tiers of shelving on the south and west walls. The original linoleum still covers the floor.

The stairway was installed here to provide access to the north attic and the rooms inserted there, apparently as additional living space for the Bie family. The construction involved the creation of an opening in the upper west wall that allowed the upper run of the stair to pass through the coat closet (101A) adjacent to the entry (101).

No mention of this space is made in the 1945 inventories, and there are no known photographs that record its appearance.

Stair (113), 1997. View from bottom of stairway constructed c. 1940-41. Photograph by JGWAA.

Floor: The floor is finished with the original, marble-patterned sheet linoleum. The staircase, a later insertion, rests on top of this surface.

Walls: All four walls are finished with a skim coat of smooth white plaster on Rocklath (a gypsum-board lath). The painted outlines of the missing shelving can be seen on the west wall.

Ceiling: At the first-floor level, the plaster on Rocklath (a gypsum-board lath) ceiling is approximately 9 feet 9 inches above the floor. The south portion of the original ceiling was removed when the stair was installed in 1940-41.

Baseboard: The original 4¾-inch-high baseboard is composed of a fascia and a filleted quarter-round cap molding.

Door: The original doorway in the north wall is framed by a plain wood casing.

Stair: The simple, closed stringer wood stair was installed in 1940-41, when rooms were created in the north attic, and may have been constructed by Christian Bie. The stair begins with eight risers ascending south to a landing in the southeast corner of the room and continues west with eight risers to the second-floor hall (205). The risers are 8⅛ inches high (with the exception of the second flight's first riser, which is 6 inches high), and the bullnosed treads are approximately 8½ inches deep. The stair is painted, and black rubber nonskid mats have been installed on the treads. Wood handrails are mounted to the east and south walls with brass brackets. Mortise holes in the first tread of the upper run and at the second-floor landing are evidence for a former handrail supported on newels.

Heating: A sheet-metal duct, extending from the crawl space up along the west wall to the second floor, was installed sometime after the rooms were created in the attic.

Lighting/Electrical: The space is lit by an incandescent bare-bulb fixture, hung from a hook on the ceiling at the first-floor level. The light switch is in the east wall.

Furnishings and Fittings: Originally, this room was finished with built-in shelving along the south and west walls, probably for the storage of kitchen equipment and food supplies. Currently there are three tiers of shelves on the south wall, with evidence for an upper, fourth shelf that was removed when the stairway was installed. The shelf supports match those used in the entry hall closet (101A). There is paint evidence for additional shelving that extended along the full length of the west wall.

Currently a wood rail with five chrome-finished brass hooks is mounted to the west wall. This fitting was installed after the shelving was removed, probably when the staircase was constructed. Subsequent to the installation of the rail, a sheet-metal heating duct was installed. The south end of the rail was cut to accommodate the duct. This work was probably carried out prior to 1945.

Attics (Second Floor)

The steeply pitched gabled roofs above the central block of the house and above each of the flanking wings shelter substantial attic space. As originally completed these were essentially unfinished spaces, although there is an indication that rough flooring was installed in at least two spaces. The area above the living room was to be used for the storage of trunks, with access through the "door" in the north gable of the central block. A hatch in the ceiling of the former closet north of bedroom 105 provided access to the attic in the south wing. A hatch in the ceiling of one of the north wing rooms, possibly the former kitchen pantry (stair 113), may have provided access to the attic in the north wing. Originally, there were no dormers or gable window openings in the two wings.

The current room arrangement of the two finished attics is the result of two distinct efforts to provide additional bedroom space in the cottage.

Work in the north attic was carried out in 1940-41 with the intent of creating additional space for the caretaker, Christian Bie, and his family. The work included the insertion of a large window opening in the north masonry gable; the construction of the west dormer; and the creation of two rooms, a stair hall, and a small toilet room, within the attic space. The rooms were very simply finished with fiberboard (Celotex), a material first developed in 1920.

The creation of the rooms in the south attic was carried out in a more substantial manner. This work was accomplished in 1942-43 and included the creation of two bedrooms, a toilet room, and a narrow stair hall. Windows were inserted in the north and south masonry gables of the wing. The bedrooms were finished with vertical chestnut boards. Plywood was used to finish the hall and toilet room.

No significant modifications were made to the attic rooms during the period that Elliott Roosevelt occupied the house.

The Potter family, who occupied the house beginning in 1952, made additions to these rooms that affected the external appearance of the cottage. Prominent dormer windows were added to the wings: a single east dormer on the north wing and three dormers on the south wing (two on the east elevation and one on the west elevation). Minor changes included the placement of a metal shower stall in the north wing and the conversion of the second-floor toilet room in the south wing to a full bathroom (203).

Stair Hall (201)

As originally planned and constructed, the spacious south attic did not include finished rooms or a stairway to access the area. The attic may have had flooring; a November 1938 letter refers to "additional rough flooring in attic wings." There was an access hatch in the ceiling of the former closet north of bedroom 105.

At the beginning of 1940, Henry Toombs and the President were studying various schemes for the location of a stairway and the arrangement of rooms in the south attic; however, it is not known who was responsible for the final design. As constructed, the alterations do not conform to Toombs' surviving sketches.

Margaret Suckley records that in August 1943, beds and mattresses were moved to the second-floor bedrooms "just made by Mr. Bie." Perhaps Christian Bie devised the clever manner in which the stair was inserted into the existing plan.

The long, narrow hall is positioned under the west slope of the roof and includes full doorways in the south and east walls and a small access door in the west knee wall. The stair rises up into the space; the stairwell fills the north half of the hall.

Floor: The floor is finished with 3¼-inch-wide pine floorboards, running north/south, installed in 1942-43. It seems unlikely that this surface is the "rough flooring" installed in 1938.

Walls: The walls are finished with painted plywood panels, installed in 1942-43.

Ceiling: The ceiling is 6 feet 8¼ inches above the floor and is finished with painted plywood, installed in 1942-43.

Baseboard: The base of the wood paneling is trimmed with a 4½-inch-high chamfered wood fascia and an ogee shoe molding.

Doors: There are three door openings in this hall: one in the south wall (D2021), one in the east wall (D2041), and a small opening in the west wall (D2011) that accesses an undereave

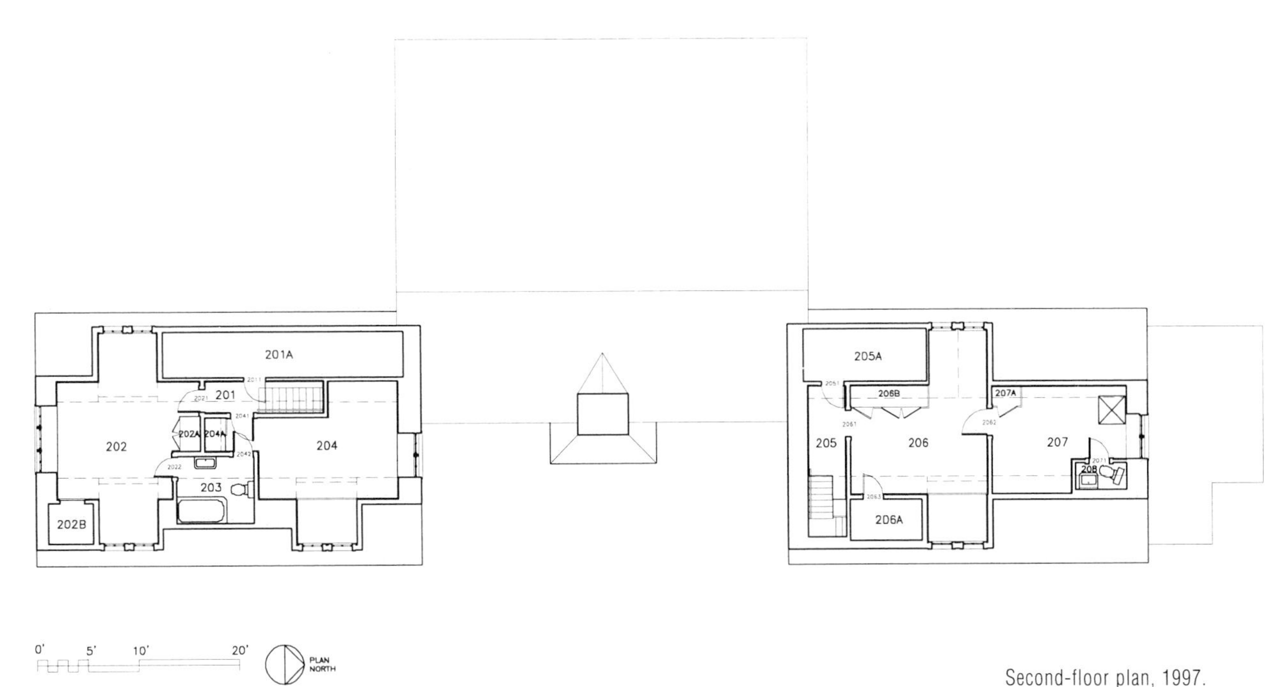

Second-floor plan, 1997.
Drawing by JGWAA.

storage space (201A). The south and east openings are framed by a 4-inch-wide fascia trimmed with a flattened bead along the outer edge. Door D2011 has a plain wood casing.

D2011: The 2-foot 2-inch-wide by 3-foot 9¼-inch-high by 1⅛-inch-thick stile-and-rail plywood door has one recessed panel and chamfered stiles and rails. Hardware consists of one pair of 3-inch-high brass-finished butt hinges, and a small brass-finished mortised latch. The door and hardware date to 1942-43.

Stairs: The enclosed stair ascends south from the first floor in a straight run of fifteen risers to the attic hall floor. The risers are 8½ inches high, and the treads are 9½ inches deep. An oak handrail is supported by brass-finished iron brackets attached to the east wall. There is evidence on the walls and ceiling at the foot of the stairway for the rear wall of the original bathroom linen closet.

Lighting/Electrical: The hall is lit by a utilitarian bare-bulb incandescent ceiling fixture. There is a switch in the west wall. These fittings date to 1942-43.

Storage (201A): This storage space extends from the north masonry wall of the south wing to the west dormer in 202. The floor is finished with 7-inch-wide floorboards, running north/south. The walls are unfinished. The north wall is the masonry of the exterior wall; the east and south walls are made up of wood studs supporting wood boards and plywood paneling; and the steeply pitched surface to the west is made up of the framing and sheathing for the roof, with 1¾-inch-thick by 5½-inch-high wood rafters, spaced approximately 1 foot 4 inches to 1 foot 4½ inches apart, supporting 5-inch-wide tongue-and-groove sheathing.

Original 1938-39 materials include the roof framing, the masonry wall, and possibly the unfinished flooring. The other materials date to 1942-43 and the Potter era.

The original cast-iron plumbing vent at the north end of the space serves the south bathroom (106) and the replacement lavatory installed by the Potters in bathroom 203.

Electrical rigid conduit runs north/south to a junction box at the south end of the space; armored cable runs from this box into the adjoining rooms. The rigid conduit spans the opening of the access door.

Bedroom (202)

This room, located in the south wing of the house, is positioned beneath the south end of the roof. In plan, the room includes a triple window in the south gable, large walk-in dormers with double windows in the east and west walls, and two doorways in the north wall. A built-in closet is positioned between the doors.

Room (202), 1997.
View looking southwest.
Photograph by JGWAA.

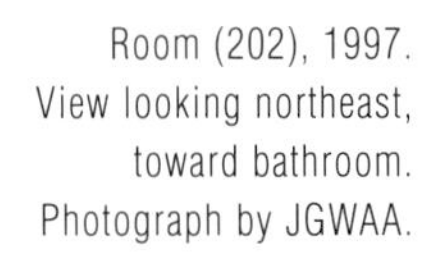

Room (202), 1997.
View looking northeast,
toward bathroom.
Photograph by JGWAA.

The room, along with the adjoining spaces in the south attic, was created in 1942-43 to provide additional space in the compact cottage for family members and guests. As originally completed for FDR, the room was paneled in vertical chestnut boards and had a window opening cut through the masonry gable at the south end of the room. The doors in the north wall opened to the stair hall (201) and a toilet room (later bathroom 203) that was shared with the room (204) at the north end of the attic. The closet between these doors appears to postdate the construction of the room.

Later, after the house was purchased by the Potters, the two dormers were constructed, greatly expanding the room and adding considerably more natural light. The expansion made use of knotty pine boards for the wall surfaces, rather than the chestnut used in the original portion of the room. Elliott (Tony) Roosevelt, Jr., who spent the summers of 1948 through 1950 at the cottage, recalled that there were no dormers in the south wing attic rooms.

The May 5, 1945, inventory makes reference to the south attic rooms: "2nd floor bedrooms - not listed," which indicates that this space functioned as a bedroom. Although the rooms were not specifically inventoried, the function of the attic space was identified. A Poughkeepsie newspaper article dated April 20, 1952, notes that "Original plans of the house were for only one floor. When the need was evident, the President had bedrooms and baths added under the Dutch roof."

This room and the other south attic room served as bedrooms for the Potter children, according to Owen Potter.

There are no known photographs that record this room as used by the various owners of the cottage.

Floor: The floor is currently covered with wall-to-wall carpet. Beneath this carpet, 3¼-inch-wide pine floorboards dating to 1942-43 run north/south.

Walls: The walls are finished with 6-inch-wide vertical chestnut tongue-and-groove boards with beveled joints, installed in 1942-43. The dormers are paneled with 6½-inch-wide pine boards contemporary with the addition of the dormers by the Potters.

Ceiling: The central part of the ceiling is 6 feet 8¼ inches above the floor and is finished with a roughly textured surface on gypsum board, installed by the Potters, over the original fiberboard ceiling panels. Paint evidence indicates that battens on the fiberboard ceiling were removed to install the gypsum board ceiling. The sloping ceiling planes at the east and west ends of the room are covered with 6-inch-wide chestnut boards, and meet the knee walls approximately 4 feet 7¼ inches above the floor. These surfaces were installed in 1942-43.

The roughly textured ceiling surfaces within the dormers date to the construction of the dormers by the Potters.

Baseboard: The base of the wood paneling is trimmed with a 5-inch-high chamfered wood fascia and a quarter-round shoe molding. The base is contemporary with the creation of the room in 1942-43. Salvaged or matching material was used in the dormer alcoves when they were created.

Cornice: The top of the wood paneling is trimmed with a quarter-round molding. In the dormers, the panels are capped by a 1½-inch-high wood cavetto and quarter-round molding. A simple wood ogee molding covers the joint between the wood paneling on the sloping ceiling planes and the flat ceiling.

Doors: There are two door openings in the north wall (D2021 and D2022). Each doorway dates to 1942-43, and is framed by a 4-inch-wide fascia trimmed with a flattened bead along the outer edge.

D2021: The 2-foot 2½-inch-wide by 6-foot 3½-inch-high by 1¼-inch-thick pine stile-and-rail door has two recessed panels. The stiles and rails are chamfered. The upper west corner of the door is angled to fit beneath the sloping ceiling. The hardware consists of one pair of 3½-inch-high brass-finished butt hinges with ball finials; and a 5¼-inch-high brass-finished mortise lockset with brass-finished knobs and decorative escutcheon plates. The door and fittings date to 1942-43.

D2022: The 1-foot 11¾-inch-wide by 6-foot 3½-inch-high by 1⅜-inch-thick pine stile-and-rail door has two recessed panels. The upper panel is glazed with textured glass; the lower panel has chamfered reveals. The hardware consists of one pair of 3½-inch-high brass-finished butt hinges with ball finials; and a 5¼-inch-high brass-finished mortise lockset with brass-finished knobs and decorative escutcheon plates. The door and fittings date to 1942-43.

Windows: The window opening in the south wall is deeply set into the masonry, with plywood reveals and a simple sill. The three 4-over-4 sash are separated by 3⅜-inch-wide mullions. The sashes slide in spring-loaded metal tracks, and have 9⅝-inch-wide by 11⅝-inch-high panes, ½-inch muntins, and brass-finished thumb latches. The opening and sashes date to 1942-43, when the attic rooms were created.

The dormers in the east and west walls were installed by the Potters. Each dormer has two window openings framed by 4³⁄₁₆-inch-wide architraves, similar to the beaded fascia used at the door openings. The stained pine 4-over-4 rope-hung sashes have 9-inch-wide by 11½-inch-high panes, ¾-inch muntins, and brass-finished thumb latches. The stamped metal pulleys are manufactured by Stanley.

Heating: There is a metal heating register with operable louvers in the east wall that is contemporary with the creation of the room. A General Electric air-conditioning unit has been inserted in the center window in the south gable.

Lighting/Electrical: A Potter-era fluorescent light fixture is surface-mounted to the ceiling of the west dormer. Wiremold surface-mounted conduit runs from this fixture to a surface-mounted duplex receptacle on the west wall and a switch in the west dormer. There is an additional surface-mounted duplex receptacle in the east dormer, as well as duplex receptacles in the east and west walls of the room. The two latter receptacles are original fittings from 1942-43.

Equipment: There is a security-alarm horn inserted through the wall of the east dormer; a telephone jack on the south wall; and a junction box with coaxial television cable in the west dormer. All of these fittings date to after the FDR era.

Closet (202A): A plywood partition and a pair of pine doors enclose a built-in closet east of door D2021. The doors are similar to the other two doors in the room, with two recessed panels and chamfered stiles and rails. The hardware includes pairs of 2½-inch-high brass-finished hinges with ball finials, as well as a brass-finished latch. The closet is outfitted with a wood shelf and a clothes rod. The closet appears to postdate the construction of the room. An oxidation line at the base of the closet suggests that a base molding was removed for the installation of the closet. Additionally there is a duplex electrical receptacle on the rear (north) wall of the closet; it is unlikely that an outlet would have been installed in a closet.

Storage (202B): The storage space under the eaves in the southeast corner of the room is accessed via a board-and-batten panel in the east wall. The panel is made up of chestnut boards like those in the wall paneling, fastened to two horizontal battens. There are two flush, brass-finished pulls on the panel. The storage area remains unfinished; unlike the other undereave storage spaces in the house, there are no floorboards. A large wood box is stored in this space. These conditions date to 1942-43.

Furnishings and Fittings: It is not known for certain how this room functioned during the FDR era, but references generally indicate that the attic spaces served as bedrooms for family and guests. This may be one of the rooms into which beds and mattresses were moved in August 1943.

Finishes Investigation: The chestnut, pine, and plywood wall surfaces have never been painted. A medium brown oil-based stain was used to finish the surfaces. The only painted surfaces are the ceiling and the sashes in the south window opening.

Bathroom (203)

The small bathroom is positioned between the two larger rooms in the south attic and is accessed directly from them. In plan, the bathroom includes single narrow doors in the south and west walls. The slope of the roof restricts the headroom along the east side of the room.

The room was constructed in 1942-43 when habitable spaces were created in the attic of the south wing. The toilet along the north wall survives from that era; however, the Potters modified the space, turning it from a toilet room into a bathroom. A tub was added in the southeast corner, and a new lavatory of shallower depth was installed in place of the original lavatory on the west wall.

Bathroom (203), 1997. View of bathroom looking north. Photograph by JGWAA.

With the removal of the south dormer on the east elevation of the south wing (added during the Potters' residency), the underside of the existing tub became accessible, exposing several critical pieces of evidence. The original floor surface was a mottled blue linoleum. The original finish on the east wall behind the tub was painted plywood with a wood baseboard. The baseboard was removed and used as a ledger board to support the edge of the tub. The tub was shimmed with newspaper dated 1956. Had a tub originally been located in the southeast corner of the space, the baseboard probably would not have been installed along the east wall.

Other modifications made here after 1945 include the installation of the plastic tile wainscot, the application of plastic laminate above the tub, and a change in the floor finish.

Floor: The floor is covered with 9-inch-square green composition tiles that probably date to 1956, when the Potters reconfigured the space. The original floor finish consisted of mottled blue linoleum dating to the 1942-43 second-floor modifications.

Walls: The walls are finished with painted plywood panels dating to 1942-43. A 4-foot 3½-inch-high wainscot made of green plastic "tiles" was installed by the Potters over an earlier, painted finish.

Ceiling: The 1942-43 plywood ceiling is 6 feet 8 inches above the floor at the west end of the room, and slopes steeply downward toward the east wall. Above the bathtub, the south end of the sloping ceiling is covered with plastic laminate panels installed by the Potters over the plywood surface.

Baseboard: A small, coved vinyl base covers the bottom edge of the plastic wainscot and is probably contemporary with that surface.
Cornice: A small wood ogee molding trims the top edge of the plywood walls.
Doors: There are two door openings in this room: one in the south wall (D2022) and one in the west wall (D2042). Each doorway is framed by a 4-inch-wide fascia trimmed with a flattened bead around the outside edge. These openings date to 1942-43. The glazing in the doors allows some natural light to enter the windowless bathroom.
Plumbing: The bathroom fittings include a porcelain-enameled cast-iron bathtub along the east wall (labeled "Baltimore, Made in the United States of America by American Standard Radiator & Sanitary Corporation, 5 FT, Master Pembroke," and dated "4 8 55"); a vitreous china lavatory on the west wall (labeled "Made in USA, American Standard, This Plumbing Fixture Made By Members of the International Brotherhood of Operative Potters," and dated "AUG 29 1955"; there is additional numbering that may indicate the model number: "171305 18," and "M55"); and a vitreous china Standard toilet on the north wall.

The chrome fittings on the bathtub are probably contemporary with the 1956 modifications.
Heating: There is a metal heating register with operable louvers in the east wall, as well as a Honeywell Holland thermostat on the west wall. These fittings date to the FDR-era creation of the room.
Lighting/Electrical: The bathroom is lit by a single-bulb incandescent fixture mounted to the west wall. The fixture has a chrome-finished bracket; the shade is missing. This fixture is contemporary with the creation of the bathroom.
Furnishings and Fittings: The bathroom is outfitted with chromium towel rods on the north, south, and west walls; a chromium toilet-paper holder on the north wall; a chromium toothbrush holder on the west wall; and a chromium soap holder on the east wall. A mirrored, metal medicine cabinet is mounted to the west wall and may date to the FDR era.
Finishes Investigation: There is a yellowish white painted wall surface behind the plastic tile wainscot.

Room (204)

This room is located at the north end of the attic in the south wing. The irregularly shaped room includes a double window in the north wall, a dormer and double window centered on the east side of the room, and single doors in the east and west walls of the south extension of the room. A small closet is positioned at the far south end of the space.

A November 1938 letter indicates that rough flooring was installed in the attics of the wings; perhaps flooring was installed here and in the adjoining space at that time. Various schemes devised by Henry Toombs and the President in addition to a heating layout plan dated July 3, 1942, reveal solutions for the placement of a stairway to the south attic. All of the proposed solutions provided access to the attic through the north end. There is no physical evidence that any of these proposals was carried out.

This room, as created in 1942-43, did not include the dormer on the east elevation. The only window opening was the one created in the north gable.

This is probably one of the second-floor bedrooms to which beds and mattresses were moved in August 1943. Margaret Suckley indicated that these bedrooms were ". . . just made by Mr. Bie . . . " and perhaps he devised the clever arrangement of the spaces in the south attic.

The room was modified by the addition of the large dormer in the east wall. This work was probably carried out for the Potters; Elliott (Tony) Roosevelt, Jr., does not recall a dormer in this location when he stayed at the house between 1948 and 1950. The walls within the dormer were constructed using original chestnut boards and new knotty-pine boards. The raised floor in the dormer accommodates the heating duct that was located behind the earlier knee wall. As originally constructed, the closet at the south end of the room had no doors; the existing doors were installed by the Potters.

No known photographs record this room as it appeared when occupied.
Floor: The floor is finished with 3¼-inch-wide pine floorboards, running north/south and dating to 1942-43. In the east dormer, the floor is raised 1 foot 1 inch and consists of similar floorboards. This floor is contemporary with the construction of the dormer.

Room (204), 1997.
View looking northeast.
Photograph by JGWAA.

Room (204), 1997.
View looking south.
Photograph by JGWAA.

Walls: All four walls are finished with 6-inch-wide vertical chestnut tongue-and-groove boards with beveled joints, similar to those in the south bedroom (202), and dating to 1942-43. The north wall of the dormer is paneled with larger, 7¼-inch-wide pine boards installed when the dormer was added. The chestnut boards on the south wall of the dormer were probably salvaged from the earlier knee wall construction.

Ceiling: The central part of the ceiling is 6 feet 8¼ inches above the floor and is finished with a roughly textured surface on gypsum board, installed by the Potters, over the original fiberboard ceiling panels. Paint evidence indicates that battens on the fiberboard ceiling were removed to install the gypsum board ceiling. A portion of the fiberboard ceiling near the center of the room was torn away to provide access for the installation of a 2-inch-diameter galvanized vent pipe running between the lavatory in bathroom (203) and the original cast-iron vent pipe for bathroom (106), located beneath the west slope of the roof. It appears that the vent piping was modified c. 1956, when the Potters made changes in bathroom (203).

The sloping ceiling planes at the east and west ends of the room are covered with 6-inch-wide painted chestnut boards; they meet the knee walls approximately 4 feet 7¼ inches above the floor. The sloping ceiling planes are contemporary with the wall surfaces. Originally, they were unpainted.

A portion of the original 1942-43 ceiling remains in the closet (204A). This ceiling is constructed of fiberboard panels with wood battens, and it is approximately ½ inch above the height of the ceiling in room 204.

Baseboard: The base of the wood paneling is trimmed with a 5-inch-high chamfered wood fascia and a quarter-round shoe molding dating to 1942-43. In the dormer, all three walls have a pine fascia baseboard dating to the construction of the dormer.

Cornice: The top of the paneling is trimmed with a wood ogee molding.

Doors: There are two door openings in this room, both located in the small entry space at the south end of the room. The west opening (D2041) and east opening (D2042) are each framed by a 4-inch-wide wood fascia trimmed with a flattened bead along the outside edge and date to 1942-43.

D2041: The 2-foot 2½-inch-wide by 6-foot 3½-inch-high by 1⅜-inch-thick pine stile-and-rail door has two recessed panels and chamfered stiles and rails. The hardware consists of one pair of 3½-inch-high brass-finished butt hinges with ball finials, marked Stanley; and a 5½-inch-high brass-finished mortise lockset with brass-finished knobs and decorative escutcheon plates. The door and hardware date to 1942-43.

D2042: The 1-foot 11¼-inch-wide by 6-foot 3½-inch-high by 1⅜-inch-thick pine stile-and-rail door has two recessed panels. The upper panel is glazed with textured glass; the lower panel has chamfered reveals. There is one pair of 3½-inch-high brass-finished butt hinges with ball finials; and a 5¼-inch-high brass-finished mortise lockset with brass-finished knobs and decorative escutcheon plates. The door and hardware date to 1942-43.

Windows: The window opening in the north wall is set deeply into the masonry, with plywood reveals and a simple sill. The two 4-over-4 sashes are separated by a 3⅜-inch-wide mullion. The sashes slide in spring-loaded metal tracks, and have 9⅝-inch-wide by 11⅝-inch-high panes, ½-inch muntins, and brass-finished thumb latches. The opening and sashes date to 1942-43 when the attic rooms were created.

The dormer in the east wall has two window openings framed by 4³⁄₁₆-inch-wide architraves, similar to the beaded fascia used at the door openings. The 4-over-4 rope-hung sashes have 9½-inch-wide by 11½-inch-high panes, ¾-inch muntins, and brass-finished thumb latches. The dormer was installed for the Potter family.

Closet (204A): A small closet at the south end of the room is enclosed with a pair of sliding doors of flake-board construction with flush, brass-finished pulls. The closet is outfitted with a clothes rod and tongue-and-groove shelving that may be contemporary with the creation of the room. The sliding doors were installed sometime after 1945.

Heating: There is a 1942-43 metal heating register with operable louvers in the east wall, beneath the raised floor of the dormer. An air-conditioning unit has been inserted in the east window of the north gable.

Lighting/Electrical: Electrical elements include duplex receptacles with metal cover plates in the east and west walls, as well as in the closet (204A). These receptacles may be contemporary with the creation of the room in 1942-43.

Finishes Investigation: The wall surfaces retain their original stained, but unpainted, finish. The sloped wood ceiling surfaces that are now painted originally matched the wall surfaces. The textured ceiling finish was added by the Potter family.

Stair Hall (205)

This narrow hall includes a single door opening in the north wall and a closet door in the west wall. A stairway descends to the first floor in two runs at the east end of the space. An exposed sheet-metal heating duct enters the hall from the stairwell and then extends into the adjoining space to the north.

The stair and hall were created in 1940-41 when the north attic was converted into living space for Christian Bie and his family. This area remains essentially as constructed, except for the removal of a handrail that was positioned on the north side of the upper stair run and the addition of paint to the wall and ceiling surfaces. The handrail was probably removed so that furniture could more easily be transported up the narrow stairway. There is no evidence that a door was ever placed in the opening in the north wall.

The carriage for the upper stair run passes through the upper portion of the entry hall closet (101A). The original unpainted wall finish of the closet can be seen behind the small triangular wall panel at the south side of the upper stair run.

The sheet-metal heating duct may not have been installed at exactly the same time as the stairway, but it predates May 1945.

No known photographs record this narrow dark hall as it appeared in the past.

Floor: The floor is finished with 3¼-inch-wide pine boards, running north/south, and dating to 1940-41. The stairwell is located at the east end of the hall. This opening is contemporary with the creation of the finished attic rooms of the north wing.

Walls: The north, south, and west walls are finished with fiberboard panels, grooved to resemble vertical wood paneling with beveled joints. A quarter-round wood molding has been installed along the north base, to either side of the door opening.

Documentation indicates that the fiberboard may be Celotex, a product manufactured from cane fiber.

Ceiling: The central flat portion of the ceiling is finished with wood battens and fiberboard panels, approximately 6 feet 8 inches above the floor. At the east and west ends of the hall, the ceiling plane follows the slope of the roof; these surfaces are finished with fiberboard paneling like that used on the walls. These finishes were installed in 1940-41.

Baseboard: The base of the fiberboard panels is covered by a 5⅝-inch-high plain wood fascia. On the north wall, there is also a small quarter-round shoe molding.

Cornice: An original small wood ogee molding covers the joints between the wall and ceiling paneling.

Doors: There are two doorways in this hall: one in the north wall (D2061) framed by a 4⅛-inch-wide fascia with a flattened bead around the outside edge; as well as a smaller opening in the west wall (D2051) framed by a plain wood casing.

D2051: This small, 2-foot 2-inch-wide by 4-foot 5-inch-high by 1-inch-thick stile-and-rail door has two recessed plywood panels. The door provides access to an undereave storage space (205A). The hardware consists of one pair of 3¼-inch-high butt hinges, and a small mortised bolt with an ovoid brass-finished knob. The door and hardware are contemporary with the construction of the attic rooms in 1940-41.

Lighting/Electrical: The hall is lit by a single-bulb incandescent ceiling fixture with a brass base and a small glass collar. This fixture was installed at the time the hall was created. There is a switch on the north wall and on the east wall at the base of the stair.

Storage (205A): This storage space extends from the north masonry wall of the central block to the west dormer in (206). The floor is finished with 5¼-inch-wide floorboards, running north/south. The walls are unfinished. The south wall is of masonry construction (with an asphalt coating); the east and north walls are made up of wood studs supporting fiberboard paneling; and the steeply pitched surface to the west consists of framing and sheathing, with 1¾-inch-thick by 5⅝-inch-high wood rafters, spaced approximately 1 foot 4 inches to 1 foot 4½ inches apart, supporting 5⅛-inch-wide tongue-and-groove sheathing.

Generally, the materials forming the south and west sides of the storage space date to 1938-39, while the conditions at the north and east sides were created in 1940-41. The unfinished flooring may be some of the "rough flooring" installed in the attics in 1938.

Furnishings and Fittings: This hall is not mentioned in either of the 1945 inventories, and it is unlikely that furniture was placed here.

Finishes Investigation: The fiberboard wall and ceiling surfaces remained unpainted until sometime after 1945.

Room (206)

In plan, this room has single doorways in the north and south walls, as well as large dormers with double windows extending east and west from the north end of the room. A built-in closet is located in the southwest corner, and an undereave storage area is located in the southeast corner, beneath the roof.

Room (206), 1997.
View looking north.
Photograph by JGWAA.

This room is probably part of the "new quarters occupied by Bie & Company" (the Bie family) that are referred to by Hall Roosevelt in a letter dated February 16, 1941.

As originally completed, the room included only the west dormer. The fiberboard (Celotex) walls and ceiling remained unpainted. The closet in the southwest corner was added at a later date.

The east dormer was added sometime after 1945, probably by the Potter family. Apparently, the floor level in the dormer had to be raised to accommodate an existing sheet-metal heating duct.

There is no documentation on how the Bie family used this room. According to Elliott (Tony) Roosevelt, Jr., the family cook and her daughter and son-in-law occupied the north wing rooms. Owen Potter remembers that the second-floor rooms in the north wing were guest rooms. There are no known photographs that record the room during the various periods of occupancy.

Floor: The floor is finished with 3¼-inch-wide pine boards, running north/south and dating to 1940-41. In the later east dormer, the floor is raised 1 foot 1½ inches above the adjoining floor surface to accommodate a heating duct that services the adjoining room (207).

Walls: All four walls and the walls forming the west dormer are finished with fiberboard panels, grooved to resemble wood paneling with beveled joints. This material, possibly Celotex, was installed in 1940-41. In the east dormer, the pattern of the grooves in the fiberboard is slightly different. This material is contemporary with the later construction of the dormer by the Potter family.

Ceiling: The central flat portion of the ceiling is finished with wood battens and fiberboard panels, approximately 6 feet 8 inches above the floor; the same material covers the gabled ceiling of the west dormer. The sloping ceiling planes above the knee walls are finished with fiberboard paneling like that used on the walls. All of this material dates to 1940-41. The east dormer has a flat ceiling, approximately 4 inches higher than the ceiling in the room. The dormer ceiling is made up of two large fiberboard panels with molded battens.

Baseboard: The base of the fiberboard panels is covered by a 5⅝-inch-high plain-wood fascia trimmed with a small quarter-round shoe molding. In the east dormer, the baseboard is a 5¾-inch-high wood fascia with a shoe molding on the north and east walls.

Cornice: A variety of small moldings, including ogees, quarter-rounds, and cavettos, are used at the junctures of the ceiling and wall planes. These moldings are contemporary with the installation of the fiberboard. A more complex cavetto and quarter-round molding is used in the east dormer and on the closet in the southwest corner.

Room (206), 1997.
View looking southwest.
Photograph by JGWAA.

Room (206), 1997.
View of west dormer
constructed c. 1940-41.
Photograph by JGWAA.

Doors: There are three door openings: one in the south wall (D2061), one in the north wall (D2062), and a smaller opening in the east wall (D2063). The north and south doorways are each framed by a 4⅛-inch-wide fascia with a flattened bead around the outside edge, while the east doorway is framed by a plain wood casing. These openings are contemporary with the construction of the room.

D2061: There is no evidence that a door was ever positioned in this opening.

D2062: The 2-foot 6-inch-wide by 6-foot 4¼-inch-high by 1⅜-inch-thick stile-and-rail door has two recessed panels. The hardware consists of one pair of 3½ inch-high steel butt hinges with ball finials; and a 5¼-inch-high mortise lockset with brass-finished knobs and rectangular escutcheon plates. The door and hardware are contemporary with the opening.

D2063: This small, 2-foot-wide by 4-foot 6-inch-high by 1⅛-inch-thick stile-and-rail door has two recessed panels and provides access to an undereave storage space (206A). The hardware consists of one pair of 3¼-inch-high steel butt hinges, and a small mortised latch with an ovoid brass-finished knob. The door and hardware are contemporary with the opening.

Windows: The west dormer has a gabled ceiling and has the same finishes on the walls, ceiling, and floor as the rest of the room. The two window openings in the west wall of the dormer are framed by an architrave matching the fascia with a rounded inner edge and flattened bead profile used at the door openings. Each window has 4-over-4 rope-hung wood sashes with 9⅜-inch-wide by 11⅜-inch-high panes, ¾-inch muntins, and a steel thumb latch. All of the conditions here are contemporary with the creation of the room in 1940-41. An access panel located at the east end of the gabled ceiling in the west dormer opens to the remaining attic space above the rooms of the north wing.

The two window openings in the east dormer are framed by an architrave similar to the architraves at the doors and the west windows, but the fascia has a sharp inner edge, and there is an additional ogee stop molding. Each window has 4-over-4 rope-hung wood sashes with 9½-inch-wide by 11½-inch-high panes, ¾-inch muntins, and a brass-finished thumb latch. The east dormer was constructed after 1945; it was probably created for the Potter family.

Closet (206B): The built-in wood closet in the southwest corner of the room was inserted sometime after the completion of the room, but probably before May 1945. The closet is outfitted with five wood storage bins on the north wall, as well as a metal clothes rod. The three closet doors each have two recessed panels and are hung on pairs of 3-inch steel butt hinges.

The single south door is secured with a key-operated latch, and the double doors share a brass-finished slide bolt.
Heating: A metal register is located in the east wall, near the floor; it was installed during, or soon after, the creation of the room. The duct for this register continues behind the east wall into the adjoining room (207).
Lighting/Electrical: The room is lit by a three-bulb incandescent ceiling fixture with a brass base and small glass collars at each bulb. Other electrical elements include switches in the north and south walls, as well as duplex receptacles in the east wall, in the west wall (now in the closet), and in the south wall of the west dormer. All of these elements are contemporary with the construction of the room.
Storage (206A): This small undereave storage space is located between the stair hall (205) and the east dormer. The floor and walls are similar to those in the west storage area (205A), but they have been covered with building insulation and paper. The sheet-metal duct from the first floor runs along the base of the west wall. The space is lit by an incandescent porcelain utility fixture.

Prior to the construction of the east dormer, this space originally extended to the north masonry wall of the wing.
Furnishings and Fittings: No mention of this room is made in the 1945 inventories.

The absence of a door in the opening to the stair hall may indicate that the room was never intended to serve as a bedroom. It is necessary to pass through this space to reach the rooms to the north. The built-in closet on the west wall is a later addition; the type of closet doors and hardware seem to indicate that it was added before the end of the FDR era.
Finishes Investigation: The fiberboard wall and ceiling surfaces remained unpainted until sometime after the construction of the east dormer. The Celotex sheets had a natural beige-colored surface that can still be seen inside of the west closet. The various wood moldings and the baseboards were painted prior to installation in a yellow-white color. The fiberboard was first painted a light blue, followed by the current white finish.

Room (207)

To reach this room, one must pass through the adjoining room (206). The space has a large double window in the north wall and a single doorway in the south wall. A toilet room is located in the northeast corner. A built-in closet is situated in the southwest corner. A freestanding metal shower stall is located near the north end of the room; it partially conceals the window.

The room remains much as it was upon completion in 1940-41. The small closet may have been inserted a short time after the room was finished; it was definitely installed before the end of the FDR era.

Originally, the walls and ceilings were unpainted. The room was painted sometime after 1945. The shower stall dates to the Potter's occupancy.

This space is not included in the 1945 inventories. At that time, it probably served as a bedroom for the Bie family. Elliott (Tony) Roosevelt, Jr., recalled that a family cook and her daughter and son-in-law occupied the rooms in the north wing.

There are no known photographs that record the room as it was used.
Floor: The floor is finished with 3¼-inch-wide pine boards, running north/south, and dating to 1940-41.
Walls: All of the walls are finished with fiberboard (Celotex) panels, grooved to resemble vertical wood paneling with beveled joints and installed in 1940-41.
Ceiling: The flat portion of the ceiling is finished with wood battens and fiberboard panels, approximately 6 feet 8 inches above the floor. The sloping planes of the ceiling are finished with fiberboard paneling like that used on the walls. These surfaces date to 1940-41.
Baseboard: The base of the fiberboard panels is covered by a 5⅝-inch-high plain wood fascia trimmed with a small quarter-round shoe molding. The baseboard is contemporary with the construction of the room.
Cornice: A variety of small ogee moldings are used at the junctures of ceiling and wall planes.
Doors: There are three door openings in this room: one in the south wall (D2062), one in the east wall (D2071), and an opening to the closet in the southwest corner (D2072). All three

openings are framed by a 4⅛-inch-wide fascia with a flattened bead around the outside edge. The south and east openings are contemporary with the construction of the room. The closet may have been constructed a short time after the room was finished.

D2071: The 2-foot-wide by 6-foot 5-inch-high by 1⅜-inch-thick stile-and-rail door has two recessed panels. The hardware consists of one pair of 3½-inch-high butt hinges with ball finials and a 5¼-inch-high mortise lockset with brass-finished knobs and rectangular escutcheon plates. The door and hardware are contemporary with the opening.

Room (207), 1997. View looking northwest, showing the shower stall. Photograph by JGWAA.

D2072: The 2-foot 6-inch-wide by 6-foot 5-inch-high by 1⅜-inch-thick stile-and-rail closet door has two recessed panels. The hardware consists of one pair of 2½-inch brass-finished butt hinges with ball finials and a key-operated latch.

Window: The window opening in the north wall is framed with a small quarter-round molding and has plain wood reveals and a bullnosed shelf. The 4-over-4 sashes in the two windows slide in spring-loaded metal tracks and have 9¾-inch-wide by 11½-inch-high panes, ½-inch muntins, and thumb latches. The track mechanism is labeled Curtis Silentite. The opening and sash date to the 1940-41 construction of the north attic rooms.

Closet (207A): A built-in closet in the southwest corner of the room is made of narrow beaded boards (floorboards) screwed to wood battens. Within the closet, the walls are trimmed with an ogee crown molding and a fascia baseboard with a shoe molding. A patch of vinyl flooring is nailed to the south wall. The closet is outfitted with a clothes rod and ledgers for three tiers of shelving (now missing). This closet was either original to the room or a very early addition (pre-1945).

Plumbing: A metal shower stall at the north end of the room has a door fitted with a single panel of textured clear glass. The copper pipes to the shower are routed through the floor from the first-floor closet (111). The shower was installed by the Potters.

Heating: A metal heating register is located in the east wall, near the floor. There is a Holland thermostat on the east wall, near the outside corner of the toilet room (208). These fittings are contemporary with the construction of the room.

Lighting/Electrical: The room is lit by a three-bulb incandescent ceiling fixture with a brass base and small glass collars at each bulb. Other electrical elements include a duplex receptacle in the west wall. These fittings are contemporary with the construction of the room.

Furnishings and Fittings: It is likely that this space served as a bedroom during the FDR-era; however, the type of furnishings that were placed here remains unknown. At that time, there was no shower stall in the room.

Finishes Investigation: The wall and ceiling surfaces were originally unpainted; the natural beige color of the fiberboard (Celotex) served as the finish. The wood trim elements, including the baseboard, were painted in a yellow-white prior to installation.

Later (after 1945) the walls were painted in a light blue, followed by the current white finish.

Toilet Room (208)

This very small room is tucked into the northeast corner of the north room (207). The rectangular space includes a doorway in the west wall. The toilet and wall-mounted lavatory completely fill the space. The crude appearance of the construction of this room may indicate that it was not a part of the 1940-41 construction work in the north attic. It is possible that it was hurriedly constructed as an afterthought. The toilet room was definitely in place well before the end of the FDR era.

All of the original fittings survive. The only modifications include the floor covering, the painted surfaces, and possibly the wood shelving.

Floor: The floor is finished with sheet vinyl from the Potter era.

Walls: All four walls are finished with fiberboard panels, grooved to resemble vertical wood paneling with beveled joints. This finish was installed when the room was constructed.

Ceiling: The central portion of the ceiling is finished with a flat fiberboard panel, approximately 6 feet 8 inches above the floor. The sloping east plane of the ceiling is finished with fiberboard paneling that matches the material used on the walls.

Baseboard: The base of the wall paneling is covered by a 5⅝-inch-high plain wood fascia trimmed with a small quarter-round shoe molding.

Plumbing: The bathroom is fitted with a vitreous china toilet set diagonally in the room. The tank is marked "13". The green decorative plastic seat dates to the Potters' residency. A porcelain-enameled cast-iron lavatory on the east wall has chrome fittings. "2815, 22 x19, USA [illegible date]" is cast into the bottom of the basin. These fittings are original to the construction of the room.
Heating: There is a register in the ceiling above the toilet, as well as a return-air grille in the east wall. Both are contemporary with the construction of the room.
Lighting/Electrical: The room is lit by an incandescent light fixture above the medicine cabinet on the south wall. The fixture is original to the room; it has a porcelain bracket with a convenience outlet, and a white opal glass shade.
Furnishings and Fittings: A mirrored, metal medicine cabinet recessed in the south wall is labeled "Lawco, Est. 1816". Other bathroom fittings include a chrome towel rod, a chrome toilet-paper holder, a chrome soap holder, and a chrome toothbrush/tumbler holder on the east wall, all of which appear to be original. There are three tiers of plywood shelving on the north wall that may have been installed after the construction of the room.

CONSERVATION ASSESSMENT

View of the cottage from the southeast, June 1939. Courtesy of the Franklin D. Roosevelt Library, Hyde Park, New York.

AFTER PRESIDENT ROOSEVELT'S DEATH IN APRIL 1945, Top Cottage remained in nearly continuous use as a private residence, first for the President's son Elliot and since 1952 as the residence of the Potter family. The building was maintained through this continued residential use, and it was not subjected to the wear and tear that public visitation would impose. However, modifications were made to accommodate family use and the particular needs of the residents. Some of these changes had an adverse effect on the historical character of the house. In other instances, time and deferred maintenance resulted in deterioration of the house.

As one of the first steps in the process of ensuring the long-term survival of the building, a thorough survey was made of the house to record the problems of repair. While the quality of the original construction served the building well, a curatorial approach was needed to arrest deterioration and preserve the original building fabric.

Problems had developed at Top Cottage that were normally associated with structures of its age. These included settlement cracks in the masonry and plaster; deterioration of exterior wood elements; obsolete building systems, including the mechanical, electrical, and plumbing systems; and modifications of the original construction that involved adding, removing, or covering building elements. These problems are listed below.

Exterior

East Elevation South Wing

–The paint on the cornice was peeling, and the wood substrate was exposed.
–A hole was cut in the east elevation of the south dormer to install a security-alarm horn.
–The patina on the copper sheet-metal flashing at the base of the dormers was variegated and missing in places. The flashing had been face-nailed, creating the potential for leaks.
–The paint on the first-floor windows was peeling, and the wood substrate was exposed.
–The aluminum storm windows, screens, and tracks at each window opening were historically inappropriate and visually obtrusive.
–The steel brackets for a window box at the first-floor north window were rusted.
–The cast-iron foundation vent located beneath the first-floor north window was rusted.
–The south shutter at the first-floor south window was no longer attached to the shutter hinge.
–The air-conditioning unit in the first-floor south window was historically inappropriate and visually obtrusive. The steel cabinet was rusted. Electrical cabling for the air conditioner had been routed up the face of the exterior wall and through a hole drilled in the window sill. The steel cable anchors in the masonry were rusted.
–Ivy vines were growing on the surface of the masonry. The vines were retaining moisture that may have accelerated the deterioration of the masonry. The adjacent shrubbery was overgrown; it obscured the lower elevation of the wall.

Rotted wood sill at second-floor window on north elevation of south wing, 1997. Photograph by John G. Waite Associates, Architects.

North Elevation South Wing

–The paint on the window sills was peeling, and the wood substrate was exposed. The second-floor window sill was completely rotted.
–Algae were growing on the first-floor window shutters, and the paint was peeling. Wood rot was visible on the shutters.
–The aluminum storm windows, screens, and tracks at each window opening were historically inappropriate and visually obtrusive.
–The air-conditioning unit in the second-floor window was historically inappropriate and visually obtrusive.
–Electrical cabling was routed along the base of the wall at grade. The cable continued along the east elevation of the south wing to the air-conditioning unit in the first-floor south window. The cable originated at the basement entry in the south face of the chimney mass. The same type of cable extended from the basement entry, up the east elevation of the central block, and then south along the cornice, and it was attached to the second-floor window sill on the north elevation of the south wing. This cable serviced the air-conditioning unit in the second-floor window. The exposed electrical cable was visually obtrusive, and the installation did not meet the requirements of the National Electrical Code.

–Ivy vines were growing on the surface of the masonry.
–A crack following mortar joints in the masonry wall extended from the upper west corner of the first-floor window opening to the lower west corner of the second-floor window opening.
–Mortar was missing beneath the south end of the gutter on the east elevation of the central block and adjacent to the lower east corner of the second-floor window opening.

East Elevation
Central Block

–The paint on the cornice was peeling, and the wood substrate was exposed and beginning to rot.
–The aluminum downspout at the north end of the elevation was historically inappropriate. Galvanic corrosion was occuring at the juncture of the gutter and downspout as a result of using dissimilar metals for the gutter (copper) and downspout (aluminum). Similarly, galvanic corrosion was occurring along the gutter, where an aluminum splash shield had been screwed to the copper gutter with steel screws. The plastic tile extension that was attached to the base of the downspout, and laid on grade, was visually obtrusive. The original in-ground drain shoe for the downspout was filled with leaves.
–Electrical cabling protruded from the ground adjacent to the north downspout. The cable was cut and the conductors were exposed, creating a potential electrical-shock hazard.
–The paint on the south downspout was peeling.
–The air-conditioner condenser located at the inside corner of the central block of the house and the south wing was historically inappropriate and visually obtrusive.
–The aluminum door and pressure-treated wood doorframe at the basement entry, located in the south face of the chimney mass, were historically inappropriate. The steel screws in the aluminum door were rusting as a result of galvanic corrosion between the two dissimilar metals. The basement sump drain pipe, the electrical cabling and copper refrigerant tubing connected to the air-conditioner condenser, and the electrical cabling routed on grade and over the face of the masonry to service individual room air-conditioning units were historically inappropriate and visually obtrusive. The electrical and plumbing lines were all routed through the base of the doorframe to the basement.
–The weatherproof electrical receptacle located to the south of the chimney did not meet the requirements of the National Electrical Code; it did not have ground-fault circuit-interrupter (GFCI) protection, and it had no ground conductor.

Loose and missing stone at southeast shoulder of chimney, 1997. Photograph by JGWAA.

–The stone veneer at the shoulder of the chimney was loose, and some of the stone was missing from the southeast corner. It appeared that water had infiltrated the masonry through the wide mortar joints and had undergone freeze/thaw cycling. The freezing process jacked the stone veneer off the concrete substrate. An ineffectual attempt had been made to reinstall displaced stone and repoint the mortar. Ivy, moss, lichen, and algae were growing over much of the masonry surface of the chimney.
–The lead lantern on the east face of the chimney had a badly rusted ferrous metal base as the result of galvanic corrosion between the dissimilar metals. The PVC electrical conduit, extending from the junction box behind the lantern to grade, was historically inappropriate.
–The tree and shrubbery growing in front of this elevation obscured the house.

South Elevation
North Wing

–Where the raking cornice of the north wing abuts the roof of the central block, the paint on the cornice molding was peeling. The wood substrate was exposed and was beginning to rot.
–Ivy vines were growing on the surface of the masonry.
–To the east of the entry, a steel bracket for a hanging plant and a decorative wooden eagle had been attached to the masonry wall. The bracket was rusting and the carved eagle was missing detail; the painted finish on the eagle was eroded.
–The paint on the entry door and frame was peeling.
–Screw holes and hinge mortises remained in the doorframe where a storm/screen door had been removed.
–A keyed switch and indicator lights for an electronic security system had been mounted on the east jamb of the entry door. These devices were historically inappropriate.
–The modern steel post light located off the southeast corner of the north wing was historically inappropriate.

East Elevation North Wing

–The paint on the cornice was peeling, and the wood substrate was exposed.
–The patina on the copper sheet-metal flashing at the base of the dormer had been partially eroded. The flashing had been face-nailed, creating the potential for leaks.
–The paint was peeling from the clapboard siding on the north elevation of the dormer, where the siding abutted the roof. Paint was also peeling around the windows and at the northeast corner of the dormer.
–The paint on the first-floor window shutters was peeling, and the wood substrate was exposed.
–The aluminum storm sash at the windows were historically inappropriate. The paint on the wood window sills was peeling.
–There were settlement cracks in the masonry joints above and below the first-floor windows.
–Telephone station wiring extended along grade between the north window and the northeast corner of the north wing. At the window, the wire was routed up the face of the masonry and through a hole drilled in the south architrave. The wiring was historically inappropriate and visually obtrusive.
–Ivy vines were growing on the surface of the masonry. The adjacent shrubbery was overgrown; it obscured the lower elevation of the wall.

North Elevation North Wing

–The abandoned electrical service hood adjacent to the second-floor windows was rusting.
–At the northeast corner of the enclosed porch, two surface-mounted electric meters, a 100-amp electric service disconnect, and two telephone service networks had been attached to the face of the building. Electric service wiring was attached to the raking cornice and routed down the northeast corner of the house to the electric meters. The equipment and wiring was visually obtrusive and historically inappropriate.
–The aluminum storm sash at the second-floor windows were historically inappropriate.
–At the inside corner adjacent to the northeast entry of the enclosed porch, the wood cornice molding of the porch was rotted.
–A 20-pound propane gas bottle with a regulator and piping rested on grade at the northeast corner of the house. The gas was used for a range located on the enclosed porch. The steel gas bottle was significantly rusted.
–At the northeast corner of the enclosed porch the protruding perimeter window sill was rotted. An unsuccessful attempt was made to repair the deterioration with epoxy.
–Algae were growing on the wood siding adjacent to the northeast entry of the enclosed porch. The base of the siding was rotted. The bottom tread of the stone steps was chipped.
–The horizontal wood window mullion on the east elevation of the enclosed porch was rotted.
–The vertical wood siding on the enclosed porch was generally split at its base.
–Paint was peeling from the woodwork of the enclosed porch. This condition was visible on the soffit and on the plywood infill panel located on the north elevation.
–The plywood infill panel installed on the north elevation of the enclosed porch, for an exhaust fan, was visually obtrusive.

Visually obtrusive and historically inappropriate electrical wiring and plumbing at northwest corner of north wing, 1997. Photograph by JGWAA.

West Elevation North Wing

–The roof shingles in the shade of the central block of the house had algae growing on them.
–The paint on the window architraves, sills, and clapboards of the dormer was peeling.
–The paint on the cornice was peeling. The television coaxial cable and the electrical cabling stapled to the cornice were visually obtrusive.
–The masonry at the inside corner of the north wing and the central block was stained green from the copper down conductor of the lightning-protection system.
–The steel tower for a television antenna, located near the northwest corner of the house, was rusting. The tower was braced with steel brackets anchored to the stonework and to the cornice of the house. The tower was historically inappropriate.
–The plumbing vent located at the northwest corner of the house was historically inappropriate.
–The exposed steel vent pipe, installed for the plumbing fixtures on the enclosed porch, was rusting.
–Electrical service wiring was routed through the wood siding on the west elevation of the enclosed porch, up the exterior face of the porch to the northwest corner of the house, where

it was terminated at electrical service hoods. From the service hoods, overhead wiring was strung to the caretaker's cottage (pony barn or horse stable), located to the southwest of the house. This wiring was historically inappropriate and visually obtrusive.
–The plywood shed located at the inside corner of the enclosed porch and the north wing of the house was historically inappropriate. The plywood doors and the sheathing beneath the rolled asphalt roofing were rotting. One of the door hinges was detached.
–The aluminum storm sash at the windows were historically inappropriate.
–The cast-iron foundation vent located at the south end of the north wing was rusted. The areaway for the vent was filled with leaves.
–Moss was growing on the masonry at the base of the west elevation.
–Ivy vines were growing on the surface of the masonry.

North Elevation Central Block

–The anemometer mounted at the north end of the gabled roof, as well as the attendant wiring attached to the raking cornice and to the clapboard siding of the enclosed porch, was historically inappropriate.
–The west end of the raking cornice on the enclosed porch was rotted.
–The abandoned steel antenna mast mounted to the horizontal siding of the enclosed west porch, just below the roofline, was historically inappropriate. The mast was rusting. A copper down conductor for the lightning-protection system was attached to the mast and routed horizontally to the inside corner of the north wing and the central block of the house. The down conductor was visually obtrusive.
–The paint on the horizontal board siding beneath the roofline of the enclosed porch, and on the clapboard siding below, was peeling.
–The electrical cabling stapled to the cornice of the north wing was routed up the face of the masonry on the central block of the house to the framed opening in the gable of the north elevation. The wiring was visually obtrusive, and a taped splice in the wiring was a potential electrical-shock hazard.
–The framed opening in the gable was obscured by a flake-board panel that was historically inappropriate.
–The aluminum storm sash at the first-floor window were historically inappropriate.
–The cast-iron foundation vent was rusted. The areaway for the vent was filled with leaves.
–The electrical conduit routed along the base of the north elevation, from the enclosed porch to the foundation vent opening, was rusted. The conduit was historically inappropriate.
–Ivy vines were growing on the surface of the masonry.

West Elevation Central Block

–The paint on the siding, windows, and fascia was peeling, and the wood substrate was exposed.
–The window glazing putty was cracked and missing.
–An electrical heating cable (to melt ice) was lying in the gutter. The wiring hung down from the north end of the gutter; it was plugged into a grounded, weatherproof receptacle beneath the ledge of the porch paving. The wiring was visually obtrusive, and there was a potential electrical-shock hazard. The electrical receptacle did not meet the requirements of the National Electrical Code; there was no ground-fault circuit-interrupter (GFCI) protection.
–Near the northwest corner of the enclosed porch, electrical conduit had been mounted beneath the ledge of the porch paving. The conduit had been routed up the wall and through the clapboard siding of the porch. The conduit was historically inappropriate, and it was rusted.
–Electrical cabling, terminated with a plug, had been connected to the electrical receptacle near the northwest corner of the porch and strung across the base of the west elevation, to the southwest corner of the porch. Television coaxial cable had been stapled to the siding. The wiring was historically inappropriate and visually obtrusive.
–The masonry base of the porch had been stained green by the rainwater runoff from the copper flashing at the base of the clapboard siding.
–Near the center of the west elevation, the masonry base of the porch was deteriorated; some of the mortar was missing.
–On both the east and west elevations, previously buried electrical cabling had come to the surface of the ground.

South Elevation Central Block

–The paint on the porch windows was peeling. The glazing putty was cracked and missing.
–A surface-mounted weatherproof switch and electrical receptacle had been attached to the clapboard siding of the porch. Electrical cabling had been fastened to the face of the siding, to the window architrave, and to the fascia and carried overhead, to the southwest of the house, for yard lighting. The wiring was historically inappropriate and visually obtrusive.
–An aluminum bracket for a hanging plant had been attached to the southwest post of the enclosed porch. The bracket was historically inappropriate.
–The masonry base of the enclosed porch had been stained green by the rainwater runoff from the copper flashing at the base of the clapboard siding.
–Moss was growing in the mortar joints of the stone steps, and mortar was falling out of the joints.
–The aluminum storm sash at the east window were historically inappropriate.
–The paint on the window shutters was peeling.
–Steel window-box brackets at the east window were rusted.
–The cast-iron foundation vent beneath the east window was rusted.
–The masonry at the inside corner of the central block and the south wing of the house had been stained green from the copper down conductor of the lightning-protection system. At the base of the wall mortar was missing from the joints in the stonework; moss and algae were growing on the masonry.
–Coaxial television cable and telephone station wire had been strung across the south elevation at the head height of the east window. The wiring was visually obtrusive.

Settlement crack in stone masonry beneath south window on west elevation of south wing, 1997. Photograph by JGWAA.

West Elevation South Wing

–Coaxial television cable and telephone station wire were stapled to the soffit. The wire had been routed up the west elevation of the dormer and through holes drilled in the siding. The wiring was historically inappropriate and visually obtrusive.
–The copper flashing at the base of the dormer had been face-nailed, creating the potential for leaks.
–The aluminum storm sash at the windows were historically inappropriate.
–Settlement cracks were visible in the masonry. The cracks extended from the lower south corner of the north window and from the lower north corner of the south window to grade. Generally, the cracks followed the mortar joints.
–Moss and algae were growing along the base of the masonry wall; mortar was missing from joints in the stonework.
–The cast-iron foundation vent beneath the north window was rusted.
–The terrace paving at the inside corner of the central block and south wing of the house had cracked mortar joints and relatively few cracked paving stones. Salt deposits were visible along the mortar joints, and moss was growing in some joints.
–The steel post light located off the southwest corner of the house was historically inappropriate.

South Elevation South Wing

–The paint on the louvered gable vent and on the trim at the eaves of the roof was peeling.
–The paint on the window frames, sills, and shutters was peeling, exposing the wood substrate.
–The aluminum storm sash at the windows were historically inappropriate.
–The air-conditioning unit in the second-floor window was historically inappropriate and visually obtrusive. The steel cabinet of the air conditioner was rusted.
–A settlement crack had developed in the masonry; it extended between the lower east corner of the first-floor window and the grade to the east of the window.
–Ferrous inclusions in the stonework had caused rust staining on the masonry near the southeast corner of the house.
–The cast-iron foundation vent was rusted, and the mortar setting bed was partially missing.
–The shrubbery adjacent to the house was overgrown; it obscured the lower elevation of the wall.

Interior

Furnace Room (B01)

–The concrete ceiling at the base of the furnace room stair was partially missing. The concrete was disintegrating, and rusted steel reinforcing bars were exposed. A steel plate had been laid on the reinforcing bars, covered with polyethylene, and concealed with dirt fill. The steel plate was rusted. It appeared that the concrete may have been removed to create an access hole for the replacement of mechanical equipment in the basement. The deterioration of the concrete was probably accelerated by a leak in the underground drainage system connected to the north downspout on the east elevation of the central block. This would explain why the downspout was no longer connected to the drainage system and why it had been supplemented by a plastic extension laid on grade. The repairs that had been undertaken were temporary and inadequate.
–The steel jacket of the oil-fired hot-water heater was significantly rusted as a result of a leak in the hot-water outlet piping. The leak was active; water flowed over the jacket, making contact with an electrical junction box used for the hot-water heater cut-off switch.
–At the north end of the furnace room, water was dripping from a drain on a valve in the domestic water piping. The floor below the valve was visibly wet.
–The domestic plumbing generally consisted of brass and copper piping. Most of the valves were corroded.
–The steel sheet-metal enclosures of the two oil-fired furnaces were significantly corroded; the bases were rusted where they came in contact with the concrete floor.
–The copper tubing used for supplying fuel oil to the furnaces and hot-water heater had been routed through the crawlspace and laid on the concrete floor of the furnace room, with no provision made to protect the tubing from damage.
–The electrical wiring was supplemented over time in an ad hoc manner. Armored cable, electrical metallic tubing (EMT), and nonmetallic sheathed cable coexisted in a confused array.

Entry (101)

–The finished surface of the plaster on Rocklath (a gypsum-board lath) ceiling was cracked along the lines of the joints in the lath. An attempt to repair the cracks with joint tape had failed.
–Sheet-vinyl flooring obscured the original oak flooring. The transverse seam in the vinyl flooring at the east end of the room was covered with an aluminum edge strip, and the perimeter of the vinyl flooring was secured with wood shoe molding. The vinyl flooring, metal edging, and wood shoe molding were historically inappropriate. The metal edge strips at the interior door thresholds had been removed, and the vinyl flooring had been peeled back.
–Telephone wiring had been attached to the surface of the baseboard at the west end of the room.
–The glazing in the aluminum storm sash at the west window was cracked.
–The cotton sash cord in the west window was at the end of its serviceable life; it required replacement.
–The exterior door was binding on the doorjamb.
–The closet doors at the east end of the room were binding on the floor.
–The two generations of controls for electronic building-security systems, mounted to either side of the exterior door, were historically inappropriate.

Closet (101A)

–The vinyl floor tiles obscured the original oak flooring.
–A horizontal hairline crack had developed in the wall plaster on the east elevation of the closet. The crack corresponded with the lower edge of the opening cut for the passage of the stair to the second floor of the north wing.
–The electronic building-security system with a radio transmitter had been mounted on the south wall of the closet. The wiring for the security system had been stapled and adhered to the wood moldings in the closet, and holes had been drilled in the floor and baseboard for the wiring.

Living Room (102)

–The painted wall surfaces were dirty.
–The oak strip flooring was uneven and slightly cupped. This condition appears to have been

the result of inefficient crawlspace ventilation and high humidity levels in the basement. The flooring was discolored in two rectangular areas, perpendicular to and flanking the fireplace.
–The button for the house call-bell system, located on the east wall, south of the fireplace, was covered with paint and was inoperable.
–The plaster on the east wall, flanking the fireplace, was cracked. The cracks extended vertically to the ceiling. A horizontal crack extended from the north wall to the fireplace opening. The cracks appeared to be the result of differential settlement between the chimney mass and the house.
–There were minor hairline cracks in the plaster adjacent to the southeast door. The cracks appeared to follow the joints of the gypsum-board lath.
–The cotton sash cord at the south window had been pulled loose or broken. The glazing in the aluminum storm sash had separated from its frame, and the frame was bent.
–The metal HVAC grille beneath the south window had been displaced; it was no longer flush with the surrounding wood molding.
–The baseboard electrical receptacles and two of the four floor receptacles were two-wire, non-grounded outlets. These receptacles were historically correct, but they did not comply with current requirements of the National Electrical Code.
–There were hairline cracks in the plaster on the west wall. The cracks appeared to follow the horizontal joints of the gypsum-board lath. A single horizontal crack extended from the north end of the room to the south end of the room along the line of the window and door headers. A significant vertical crack had developed in the plaster above the opening for the sliding doors. The crack, located near the south end of the door opening, extended vertically to the plane of the sloped ceiling and continued along the sloped ceiling surface.
–The wood moldings that were used to conceal the overhead door track and flanking door pockets of the sliding doors when the west porch was enclosed had been partially removed.
–The original double-hung sash were missing from the window openings on the west wall. They were removed sometime after the west porch was enclosed. The blank panels that had been installed to obscure the original sash weight pockets, the dados for the parting stops, and the mortised holes for the sash pulley mechanisms had been partially removed.
–Historically inappropriate telephone wiring had been attached to the surface of the baseboard on the west wall, between the door opening and the north window.
–A vertical plaster crack extended upward from the northeast door opening, and horizontal hairline cracks had developed in the wall plaster adjacent to the door. The horizontal cracks appeared to follow the joints of the gypsum-board lath.
–The northeast door was binding on the floor.
–The thermostat on the north wall, adjacent to the northeast door, was historically inappropriate.

Fiberboard acoustical tile stapled to original tongue-and-groove ceiling boards of west porch, 1997. Photograph by JGWAA.

West Porch (102A)

–The original tongue-and-groove wood ceiling had been covered with historically inappropriate acoustic tile. The tile had been partially removed.
–The electrical receptacles on the east wall were two-wire, nongrounded outlets. The receptacles were historically correct, but they did not comply with current requirements of the National Electrical Code.
–The frame construction of the north, west, and south walls that was used to enclose the porch was historically inappropriate. The glazing putty on the casement sash in these walls was significantly deteriorated. Much of the glazing putty was missing, and the muntins were water stained. The two-wire, nongrounded electrical receptacles in the outer walls did not comply with current requirements of the National Electrical Code. The surface-mounted telephone and television wiring detracted from the historic character of the space.

Hall (103)

–The north door was binding on the doorjamb.
–The plaster wall surfaces were slightly irregular where shelving had been removed and where a door opening in the east wall was filled when the door to bedroom 105 was relocated to the south. Along the south side of the filled door opening a vertical crack in the wall plaster extended from the ceiling to the baseboard. Fasteners and repaired holes remained in the walls where picture hangers were once installed.

–The painted plaster finishes were dirty.
–The rubber bumper was missing from the north doorstop. As a result, the north door was scarred.
–The original cotton sash cord at the window had been replaced with steel chain.

Bedroom (104)

–The oak flooring was obscured by carpeting.
–The northwest door was binding on the doorjamb. The rubber bumper was missing from the northwest doorstop. As a result, the door was scarred.
–Over much of the plaster wall surfaces the paint was peeling and flaking in small fragments.
–There were horizontal hairline cracks in the wall plaster that appeared to follow the joints of the gypsum-board lath.
–The finished surface of the plaster on gypsum-board lath ceiling was cracked along the lines of the joints in the lath. An attempt to repair the cracks with joint tape had failed.
–The original cotton sash cord at the south and west windows had been replaced with steel chain.
–Minor deterioration had occurred at the south and west windows as a result of condensation. Two lights in the upper sash of the south window were cracked. The glazing was missing from the aluminum storm sash at the south and west windows.
–The window air-conditioning unit at the east window was visually obtrusive. The increased exposure of the window sash created by the installation of the air conditioner had caused moderate deterioration of the wood sash. Condensation had contributed to the deterioration. A historically inappropriate, surface-mounted electrical receptacle for the air conditioner had been installed on the window seat.
–A vertical crack in the wall plaster extended between the baseboard and window seat of the east window.
–The electrical receptacles in the baseboard were two-wire, nongrounded outlets. The receptacles were historically correct, but they did not comply with current requirements of the National Electrical Code.
–The surface-mounted telephone wiring and what appeared to be a panic button for the previous security-alarm system, mounted near the south window, were historically inappropriate.

Bedroom (105)

–The original oak flooring was obscured by carpeting.
–The southwest door was binding on the doorjamb. The rubber bumper was missing from the doorstop. As a result, the door was scarred.
–The west door was binding on the doorjamb.
–The northeast door did not latch; the strike plate was loose. The rubber bumper was missing from the doorstop. As a result, the door was scarred.
–The cotton sash cord in the east window was at the end of its serviceable life; it required replacement. The paint was peeling from the upper sash, and the glazing was missing from the aluminum storm sash.
–The surface-mounted electrical conduit and receptacles on the north and east walls were historically inappropriate.
–A vertical crack in the wall plaster extended between the baseboard and window seat of the east window.
–The finished surface of the plaster on gypsum-board lath ceiling was cracked along the lines of the joints in the lath. An attempt to repair the cracks with joint tape had failed.
–There were hairline cracks in the plaster on the underside of the stair and above the west door.

Bathroom (106)

–Sheet-vinyl flooring obscured the earlier linoleum flooring. At the east end of the room the vinyl flooring and the linoleum had been ripped up; the linoleum was torn. The vinyl base molding had been removed from the east and south walls; adhesive residue remained on the walls.
–There were cracks in the ceiling and wall plaster that appeared to coincide with the location of a former partition wall at the east end of the room that separated the bathroom from a closet.

Rotted and partially collapsed flooring behind the toilet in bathroom (110), 1997. Photograph by JGWAA.

–A hole of approximately 4 inches in diameter had been cut in the plaster wall above the showerhead on the east wall.
–The west door was binding on the doorjamb.
–The electrical receptacle on the north wall was a two-wire, nongrounded outlet. The receptacle was historically correct, but it did not have ground-fault circuit-interrupter (GFCI) protection. This installation did not meet current requirements of the National Electrical Code.
–A towel bar had been removed from the north wall, and the pieces had been left in the window reveal.
–The cotton sash cord in the north window was at the end of its serviceable life; it required replacement. The glazing in the aluminum storm sash was cracked.
–A vertical crack had developed between the plaster on the west wall and the plywood wall construction surrounding the west door.
–A vertical crack had developed between the east jamb of the southeast door and the plaster on the east wall.
–A ceramic tile on the wing wall at the west end of the tub was cracked.

Vestibule (107)

–Carpeting in the vestibule had been torn up, exposing the linoleum flooring beneath. The linoleum was torn along its west edge. The replacement vinyl base along the north wall had been pulled loose.

Pantry (108)

–Historically inappropriate sheet-vinyl flooring and vinyl base were installed in the pantry, replacing the original floor covering. At the east and west ends of the room the vinyl flooring had been peeled back, and the vinyl base had been pulled loose.
–The painted and papered wall surfaces were dirty.
–The paint on the walls above the perimeter picture molding was peeling.
–A horizontal hairline crack in the plaster on the south wall appeared to coincide with a joint of the gypsum-board lath.
–A vertical crack in the wall plaster extended between the ceiling and the head of the south door.
–A plaster crack in the ceiling extended from north to south, passing through the cutout for the electrical junction box of the light fixture.
–The surface-mounted ringer for the telephone, mounted at the base of the wall in the southwest corner of the room, was historically inappropriate.
–The electrical receptacle in the north wall was a two-wire, nongrounded outlet. The receptacle was historically correct, but it did not comply with current requirements of the National Electrical Code.
–The cotton sash cord in the west window was at the end of its serviceable life; it required replacement. The glazing in the aluminum storm sash was cracked, and the vinyl seals had been pulled loose. A hole had been drilled in the north architrave of the window for television coaxial cable.
–The north face of the south door was scratched and abraded.

Bedroom (109)

–Carpeting and sheet-vinyl flooring obscured the original oak floor.
–The ceiling light fixture was missing; an exposed electrical junction box remained.
–Cracks in the ceiling plaster appeared to coincide with joints in the gypsum-board lath. The paint in the northeast quadrant of the ceiling was peeling; this may have been the result of plumbing leaks above.
–A diagonal plaster crack extended above the head of the southeast door. Between the east door and the southeast door, horizontal and vertical cracks were visible in the plaster above the picture molding on the east wall.
–The electrical receptacles in the baseboard were two-wire, nongrounded outlets. The receptacles were historically correct, but they did not comply with current requirements of the National Electrical Code.
–The cotton sash cord in the west window was at the end of its serviceable life; it required replacement. The glazing was missing from the aluminum storm sash.

–A vertical crack in the plaster on the west wall extended from the window seat to the baseboard.
–The northeast door was binding on the doorjamb.

Bathroom (110)

–The door was binding on the doorjamb.
–Replacement vinyl floor tiles had been pulled up, exposing the wood subfloor. The subfloor behind the toilet was dry-rotted and partially collapsed.
–Cracks were visible in the ceiling and wall plaster .
–The porcelain finish on the lavatory was worn, and the exposed cast iron was rusting.
–The cotton sash cord in the window was at the end of its serviceable life; it required replacement.
–The paint on the plaster wall surfaces behind the toilet and beneath the lavatory was peeling. Crude repairs had left the wall plaster at the north end of the tub uneven.
–The HVAC grille had been removed from the south wall.
–The plastic tile surrounding the tub was historically inappropriate.

Closet (111)

–An access hole had been cut in the oak floor and repaired with pine floorboards.
–The painted finish on the plaster walls and wood casework was dirty. The paint was peeling from the plaster in localized areas.
–Holes in the plaster on the east and west walls had been crudely repaired.
–The wood base at the north end of the closet had been pulled loose.
–The corrosion on a union in the exposed domestic water piping above the casework was evidence of a leak.

Kitchen (112)

–The sheet-vinyl flooring was historically inappropriate; it appeared to have been used to replace the original linoleum flooring. The vinyl had been peeled back at the door openings to the south and west. The vinyl base used throughout the kitchen was historically inappropriate; it had been peeled back in several places.
–A longitudinal crack in the ceiling plaster extended from north to south, along the centerline of the ceiling. The painted finish at the north end of the ceiling was peeling, probably as a result of plumbing leaks above.
–Diagonal settlement cracks in the wall plaster extended upward from the upper corners of the north and northwest door openings and from the northeast window opening.
–A crack in the plaster extended between the upper east architrave of the southeast door and the head of the southeast window opening.
–One light in the lower sash of the southeast window was cracked. The cotton sash cord appeared to be in relatively good condition.
–Historically inappropriate nylon sash cord had been used to replace cotton sash cord at the northeast window. A historically inappropriate surface-mounted telephone jack had been installed at the base of the south window architrave.
–The metal weather stripping on the bottom rail of the northeast door was scraping the aluminum edge strip of the vinyl flooring. The door was binding on the doorjamb. The exterior face of the door was eroded; it appeared to have been clawed repeatedly by a dog.
–The doorstop moldings had been removed from the head and jambs of the northwest door. This modification was made so that the swinging door, originally hung in the south door opening of the pantry (108), could be installed in the northwest door opening of the kitchen. The swinging door was binding on the vinyl flooring that had been peeled back.
–The southwest swinging door was binding on the doorjamb.
–The southeast door was binding on the vinyl flooring.
–The electrical receptacles in the kitchen were two-wire, nongrounded outlets. These receptacles did not have ground-fault circuit-interrupter (GFCI) protection. While the receptacles were historically correct, they did not comply with current requirements of the National Electrical Code. The receptacle in the east wall, adjacent to the refrigerator, had no cover plate; the wiring was exposed.
–The copper tubing used to supply water to the refrigerator ice-maker extended along the east wall, to a plumbing connection at the kitchen sink. The tubing passed in front of and below the northeast window; it was visually obtrusive.

–The plumbing beneath the kitchen sink was corroded as a result of leaks.
–The HVAC grille beneath the northeast window had been displaced.
–The thermostat on the north wall, adjacent to the electrical panel, was historically inappropriate; and the surface-mounted thermostat wiring was visually obtrusive.
–The face of one of the wooden drawers in the casework on the west wall was split.

North Porch (112A)

–The vinyl floor tiles on the porch were discolored and stained. At the southeast corner the flooring had been cut out for access to the crawl space; the adjacent vinyl tiles were chipped and broken. The vinyl tiles near the exterior door of the porch were broken, and the wood flooring was exposed. The wood was water stained.
–The bottom rail on the exterior door of the porch was rotted. The paint on the door was peeling.
–The paint on the wood-paneled wall surfaces, and on the fixed window sash, was peeling. Portions of the window sash and framing were rotted.
–The stone threshold at the door to the kitchen (112) was cracked. Unsuccessful attempts had been made to repair the crack with cement mortar; this had caused the stone to spall.
–The electrical receptacles on the porch were two-wire, nongrounded outlets. The receptacles did not comply with current requirements of the National Electrical Code. The surface-mounted electrical conduit, armored cable, junction boxes, and receptacles were visually obtrusive.
–The clothes-dryer exhaust appeared to have been ducted into the crawl space beneath the porch. The moisture in the discharge air promoted rot.
–There was paint buildup on the sheet-metal cabinet beneath the laundry sink; the cabinet was rusted. The porcelain on the cast-iron sink was stained and discolored, and chips of porcelain were missing.
–The electric resistance heating units mounted on the exterior frame walls of the porch were a fire hazard.
–The exhaust hood mounted in a fixed sash panel on the north elevation of the porch was visually obtrusive and detracted from the historic quality of the house.
–The uninsulated porch was not a practical location for plumbing fixtures and a washing machine. Freezing conditions could cause piping to burst.
–The gas stove at the southeast corner of the porch, with gas piping to an exterior tank, was visually obtrusive.

Surface-mounted electrical conduit, armored cable, junction boxes, and receptacles on the north porch are visually obtrusive and historically inappropriate, 1997. Photograph by JGWAA.

Stair (113)

–The painted finishes within the stairway were dirty.
–A horizontal hairline crack in the plaster on the east wall appeared to coincide with a joint in the gypsum-board lath.
–The bare-bulb incandescent light socket, hanging by an electrical cord from a hook on the ceiling, was historically inappropriate and noncompliant with the National Electrical Code.

Stair Hall (201)

–At the base of the stair, the wood trim at the head of the door opening had been pried loose.
–The pine stair treads were obscured by a carpet runner.
–There were cracks in the plaster on the west wall that appeared to coincide with joints in the gypsum-board lath and with crude plaster repairs that were made when the stair was installed.
–The west fascia of the stair opening at the second-floor level had been pried loose and splintered.

Room (202)

–The floor was obscured by carpeting.
–The surface-mounted electrical conduit, switch, receptacle, and fluorescent light fixture in the west dormer were historically inappropriate and visually obtrusive.
–The muntins in the lower sash of the west dormer windows were abraded. The glazing putty on the windows was cracked and had lost adhesion. The glazing in the aluminum storm sash was cracked and broken.
–The glazing putty at the three south windows was cracked and missing. The window air-conditioning unit in the south-central window was visually obtrusive; the exterior steel cabinet was rusted. The increased exposure of the window sash created by the installation of the air conditioner had caused moderate deterioration of the wood sash; the paint was peeling. The

aluminum frame for a storm window remained at the south-central window opening. The glazing in the aluminum storm windows flanking the central window was cracked and displaced from the aluminum framing. The aluminum storm sash were historically inappropriate. Two lights in the east window were cracked.

–The surface-mounted telephone wiring was visually obtrusive.
–The electrical receptacles in room 202 were two-wire, nongrounded outlets. The receptacles were historically correct, but they did not comply with current requirements of the National Electrical Code.
–The textured ceiling finish was historically inappropriate.
–One of the sash cords in the north window of the east dormer had pulled loose. There was minor deterioration of the window glazing putty at the east windows.
–A hole had been cut in the east elevation of the east dormer to install a security alarm horn.
–The west door of closet 202A was binding on the doorjamb.

Bathroom (203)

–The vinyl floor tiles beneath the toilet tank and to the north of the tub were water stained and deteriorated.
–The globe was missing from the incandescent light fixture above the lavatory. The electrical receptacle on the light fixture was a two-wire, nongrounded outlet. The receptacle did not have ground-fault circuit-interrupter (GFCI) protection. This installation did not meet current requirements of the National Electrical Code.
–The chrome-plated toothbrush holder was rusted.
–The plastic tile on the walls was historically inappropriate.

Room (204)

–The pine floorboards were scuffed and abraded.
–The textured ceiling finish was historically inappropriate.
–The glazing putty at the two north windows was cracked and missing. The window air-conditioning unit in the east window and the surface-mounted electrical receptacle installed for the air conditioner were visually obtrusive. The increased exposure of the window sash created by the installation of the air conditioner had caused relatively minor deterioration of the wood sash; the sash was water stained. The aluminum frame for a storm window remained at the east window opening. The aluminum storm sash were historically inappropriate. Two lights in the east window and one in the west window were cracked. A muntin in the upper sash of the west window was splintered.
–The glazing putty at the south window in the east dormer was cracked and missing. Water staining that could be attributed to condensation was visible on the wood sash. The glazing in the aluminum storm window to the north was cracked. The aluminum storm sash were historically inappropriate.
–The sliding doors of closet 204A were binding in the overhead track. The flake-board construction of the doors was historically inappropriate.
–The electrical wiring stapled to the floor of closet 204A, and routed through holes drilled in the baseboard and floor, was historically inappropriate and noncompliant with the National Electrical Code.
–The electrical receptacles in room 204 were two-wire, nongrounded outlets. The receptacles were historically correct, but they did not comply with current requirements of the National Electrical Code.
–Coat hooks attached to the back of the southwest door, and to the west wall behind the door, had splintered and crushed the wood construction of the door and wall paneling.

Stair Hall (205)

–The pine floorboards were scuffed, and the flooring at the north side of the stair landing had been cut out to receive a newel post that was subsequently removed.
–An electrical cord was routed across the ceiling from the light fixture to the north wall, and down to the ceiling of stair 113 for a bare-bulb incandescent light socket hanging from a hook. The wiring was historically inappropriate and noncompliant with the National Electrical Code.

–The sloped surface of the fiberboard ceiling at the east end of the space had been crushed and abraded by the movement of furniture up and down the stair.
–The door to storage 205A was binding on the doorjamb.

Room (206)

–The pine floorboards were scuffed and stained.
–The door to storage 206A was binding on the floor.
–The sash cord at the windows in the east and west dormers had been painted and required replacement. The aluminum storm sash were historically inappropriate. The glazing putty on the windows was cracked.
–The surface-mounted low-voltage electrical wiring on the baseboard was historically inappropriate.
–The paint on the wood battens and trim of the fiberboard ceiling in the west dormer was crazed. The trim to the south was water stained.
–The painted finish on the attic access panel in the west dormer was dirty and smudged.
–Some of the wood battens on the ceiling had been pulled loose.
–The fiberglass insulation laid above the second-floor ceiling in the north wing had been improperly installed with the vapor barrier facing up. This may have caused condensation to form within the insulation, ultimately leading to problems with water-damaged framing and ceiling materials.
–The electrical receptacles in room 206 were two-wire, nongrounded outlets. The receptacles were historically correct, but they did not comply with current requirements of the National Electrical Code.
–The mouse trap in closet 206B was an indication of problems with rodents.
–The intermediate support of the hanging rod in closet 206B, consisting of braided steel wire hanging from a nail, was inappropriate and insufficient.

Room (207)

–The pine floorboards were scuffed, and holes had been drilled in the flooring for the installation of a shower stall at the north end of the room.
–The freestanding steel shower stall at the north end of the room was historically inappropriate and visually obtrusive.
–The electrical receptacles in room 207 were two-wire, nongrounded outlets. The receptacles were historically correct, but they did not comply with current requirements of the National Electrical Code.
–The door to closet 207A was binding on the doorjamb and would not close.
–A hole cut in the fiberboard wall construction of closet 207A, for access to a light switch located in room 206, had been improperly repaired with a piece of vinyl flooring.
–The wood cornerbead on the outside corner of toilet room 208 was splintered.
–The door to toilet room 208 was binding on the doorjamb.
–The lower sash in one of the aluminum storm windows was out of its track.

Toilet Room (208)

–Sheet-vinyl flooring obscured the pine floorboards.
–The edge of the vinyl flooring was peeling up where the shoe mold had been removed.
–The cast-iron lavatory was rusting at the overflow drain, where the porcelain finish was missing.
–A minor leak at the lavatory drain had caused corrosion on the plumbing beneath the lavatory.
–The towel rod was missing from the south wall; the metal anchors remain.
–The electrical receptacle on the light fixture was a two-wire, nongrounded outlet. The receptacle did not have ground-fault circuit-interrupter (GFCI) protection. This installation did not meet current requirements of the National Electrical Code.

RESTORATION

View of the restored cottage from the northwest, showing the west porch and the earthen wheelchair ramp to the north of the porch, 2001. Randall Perry Photography.

THE ORIGINAL MATERIALS AND METHODS OF CONSTRUCTION used at Top Cottage had served the building well, even though modifications were later made and maintenance was deferred in recent years. Between 1999 and 2000, under the direction of John G. Waite Associates, Architects, Top Cottage was returned to its most historically significant period, that of its original construction and the subsequent alterations overseen by President Roosevelt.

The changes made during Roosevelt's lifetime, including the addition of rooms at the second-floor level of the north and south wings and the construction of the west dormer on the north wing, were respected and maintained. However, the alterations made following the President's death—including the construction of additional dormers, the construction of the north porch, and the enclosure of the west porch—were removed because these changes had altered the appearance and functional layout of the house in major ways. Interior changes that were made to accommodate successive residents, including the reconfiguration of bathroom 106, bathroom 203, and the pantry (108), were reversed.

The restoration work also addressed deferred maintenance problems. On the exterior, masonry repairs and pointing were undertaken. Consolidation and dutchman repairs were made to deteriorated wood components of the windows and trim. On the interior, the cleaning and restoration of finishes was required. To ensure safe, efficient, and problem-free service, deteriorated heating, electrical, and plumbing systems were replaced with new equipment that is sensitive to the historic character of the property. Because the removal of historic material affects the intrinsic value of the house, serious consideration was given to the long-term preservation and future use of the house before any changes were made to address immediate needs.

The restoration work required that vines and biological growth on the masonry walls of the house and the overgrown vegetation immediately surrounding the house be removed. The plants adjacent to the cottage obscured the house from view and masked many of the building's problems.

A substantial study of the overall landscape is now underway. This work will culminate in a cultural landscape report that will form the basis for future decisions regarding property development and conservation. A complete history of land ownership and site development is being undertaken as part of this work, and important elements of the site—the view to the Hudson River, the pedestrian and vehicular circulation patterns, the vegetation, and the relationship of the house to the landscape—are being studied.

The archival information reviewed in the preparation of the historic structure report was voluminous, but additional documentary research may yield more information about the property. The local newspapers may have stories about the original construction and alterations. During the course of the building restoration, William A. Faber, the son of contractor John Faber, was interviewed, and the Faber family made a significant contribution of archival material to the Franklin D. Roosevelt Presidential Library. At the FDR Library many avenues of research remain. Additional material may be found in the President's and in Eleanor Roosevelt's correspondence, the President's bank accounts, and records relating to the settlement of his personal estate. Papers and documents for the cottage generated by Elliot Roosevelt or by estate caretakers and workers may provide information on maintenance, alterations, and life at Top Cottage. Through interviews and family records, Roosevelt and Potter descendants may be able to provide additional insights on the subsequent ownership and occupation of Top Cottage. Finally, distinguished visitors may have recorded accounts of their visits to the President's hill top cottage.

The physical research at the house continued from 1998 through 2000. Investigative probes were made as construction documents were prepared for the restoration. Final determinations could then be made on the dates of installation and/or modifications for such things as the shelving in hall 103, the dressing table in bedroom 104, and the built-in closets in bedroom 105. Throughout the restoration, observations were recorded as construction progressed and hidden conditions were uncovered. These discoveries contributed to an understanding of how the building was originally constructed and how it evolved over time.

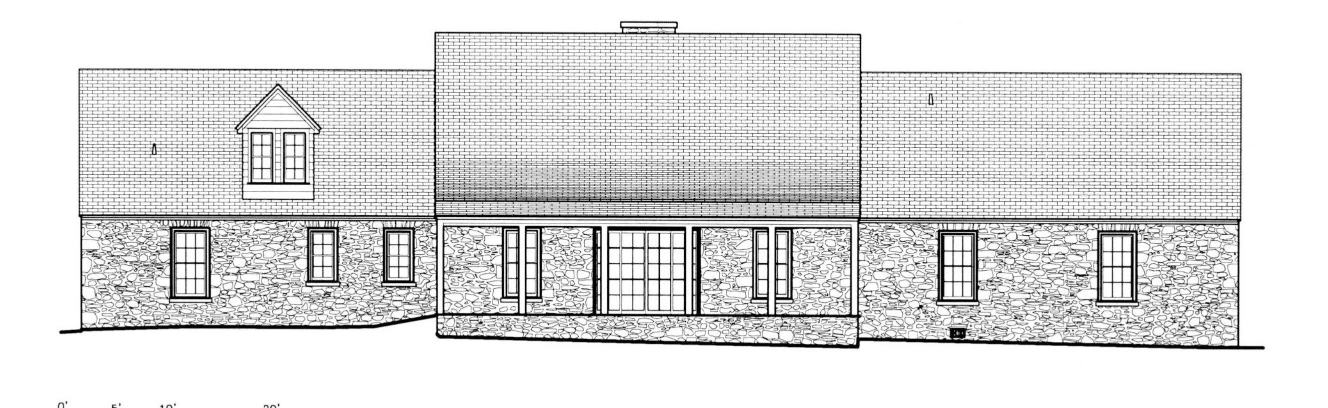

West elevation, 2001.
Measured drawing by John G.
Waite Associates, Architects.

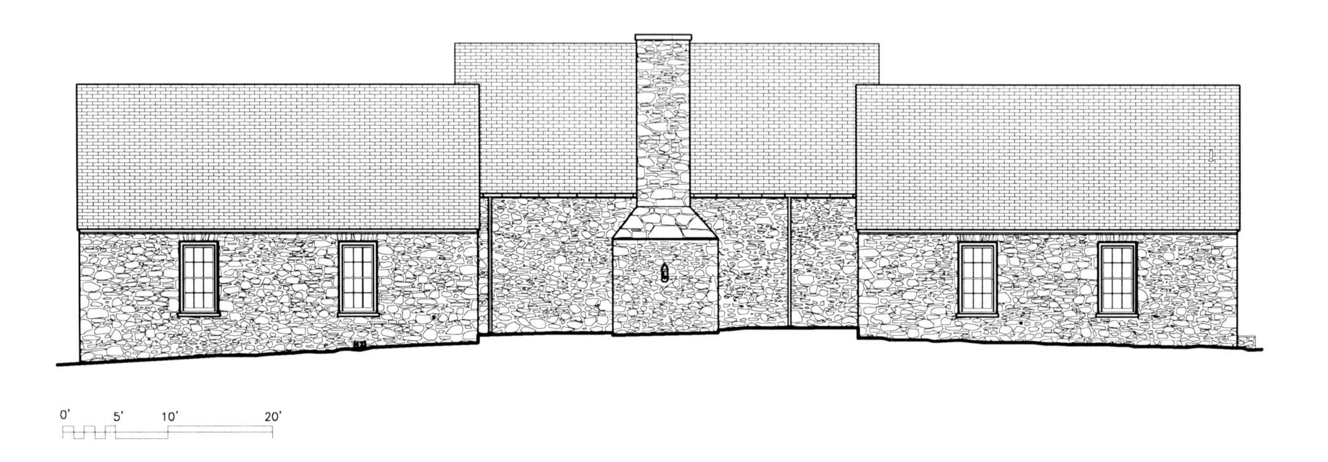

East elevation, 2001.
Measured drawing by JGWAA.

A complete set of detailed construction documents, including drawings and specifications, was prepared for the restoration. The work that was undertaken for the restoration has been outlined below.

Exterior

The window air-conditioning units and central air-conditioning condenser, located at the inside corner of the south wing and central block of the house, were removed.

All exterior telephone, television, and electrical wiring that was attached to the building, laid on grade, buried, or strung around the house was removed. The landscape lighting fixtures, located off the south and east elevations of the house, were removed.

The existing electric meters, disconnect, and overhead electric service wiring were removed. New telephone and electric service was provided for the house. It was routed through underground conduit because of its nonhistorical character and appearance. In the future, a nonfunctioning, historic electric meter and overhead electrical wiring should be installed to reestablish the appearance of the original service entry.

As originally constructed, Top Cottage had no storm windows; they were removed from the scope of work as a cost-saving measure. The exterior aluminum storm windows, installed at a

View from the southeast, showing the removal of the southeast dormers and restoration of the roof, 1999. Photograph by JGWAA.

later date, were removed during the restoration because of their nonhistorical character. However, with the current need to utilize the building during the winter months, the decision was made to install historically appropriate wood storm windows.

The wood window sash and frames were restored as required; cracked and broken glass was replaced; deteriorated glazing putty was replaced; and damaged wood components were consolidated or repaired. The existing shutters and shutter hardware were removed from the windows.

The wood trim, windows, and doors were prepared and painted.

The ivy vines that were growing on the surface of the masonry were removed. The overgrown vegetation was cut back and removed, including the shrubbery on the earthen wheelchair ramp at the north end of the west porch.

The rusted foundation vents were cleaned and painted. Where they were located below grade level on the west elevation of the house, simple stone areaways were created to replace haphazard areaways constructed of concrete blocks.

All dormers were removed, except the west dormer on the north wing, the only one constructed during President Roosevelt's lifetime. Roof rafters were repaired as required, and new blue-black asphalt shingles were installed to match the original shingles. A new copper sheet-metal roof was installed on the west porch to match the original roof.

New copper gutters and downspouts were installed on the east elevation of the house to match the original ones. A new copper gutter and downspouts were installed on the west porch to alleviate the problem of water splashing back on the porch columns. A new in-ground storm-water drainage system with a drywell was installed on the east side of the house to replicate the original system.

The stone masonry was chemically cleaned to remove algae, moss, and lichen.

The stonework was pointed where stone was loose and mortar was missing and where settlement cracks had occurred. Displaced and missing stonework was reset and replaced with stones and mortar to match the original masonry.

The aluminum storm door and pressure-treated wood door frame at the basement entry were replaced with a new wood door and frame to match the original.

The original lead lantern mounted on the east face of the chimney was rewired and refurbished.

Rotted exterior wood trim was repaired or replaced in-kind.

The north porch was removed and the original exterior kitchen entry condition was reestablished.

A new wood attic-access door was installed in the north gable of the central block. The original door was found in a rotted condition, lying against the base of the house. A new door was constructed to replicate the original.

View from the southwest during restoration,1999. Photograph by JGWAA.

Masonry restoration of the chimney, 2000. Photograph by JGWAA.

The steel television-antenna tower erected off the west elevation of the north wing was removed; the wood cornice and stonework were repaired where the mounting brackets were removed.

A new lightning-protection system with unobtrusive tinned down conductors was installed.

The rusted steel antenna mast was removed from the north end of the west porch, and the anemometer was removed from the north end of the gabled roof of the central block of the house.

The heating cable and associated electrical wiring at the eave of the west porch roof were removed.

The historical landscape of woodland duff to the southwest of the house was restored; the existing terrace paving, steps, and goldfish pond were removed.

All historically inappropriate hardware affixed to the exterior of the house was removed.

A new underground mechanical-access vault, connected to the basement, was constructed to the north of the chimney mass. This vault replaced the deteriorated portion of the concrete foundation in the furnace room that had been modified to provide access for the replacement of mechanical systems. In the future, when mechanical system upgrades are necessary, the concrete cap on the vault can be removed to provide basement access.

A new septic tank and leach field were installed to the southeast of the house.

The existing well was drilled deeper in an effort to improve the well's performance and to provide additional water storage in the well casing.

The existing underground fuel-oil tank, located adjacent to the east elevation of the house, was excavated and removed.

View of the restored cottage from the southeast, 2001. Randall Perry Photography.

View of the restored cottage, showing the east entry, 2001. Randall Perry Photography.

View of the restored cottage from the north, following the removal of the north porch, 2001. Randall Perry Photography.

View of the restored cottage from the northwest, showing the c. 1940 west dormer on the north wing and the attic access door in the gable of the central block, 2001. Randall Perry Photography.

View of the restored cottage from the southwest, 2001. Randall Perry Photography.

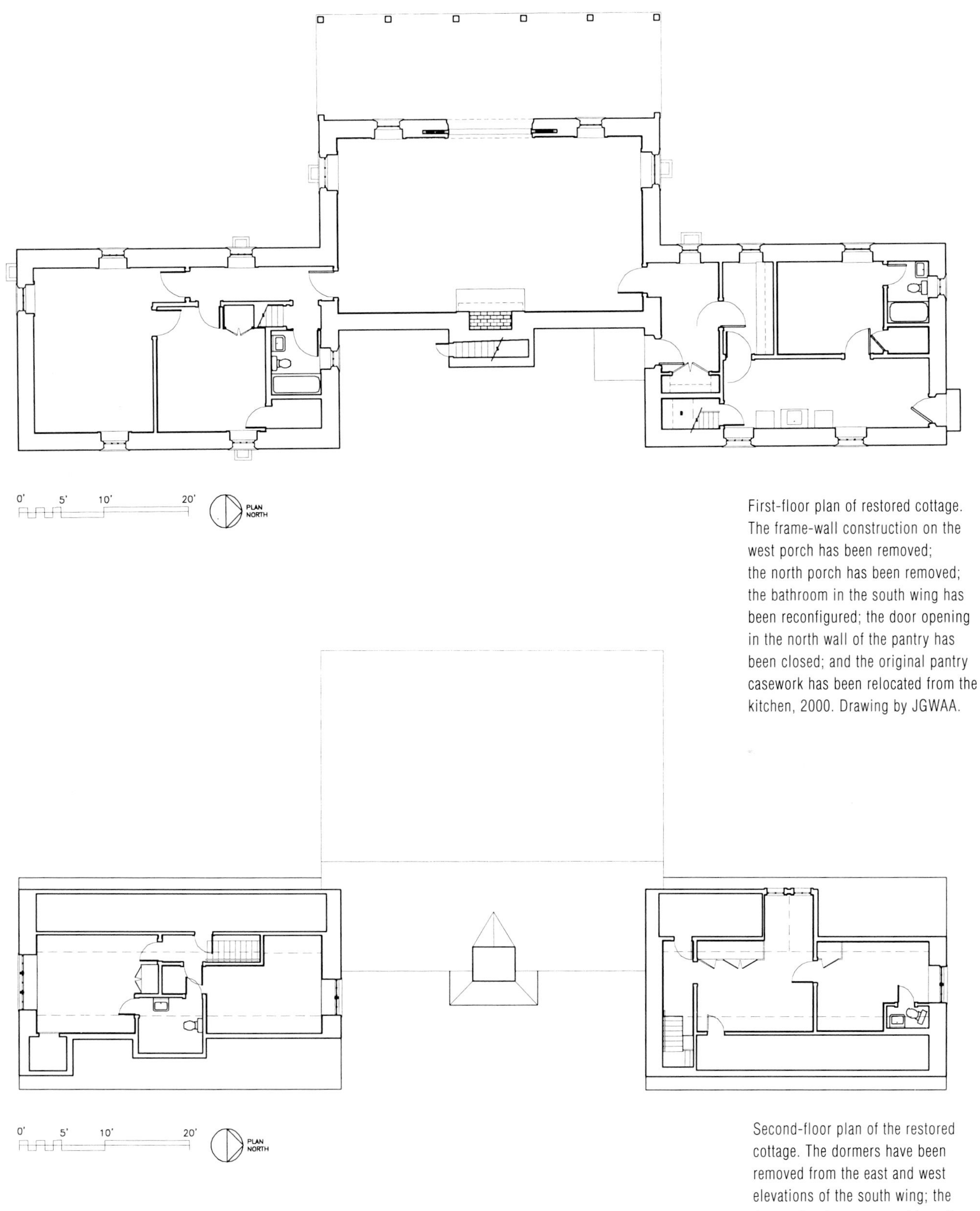

First-floor plan of restored cottage. The frame-wall construction on the west porch has been removed; the north porch has been removed; the bathroom in the south wing has been reconfigured; the door opening in the north wall of the pantry has been closed; and the original pantry casework has been relocated from the kitchen, 2000. Drawing by JGWAA.

Second-floor plan of the restored cottage. The dormers have been removed from the east and west elevations of the south wing; the dormer has been removed from the east elevation of the north wing; and the tub has been removed from the bathroom in the south wing, 2000. Drawing by JGWAA.

Interior

All building materials and debris that had accumulated in the basement crawlspaces were removed.

The furnaces and hot-water heater in the furnace room were replaced with new equipment. A new fuel-oil tank was installed in the furnace room, and new ductwork was fabricated to replace the existing.

A dehumidifier was installed and ductwork was reconfigured to alleviate problems with inefficient crawlspace ventilation and high humidity levels in the basement.

A new wireless fire-detection and security-alarm system with remotely located controls was installed in the house.

The plumbing in the house was at the end of its serviceable life; it had been compromised by ad hoc changes over time. The plumbing lines routed throughout the furnace room and crawlspaces were replaced, as were the plumbing risers to the kitchen and first-floor bathrooms. However, the new plumbing lines for the second-floor bathrooms were capped off in the crawlspaces at the base of the risers to the second floor. This was done to retain the historic plumbing lines to the second floor of the house and to minimize disruption and damage to the historic building fabric. The plumbing fixtures in the second-floor bathrooms are currently inoperable.

The original plumbing fixtures located throughout the house remain in place. A salvaged sink for the kitchen (112) and a salvaged lavatory for bathroom 203 were installed. The tub installed by the Potters in bathroom 203 was removed.

All surface-mounted telephone, television, and electrical wiring was removed.

The electrical wiring was replaced throughout the house. In many instances the wiring did not comply with the current requirements of the National Electrical Code. While it was important to upgrade the wiring to ensure safety and to prevent the possibility of fire, a concerted effort was made to maintain original fixtures and wiring devices.

To the extent that it was possible, light fixtures throughout the house were restored to their original locations and historical appearance. Historically inappropriate light fixtures were removed, and reproduction fixtures were installed in their place.

Electrical receptacles were replaced with new three-wire grounded receptacles. Ground-fault circuit-interrupter (GFCI) circuit breakers were installed for all electrical circuits used for receptacles and light fixtures in the furnace room, bathrooms, kitchen, and west porch, as well as on the exterior of the house.

The paint buildup was removed from the house call-bell buttons and annunciator, and this system was restored to working order.

The original thermostatic controls for the heating system were retained for their historic appearance. New remotely located thermostatic controls for the HVAC system were installed in the front-hall closet; temperature sensors were installed in unobtrusive locations, one within the shell of a historic thermostat and the second in a baseboard junction box adjacent to the living-room fireplace.

All cracks, chips, and holes in the plaster finishes were repaired.

All wall and ceiling surfaces were cleaned and refinished as required. Where paint was applied to the original sand-finished plaster, it could not be removed without damaging the plaster. Therefore, these surfaces were painted to match the color of the plaster as closely as possible. The only large area of sand-finished plaster that remained unpainted was the wall surface behind the vanity in bedroom 104; this finish was preserved intact.

The carpet and vinyl flooring that obscured the original hardwood and linoleum floor finishes were removed. The original flooring was repaired and refinished as required. New linoleum flooring was installed in the bathrooms, kitchen, and pantry (108) to replicate the historic flooring in these spaces. The original linoleum in the pantry space to the south of the kitchen was retained. An area of original dark-stained flooring was preserved in bedroom 104 (southeast corner) and in bedroom 105 (adjacent to the south wall).

All window sash weights were rehung with cotton sash cord to match the original. The wood windows were repaired as required and painted. New window sash were installed in the

View of the restored living room, looking northeast, 2001. Randall Perry Photography.

View of the restored living room, looking northwest, 2001. Randall Perry Photography.

two window openings on the west elevation of the living room (102); the original sash had been removed sometime after the west porch had been enclosed.

All doors were adjusted and repaired to prevent binding and to ensure proper operation.

The sheet-metal HVAC grilles were cleaned, repaired, and refinished as required.

The operation of the sliding doors in the west wall of the living room (102) was restored. The doors and overhead track were repaired as required.

The acoustical tile was removed from the original tongue-and-groove wood ceiling of the west porch (102A).

The frame-wall construction to the north, west, and south that enclosed the west porch (102A) was removed, returning the porch to its original configuration.

The perimeter shelving beneath the ceiling of hall 103 was removed.

The vanity and built-in closets in bedroom 104 were removed.

The built-in closets in bedroom 105 were removed.

Southeast corner of restored bedroom (104), 2001. The original unpainted sand-finished plaster wall surface was preserved behind the built-in cabinetry installed by Elliot Roosevelt. Randall Perry Photography.

View of restored bathroom (106), looking southeast, 2001. The east wall partition has been reconstructed, and the tub has been returned to its original location. Randall Perry Photography.

The original architectural hardware throughout the house was repaired and refurbished as required. The hardware was adjusted for proper operation.

The historic configuration of bathroom 106 was reestablished. A new wood-frame partition wall was constructed, replicating an original wall partition and separating the bathroom from a closet to the east. The bathtub was returned to its original north-south orientation against the newly constructed east-wall partition. The sand-finished plaster walls and attic access hatch in the closet were restored.

View of restored pantry, looking northwest, 2001. The door opening in the north wall has been closed, and the original pantry casework has been relocated from the kitchen. Randall Perry Photography.

The rotted wood flooring behind the toilet in bathroom 110 was replaced.

Historically inappropriate plastic tiles were removed from bathroom walls.

Historically appropriate bathroom accessories were reinstalled.

The swinging door at the northwest door opening of the kitchen (112) was returned to its original location in the south-door opening of the pantry (108).

The pantry (108) was restored to its historic configuration, closing the north door opening and returning the casework from the west wall of the kitchen to its original location along the north wall of the pantry. The wood casework was restored.

The kitchen (112) was generally restored to its historic appearance with original cabinets flanking a salvaged kitchen sink. However, the exact configuration of the kitchen remains unknown. It is anticipated that this space will function as a staging area for food preparation and catering.

Cracked, splintered, and gouged wood trim was repaired.

Coat hooks were removed from the west wall and southwest door of room 204 to prevent further damage to the wood paneling and door.

The existing insulation was removed from the attic spaces, and new fiberglass batt insulation, with an appropriate vapor barrier, was installed.

The steel shower stall and associated plumbing were removed from room 207, and the flooring was repaired.

Where dormers were removed from the south wing, new ash wall paneling was fabricated and installed at the second-floor level to match the existing chestnut paneling.

The textured ceiling finishes at the second-floor level of the south wing were removed, exposing the original fiberboard ceiling panels. Wood batten strips were reinstalled, and the fiberboard ceilings were restored.

At the second-floor level of the north wing, fiberboard wall paneling was installed where the east dormer was removed. The fiberboard was routed with grooves to match the existing wallboard.

INDEX

References to illustrations are italicized.

ACCESSIBILITY, 8–9, 15, 27, 32, 41, 61, 79, 88, 92, *144*, 147
Adams, Paul D., 35–38, 40–43, 46, 48, 53, 58, 81
Adams-Faber Company, 33, 35–42, 44–46, 48–49, 55, 77
AES Intelliset, 88
Aldrich, J. Winthrop, Jr., 10
American Builder, 51, 83
American Institute of Architects (AIA), 29, 36
American Standard Radiator and Sanitary Corporation, 121
Architectural Forum, 49
Attic, 18, 23, 41, 49, 58, *66–68*, 77, 79–80, 85, 87, 94, 98–102, 104, 106–107, 109, 115–121, 123–124, 126, 128, 147, *150*, 155

BACKER, DOROTHY, 22, 27–29, 35, 39, 60
Backer, George, 22, 27–28, 35, 60
Barker, Harry G., 54, 80–81
Barn, 64
Barrett Company, 31
Basement, 19, 23, *24*, 28–29, 31, 37, 39, 47–48, 76–77, *77*, 79, 81, 83, *83*, 84, 131–132, 136–137, 147–148, 152
Bathrooms, 19, 23, 28–29, 31–32, 40–41, 45–46, 50, 59–60, 63, *68–69*, 82, 84–85, 98–99, 104–106, 109, 116, 119, 152
  Bathroom (106), 94, 99–101, *101*, 102–104, 117, 122, 138, 145, 154, *154*
  Bathroom (110), 108, 114, *139*, 140, 155
  Bathroom (203), 116–118, *118*, 120, *120*, 121–122, 142, 145, 152
  Toilet room (208), 106, 110, 128–129, 143
Bausch and Lomb, 75, 82
Beaverkill Conservancy, 10, 64–65
Bedrooms, 9, 18–19, 23, 27–28, 32, 36, 41, 44, 51, 58–60, 62–64, *68*, 82, 85, 98, 100, 102, 106–107, 116, 119–120
  Bedroom (104), 85, 94, 96–97, *97*, 98–99, 101, 111, 138, 145, 152–153, *154*
  Bedroom (105), 85, 94–96, 98–99, *99*, 100–102, 113, 116, 137–138, 145, 152–153
  Bedroom (109), 85–86, 104, 106, *106*, 107, 139
  Bedroom (202), 117–118, *118*, 119–120, 122, 141–142
  Bedroom (204), 118, 121–122, *122*, 123, 142, 155
  Bedroom (206), 124–125, *125*, 126, *126*, 127, 143
  Bedroom (207), 125, 127–128, *128*, 143, 155
  Servants' bedroom, 23, 32, 45, 64, 84
Bendix, 62, 112
Berkshire Mountains, 7
Bie, Christian, 41, 54, 58, 60, 62, 67, 87, 91, 106–107, 115–116, 121, 123, 125, 127
Bie, Ruth, 53, 62, 112
Bie, Ruthie, *6*
Bigelow Sanford, 54, 91
Blandino, John, 59
Bock, 84
Bryant, 90
Burrowes Corporation, 31

CALIFORNIA OIL COMPANY, 63
Campbell (G. D.) Building Company, 33
Catskill Mountains, 7, 17, 61, 76, 92
Central block of cottage, 18, 27, 76–77, *78*, 79–81, 83–84, 92, 116, 124, 131–136, 146–148, *150*
Central Hudson Gas and Electric, 47
Certainteed Products, 31
Chairs, Inc., 55
Chevron, 84
Chiang Kai-shek, Madame, 7, 63
Chimneys, 18–19, *23*, 28, 30, 37, 39–41, 43–44, *76*, *77*, 80, *80*, 81, 83–84, 87, 131–132, *132*, 137, 147–148, *148*
Churchill, Winston, 7, 9, 63
Cincinnati Fly Screen Company, 30
Clay, J. E., 33
Cloister Inn, 35
Closets, 23, 29, 41, 50–51, 59, 63, *68–69*, 82, 85–88, 96–104, 115, 117–118, 121, 123–124, 127–128, 152–154
  Closet (101A), 86–87, 115, 124, 136
  Closet (111), 108–109, 128, 140
  Closet (202A), 120, 142
  Closet (204A), 123, 142
  Closet (206B), 126–127, 143
  Closet (207A), 128, 143
Coburn Trolley Track Company, 30
Connecticut, 7, 17
  New Britain, 49
Cook, Nancy, 19, 21–23, 26, 28–30, 33, 37, 39, 43, 45
Cooper Company, 45
Corbin, P. and F., 49, 86, 90, 111
Corbin, Yale and Towne, 30
Cornerite, 31
Coverts (H. W.) Company, 30
Creighton, William J., 19, 38, 46, 48
Cret, Paul, 19
Cuba, 63
Curnan, Charles, 112
Curry (P. J.) Company, 62, 87, 91, 94, 96, 98, 112
Curtis Company, 30, 33
Curtis Silentite, 128
Cutter, John, 22–23

DICKERMAN, MARION, 19, 21–22
Dining room, 21, 64, 82, 85, 104, 106–107, 109
Disabled accessibility. *See* Accessibility
District of Columbia
  Washington, 17–18, 26, 33, 50
Dodge (F. W.) Corporation, 103
Draiss, Frank, 112
Draiss, Kenneth, 112
Driveway, 18, 23, 79
du Pont de Nemours (E. I.) and Company, 35
Dutchess Hill, 7, 10, 17, 37, 42, 76

EARLY, STEVE, 9
Edwards and Company, 91, 98, 107, 111
Eisenhower, Dwight D., 63
Electric service, 32, 41, 47, 49, 81, 132–134, 146
Elizabeth, Queen (of Great Britain), 7, 53, *54*
Elmore Design Collaborative, 65
Emerson, Faye, 9, 63, 85, 96, 98
Entry (101), 29, 36–37, 40–41, 44, *56*, 62, 79, 81, 86, *86*, 87–88, 104, 109, 115, 136
Eylers, John, 26–27, 33

FABER, JOHN H., 35–39, 43–45, 145
Faber, William A., 145
Fala, *6*, *19*, *56*, *58*
Federal Reserve bank, 22
Feller, William, 33
Feller Brothers, 33

Fimble, Joseph L., 45–46, 59–60
Floor plans
  Basement plan, *83*
  First-floor plan, *17*, *22*, *24*, *66–69*, *85*, *151*
  Second-floor plan, *66–69*, *117*, *151*
Franklin and Eleanor Roosevelt Institute (FERI), 10–11, 15, 65
Furnace room (B01), 31, 83–84, *84*, 136, 148, 152

GARCIA, H. G., 87
General Electric, 53, 62, 111–112, 114, 119
George II, King (of Greece), *57*
George VI, King (of Great Britain), 7, 53, *54–55*
Georgia, 7
  Atlanta, 23, 36–37, 46, 49–50, 60
  Warm Springs, 9, 20–23, 29, 60–61
Georgia Department of Archives and History, 21, 37, 43
Georgia Warm Springs Foundation, 20, 23
Germany, 63
Goodwin, Doris Kearns, 9
Greenhouse, 64

HACKETT, HENRY T., 27
Haga, Wiley J., 81
Hall and Mack, 32, 103
Hallways, 40, 44, 59, 62, 85, 99–101
  South hall (103), 84, 90, 94–95, *95*, 96, 101, 113, 137, 145, 153
  Stair hall (201), 116–118, 141
  Stair hall (205), 115, 123–124, 127, 142
Hambley, Margaret, *57*
Hammacher Schlemmer, 54
Hammer Galleries, 63, 85
Handicap accessibility. *See* Accessibility
Hart and Cooley, 32, 86, 90, 95, 97, 100, 107, 111
Hart and Hegeman, 32
Harvard University, 36
Hering, Frank, 59
Hermidifier, 84
Hitler, Adolf, 7
Holiday, 52
Holland Furnace Company, 32, 38–39, 46–47, 49, 58–60, 84
Home Owner's Catalogs, 103
Honeywell Holland, 121
Hopkins, Diana, 55
Hopkins, Harry, 7–8, 55
Horn (C. C.) Company, 31
Hudson River, 7–10, 17, 19, 26, 62, 76, 92, 145
Hutchinson, J. C., 49

INDIANA, 51
  Carmel, 54, 80
ITE Imperial Corporation, 84

JEFFERSON, THOMAS, 8, 15, 51, 62, 91
Johns Manville Company, 31
Juliana, Princess (of the Netherlands), 7

KAY, WILLIAM H., JR., 63
Keene's Cement, 31
King, MacKenzie, 7
Kirch, 54
Kitchen (112), 18–19, *24*, 28–30, 32, 36, 38, 40, 45, 48–49, 58, 62, 64, *66–67*, *69*, 81–82, 84–86, 98, 104–106, 109–110, *110*, 111, *111*, 112–114, 140–141, 152, 155, *155*
Kloepfer, Fred, 59
Knox, George, 11
Kwikset, 93

LAFAYETTE, GENERAL MARIE JOSEPH PAUL, 62
LaGuardia, Fiorello, *16*
Lane, Frederick, 33
Larson Brothers, 49
Lawco, 129
Leahy, Admiral, 58
LeHand, Marguerite (Missy), 7, 22, 27–28, 39, 42, 46, 53–55, 58
Lehman, Herbert, 55
Lenox, 80
Lewis, Schell, 50–51, 64
Life, 48, 51
Lightning protection system, 81, 134–135, 148
Lightolier Company, 40, 81, 103, 105, 111, 114
Lila Acheson and DeWitt Wallace Fund for the Hudson Highlands, 10, 65
Linaka, Russell, 58
Little White House, 20
Living room (102), 19, 21, 23, 28–32, 37–38, 41–42, 44–45, 55, *56–57*, 59, *59–61*, 62, 64, 77, 82, 84–88, *88–89*, 90–92, *92*, 93–95, 98, 104–107, 111, 116, 136, 152–153, *153*
Look, 63
Louise, Princess (of Sweden), 7, 37
Luckey, Platt and Company, 54, 91
Lumb (W. W.) and Company, 59
Lumb Woodworking Company, 33
Lynch, E. M., 62, 79

MAGIC GENERAL CONTRACTING, 65
Magnum Alert, 87–88
Martens, Joseph, 10
Martha, Princess (of Norway), 7, *57*
Massachusetts, 7, 17
  Boston, 22, 55
  Springfield, 65
Matthews, Mr., 27
McIntire, Admiral, 58
McKim, Mead and White, 19
Michigan, 61
Miller and Gaynor Corporation, 33
Minneapolis Honeywell Regulator Company, 95, 111
Minnesota
  Minneapolis, 81
Monticello, 8, 51
Morgenthau, Mrs. Henry, *55*

NATIONAL ELECTRICAL CODE, 131–132, 134, 137–143, 152
National Gypsum Company, 31
National Park Service, 9–10, *64*, 65
National Press Club, 91
Neely, Frank, 23
New Jersey
  Elizabeth, 45
  Upper Montclair, 35–36, 51
New York, 19, 22, 38, 58, 62, 65
  Albany, 65
  Dutchess County, 9, 17, 64, 76
  Granville, 3
  Hudson Highlands, 7
  Hudson Valley, 15
  Hyde Park, 7, 10, 17, 19–20, 22–23, 26–30, 33, 35–41, 43, 48, 52–53, 62–63
    Cream Street, 47, 49
  Kingston, 26, 55
  Middletown, 51
  Mount Vernon, 45, 49
  Netherwood, 63
  New York, 26, 33, 35–36, 40, 46, 55, 62, 85, 91
  Oyster Bay, 22
  Poughkeepsie, 17, 26–27, 33, 44–49, 53–54, 63, 81, 91, 112, 119
  Red Hook, 33
  Rhinebeck, 26, 47, 62, 79
  Salem, 65
  Saugerties, 26
  Tivoli, 62, 91
  White Plains, 35, 49
New York City Plumbing Ordinance, 32
New York Fire Insurance Rating Organization, 48
New York Herald Tribune, 50
New York State Office of Parks, Recreation and Historic Preservation, 10
New York Times, 33, 37, 48, 50–51, 53, 63–64
New York Times Magazine, 58
Norway, 54
Noyes, Horace, 38

O'BRIEN BROTHERS SLATE COMPANY, 33
O'Day, Caroline, 19
Ohio
  Middletown, 103
  Wooster, 31
Olsen, Henry A., 44–45
Open Space Institute, 10, 15, 65
Osthagen, Mr., 94

PALAZZO, CLAY S., 11, 15
Pantries, 19, 28–29, 32, 40–41, 45, 49, *56*, 58, 62, *66*, *69*, 82, 84, 86–87, 105, 109, 115, *155*
  Food pantry (113), 85, 106, 109–110, 112
  Pantry (108), 85, 104, *105*, 106, 110–113, 139–140, 145, 152, 155
Patio, 79
Pencil Points, 51
Pennsylvania, 47
  Ford City, 98
  Philadelphia, 19
  Wilkes-Barre, 47
Perkins, Frances, 9
Philip Carey Company, 103
Pittsburgh Plate Glass Company, 98
Pittsburgh Press, 50
Plog, William A., 42–43, 53
Pond, 64, 79, 148
Poplar Forest, 8, 15
Porches, 9, 17–19, 27, *27*, 28, 36, 39–40, 43–45, 53–55, 58, 76, 78–79, 84, 133–134
  Dutch porch, 27–28
  Kitchen porch, 36, 40
  North porch (112A), *69*, 75, 79–82, 85, 108–109, 113–114, *114*, 141, *141*, 145, 147, *150*
  Servants' porch, 28
  West porch (102A), *6*, *19*, 28, 30, 36, 40–41, *42*, *53*, *55*, *57*, *69*, *74*, 75, 77, 81–82, 85–86, 88, *89*, 92, *92*, 93–94, 113–114, 137, *137*, *144*, 145, 147–148, 152–153
Potter, Agnes F., 64
Potter, Ellen, 64
Potter, Jean O., 64
Potter, Owen, 10, 64, 84, 104, 119, 125
Potter, Philip S., Sr., 9, 63–64, 75–76, 79–82, 84, 86–88, 90, 93–94, 96, 98–102, 104–107, 109, 111–113, 115–118, 120–123, 125, 127–129, 131, 145
Potter, Robert, 63
Potter, Robert, Jr., 79

Pratt and Lambert, 31, 48–49, 91
Previews, Inc., 64
Princeton University, 35–36
Progress, 114
Progressive Farmer, 51

QUINN, JOSEPH D., 47–48

RAMP, 147
Rich's Department Store, 23
Rising and Nelson Slate Company, 31
Robertshaw Hardwick, 114
Roosevelt, Betsey Cushing, 54
Roosevelt, Chandler, 63
Roosevelt, Christopher du P., 11, *64*
Roosevelt, Eleanor, 7, 9–10, 19–21, 23, 33, 37, 41, 45, 50, *56*, 58, 62–63, 145
Roosevelt, Elliott, 9, 62–63, 75, 77–80, 82, 84–88, 91, 93–96, 98, 101, 104, 106–107, 111–113, 115–116, 131, 145, *154*
Roosevelt, Elliott (Tony), Jr., 63, 101, 118, 121, 125, 127
Roosevelt, Franklin, Jr., 9
Roosevelt, Franklin Delano, *6*, *16–17*, *52*, *56–57*, *59*
  Correspondence, 19, 27, 37
  Drawings, 17, *17*, 21, *21–22*, 27, *27*
Roosevelt, G. Hall, 41, 49, 58, 61, 125
Roosevelt, James, 9, 54, 62
Roosevelt, John, 9
Roosevelt, Sara Delano, 7, *55*
Roosevelt Family Committee, 65
Roosevelt (Franklin D.) Library, 20–21, 37, 43, 145
Roosevelt (James) Memorial Library, 20, 33
Roosevelt-Vanderbilt National Historic Sites, 9–10
Russell Erwin Company, 31
Russia, 63

SANDFORD WOODWORKING COMPANY, 45
Seaman, Frank, 33
Sears, John F., 10–11
Security system, *52*, 87–88, 120, 132, 136, 138, 142, 152
Septic system, 23
Sewage system, 32, 41, 45, 84, 148
Shawangunk Mountains, 7, 17
Shed, 77, 80, 134
Sherwin-Williams, 31
Silverblatt and Lasker, 26, 33
Simon, Louis A., 26
Site plan, 77
Smith, Joseph Kellum, 19
Southeastern Underwriters Association, 32
Spencer-Kellogg, 31
Spivack, S. S., 54, 91
Springwood, 10, 17
Stairs, *24*, 28, 31, 58–59, *67–68*, 76, 83–85, 87–88, 94, 98–99, *99*, 100–102, 104, 109–110, 116, 121, 123–124, 136
  Stair (113), 115, *115*, 116, 141–142
Stalin, Joseph, 63
Standard Sanitary Manufacturing Company, 103, 108, 112
Stanley Works, 49, 119, 123
Storage space (201A), 117
Storage space (202B), 120
Storage space (205A), 124, 127, 143
Storage space (206A), 127, 143
Suckley, Margaret (Daisy), 7, 17–18, *18*, 19, *19*, 55, 58, 60–62, 79, 82, 87–88, 91, 96, 116, 121
Sunday New Yorker, 63
Sunday Star, 50
Sweden, 37
Swimming pool, 64

TELLER, MYRON S., 55
Terrace, 17–19, 50, 60, 77, 135, 148
  East terrace, 30, 36
The New Yorker, 48
Thompson (George E.) Company, 81
Time, 51, 63
Tock Brothers, 31
Toombs, Henry J., 7, 9, 15, 19–20, *20*, 21–23, 26–29, 33, 35–51, 53, 55, 58–60, 63, 77, 80–81, 85, 94, 113, 116, 121
  Drawings, *23–26*, 29
Toombs, Michael, 21
Toombs, Tanya, 20–21
Top Cottage, views of, *34–35*, *39–40*, *44–45*, *50–51*, *54*, *64*, *76*, *78*, *80*, *130*, *144*, *146–150*
Top Cottage Committee, 11
Treasury Department
  Procurement Division, 20, 26, 60
Truscons, 31
Tull Metal and Supply Company, 45, 49
Tully, Grace, 55

U. S. GYPSUM COMPANY, 31
United Mine Workers of America, 47
University of Pennsylvania, 19
University of Virginia, 51

VAL-KILL, 7, 9–10, 19–20, 22–23, 29, 33, 39, 47
Val-Kill Heights, 64
Val-Kill Inn, 63
Val-Kill Shop, 19
van Brookhoven, Henry, 10
Vermont, 31
  West Pawlet, 31
Vestibule (107), 101–102, 104, 139
Virginia
  Lynchburg, 15
Vulcan Anthracite Stoker Company, 47

WAITE, DIANA S., 11
Waite, John G., 11
Waite (John G.) Associates, Architects, 11, 15, 65, 145
Wallace, Henry, 7
Wallace Company, 53, 112
Ward, Geoffrey C., 8–9, 11, 15, 55
Warner Brothers, 63
Washington, George, 62, 91
Well, 28, 33, 42, 47, 148
Western Electric, 105
Western Waterproofing Company, 30
Westinghouse, 81
White House, 7, 9, 20–21, 26–28, 49
White House Signal Department Diagram, *52*
Whitney, Kate Roosevelt, 11
Wilhemina, Queen (of the Netherlands), 7
Wings, 18–19, 36, 45
  North wing, 18, 23, 27, *27*, 28, *43*, 58, 62–64, *66–67*, *69*, 75–76, 79–85, 87, 107, 113, 116, 124–127, 132–133, *133*, 134, 136, 145, 147–148, *150*, 155
  South wing, 18, 23, *24*, 27–28, 32, 38, 45, 58, 62–64, *66*, *69*, 75–76, *78*, 79–85, 88, 94, 99, 101, 116–118, 120–121, 131, *131*, 135, *135*, 145–146, 155
Wooster Products Company, 31
Works Projects Administration, 55
Wright, Frank Lloyd, 51
Wright, John Lloyd, 51